T0330350

Globalization and Equity

Globalization and Equity

Perspectives from the Developing World

Edited by

Natalia Dinello, *Principal Political Scientist*, and

Lyn Squire, *President*

Global Development Network, Washington, DC, USA

Edward Elgar
Cheltenham, UK • Northampton, MA, USA

Published by
Edward Elgar Publishing Limited
The Lypiatts
15 Lansdown Road
Cheltenham
Glos GL50 2JA
UK

Edward Elgar Publishing, Inc.
William Pratt House
9 Dewey Court
Northampton
Massachusetts 01060
USA

A catalogue record for this book
is available from the British Library

Library of Congress Cataloguing in Publication Data:

Global Development Conference (4th : 2003 : Cairo, Egypt)
    Globalization and equity : perspective from the developing world / edited by
Natalia Dinello and Lyn Squire.
        p. cm.
    "All of these papers were delivered at the Fourth Annual Global Development
Conference, held in Cairo, Egypt, 18–21 January 2003"—Introd.
        1. Developing countries—Economic conditions—21st century. 2.
Globalization—Economic aspects—Developing countries—Congresses. 3.
Globalization—Social aspects—Developing countries—Congresses. 4.
Poverty—Developing countries—Congresses. 5. Equity—Developing
countries—Congresses. 6. Equality—Developing countries—Congresses. I.
Dinello, Natalia E. II. Squire, Lyn, 1946—III. Title.

HC59.7.G563 2003
337'.09172'4—dc22

                                                                    2004061474

ISBN 978 1 84376 884 5

Printed on FSC approved paper
Printed and bound in Great Britain by Marston Book Services Ltd, Oxfordshire

Contents

List of Figures

List of Tables

Notes on the Contributors

S. IBI AJAYI is Professor of Economics at the University of Ibadan, Nigeria. He holds a doctorate in economics from Queen's University (Canada). He has consulted for the World Health Organization, World Bank, IMF and African Economic Research Consortium. His research focuses on health economic issues, macroeconomics, monetary economics and economic development issues.

ALI ABDEL GADIR ALI has a Ph.D. in economics and is an economic advisor with the Arab Planning Institute in Kuwait. His current research topics include poverty, income distribution and labor market, sustainable development issues, the social dimensions of macroeconomic policies and the role of institutions in the development process.

ROBERTO BOUZAS is an economist holding degrees from the University of Buenos Aires (Argentina) and Cambridge University (UK). He is professor at Universidad de San Andrés. Professor Bouzas has been a consultant to the Economic Commission on Latin America and the Caribbean, the UN Development Program, the Inter-American Development Bank and Argentina's Ministry of Foreign Relations and International Trade.

CHIA SIOW YUE is Senior Research Fellow at the Singapore Institute of International Affairs, and the former regional coordinator of the East Asian Development Network. She has also worked with the World Bank, the United Nations (UN), OECD Development Centre, Asian Development Bank, and ASEAN Secretariat. She holds a Ph.D. in Economics from McGill University (Canada).

NATALIA DINELLO has earned doctoral degrees from the University of Pittsburgh and the Soviet Academy of Science. As Principal Political Scientist at the Secretariat of the Global Development Network, she designs and implements strategies and programs for building research capacity in developing and transition economies. She also has an extensive publication record for her own research.

RICARDO FFRENCH-DAVIS holds a Ph.D. in economics from the University of Chicago. He is former deputy manager of the Central Bank of Chile and is currently post-graduate professor of international economics at the University of Chile. He is also principal regional advisor of the Economic Commission for Latin America and the Caribbean (ECLAC).

SISIRA JAYASURIYA is director of the Asian Economics Centre and associate professor in economics at the University of Melbourne (Australia). He obtained his Ph.D. from Australian National University. He has published on macroeconomic and trade issues, agricultural and environmental problems, and economic policymaking in developing economies, particularly in South and Southeast Asia.

GRZEGORZ W. KOLODKO is director of Transformation, Integration and Globalization Economic Research at the Leon Kozminski Academy of Entrepreneurship and Management in Warsaw (Poland). As Polish Deputy Prime Minister and Minister of Finance he played a leading role in securing Poland's entry into the OECD and European Union.

LYN SQUIRE is president of the Global Development Network. After gaining his Ph.D. from Cambridge University, he has spent his professional career at the World Bank. He has served as Chief Economist of the Middle East and North Africa Vice-Presidency, Director of the Research Department, and Director of the 1990 World Development Report on Poverty.

KSENIA YUDAEVA is director for Policy Studies at the Center for Economic and Financial Research in Moscow. She earned a Ph.D. in economics from the Massachusetts Institute of Technology. Her research interests include empirical analysis of foreign direct investment and trade, particularly FDI effects on productivity in Russian manufacturing firms.

Acknowledgments

This book is the result of the combined efforts of many individuals.

Richard Cooper, Harvard University and the GDN Governing Body; Gary McMahon, GDN Secretariat; and Hoda Rashad, the American University in Cairo and the GDN Governing Body reviewed the individual papers and provided the authors with invaluable suggestions for the final versions of the chapters.

Ann Robertson supervised the copyediting and prepared the text for publication, with help from Irina Papkov of the GDN Secretariat.

Data collection and analysis for the opening chapter was conducted with the assistance of Jim Bang, University of Illinois at Urbana-Champaign; Shaymal Chowdhury, International Food Policy Research Institute; Hadi Salehi Esfahani, University of Illinois at Urbana-Champaign; Klaus Deininger, World Bank; Branko Milanovic, Carnegie Endowment for International Peace; Irina Papkov, GDN Secretariat; Martin Ravallion, World Bank; Kristina Mihailova, GDN Secretariat, and Kareff May Rafisura, GDN Secretariat.

Introduction

Natalia Dinello and Lyn Squire

Globalization has been the topic of contentious debate over the last decade involving academics, policy-makers, business tycoons, journalists and the general public. The popular web-based bookseller, Amazon.com, returns more than 13,000 search results on the request for publications on globalization. The views of intellectuals and celebrities on the topic range from harsh condemnation of the pattern of globalization imposed on the developing world to powerful praise of globalization's potential, if not of its current reality.

In a recent controversial book, Nobel Laureate in Economics, Joseph Stiglitz, provides an unsettling insider's look at the international financial institutions that promote globalization (Stiglitz 2002). Based on his experiences as chairman of President Bill Clinton's Council of Economic Advisers and as chief economist at the World Bank, Stiglitz highlights the failure of these institutions to alleviate poverty and stimulate economic growth. In contrast, another internationally renowned economist and Stiglitz's colleague at Columbia University, Jagdish Bhagwati, proposes that globalization benefits all emerging markets by creating virtuous economic cycles of faster economic growth. He also provides evidence that, in at least some cases, growth can be successfully coupled with appropriate environmental and social safeguards and, moreover, that global economic integration can improve the lot of women and children in developing countries (Bhagwati 2004).

Academic assessments of globalization compete with no less authoritative commentaries on the phenomenon by famous businessmen and journalists. Like Stiglitz, financial guru and philanthropist, George Soros, directs his criticism at what he describes as market fundamentalism within international financial and trade institutions, and he suggests recipes for making globalization serve the poor and improve development (Soros 2002). In yet another best-seller, *New York Times* foreign affairs columnist, Thomas Friedman, describes globalization as a lasting phenomenon – an international system that has replaced the Cold War system – and goes beyond economics to highlight the tension between the modern integrated world and the age-old forces of culture, geography, tradition and community (Friedman 1999).

The difference in the views and arguments of the four above-mentioned authors cannot conceal a curious similarity: their influential analyses of the plight of the developing world in the age of globalization all come from New York. However, while the positions of leading Western spokespeople for the developing world are certainly of value, it is very important to let intellectuals from developing countries speak for themselves. The editors of this book are motivated precisely by the concern that the voices of researchers from developing and transition economies are seldom heard in the ongoing debate on globalization. This book therefore attempts to fill this void, focusing specifically on the relationship between globalization and equity across the developing and transition countries.

GLOBAL DEVELOPMENT NETWORK

This book is built around a set of papers that analyze the topics of globalization and equity from the perspectives of seven regions—the Commonwealth of Independent States, Central and Eastern Europe, East Asia, Latin America, the Middle East and North Africa, South Asia and Sub-Saharan Africa. All these chapters were delivered at the Fourth Annual Global Development Conference, held in Cairo, Egypt, 18–21 January 2003, and organized by the Global Development Network (GDN), an organization with the dual mission of building research capacity in the social sciences and of bridging research and policy, with a particular focus on the developing world. The authors represent GDN's seven network partners in developing and transition economies; they have benefited from GDN's funding and promotion of their research.

Indeed, GDN is uniquely positioned to sponsor a book highlighting the voices of intellectuals from the developing world. The organization fosters home-grown expertise in the social sciences and in policy analysis as well as encouraging the cross-fertilization of research conducted in both developing and developed countries. Consistent with GDN's mission, the Cairo Conference attracted almost 600 participants primarily from the developing world, including prominent leaders such as the president of Tanzania, Benjamin Mkapa, and a former Mexican president, Ernesto Zedillo. Many conference participants emphasized the importance of human intervention grounded in local knowledge – as opposed to advice imposed from outside – as a means of increasing the benefits of globalization and mitigating its detrimental effects (Dinello 2004, 10).

Speaking at the conference, Egypt's first lady, Suzanne Mubarak, acknowledged that 'globalization is sweeping across our nations like a storm' (2003, 3). Accepting and even welcoming globalization, most presenters from the developing world nevertheless deemed it imperative to harness the phenomenon's willful forces, to tame its negative impact and to steer globalization toward a positive and equitable course. Echoing Egyptian Prime Minister Atef Ebeid's observation that 'It is our [Egypt and other developing countries] responsibility to shape our future in globalization' (2003, 3), contributors to this book endeavor to examine the links between globalization, growth and equity and to suggest actions that could alleviate inequality and promote new opportunities. The chapters describe and analyze the principal topics and currents of discussion on globalization and equity in various regions of the world, outlining methodological approaches, the results of empirical research and their implications for policies and strategies.

THE BENEFITS OF GLOBALIZATION

Within the worldwide debate, the proponents of globalization often point to its three-fold beneficial impact, with positive implications for equity: 1) stimulating trade and economic growth, 2) reducing poverty without rise in inequality, and 3) contributing to economic and political stability. These claims are promptly supported by evidence.

First, the 2002 World Bank report *Globalization, Growth and Poverty* provides many examples of accelerated growth in those developing countries that are more integrated into the global economy. These examples are further supported by cross-country statistical analyses establishing that higher trade volumes are correlated with higher growth (World Bank 2002, 5). The Organization for Economic Co-operation and Development (OECD) study of developing countries (Little et al. 1970), as well as the National Bureau of Economic Research project (Bhagwati and Krueger 1973; Srinivasan and Bhagwati 1999), both offer evidence of the positive relationship between increased trade and growth. In a more recent study, David Dollar and Aart Kraay demonstrated that if the share of trade in GNP is used as a criterion of globalization, globalizers have enjoyed higher growth rates than non-globalizers (2001).

Second, the potential for global integration to reduce poverty and advance social welfare is well illustrated by the cases of such globalizers as Uganda and Vietnam. In Uganda, poverty fell about 40 per cent during the 1990s, while school enrollment doubled. In Vietnam, the income of the poor has risen dramatically, and the level of absolute poverty has been cut in half in ten years

(World Bank 2002, 6). As the most powerful evidence of the favorable effect of globalization on well-being and equity, the studies of Dollar and Kraay (2001, 2002, 2004) show that integration in the global economy benefits all social groups in a given country. In particular, they show that globalization and economic growth raised the incomes of the poor in developing countries by about as much as they raised the incomes of the non-poor for the time period under study.

Some contributors to this book further explore the findings of Dollar and Kraay (2001, 2002, 2004). Based on her comparison of Central and Eastern Europe and the Commonwealth of Independent States as well as an analysis of various regions within Russia, Ksenia Yudaeva corroborates the positive relationship between globalization, growth, and poverty reduction. In particular, she highlights some evidence that globalizers grow relatively faster and even more convincing evidence that although poverty has increased in transition economies, the rate of this increase is lower for 'active' globalizers compared to 'passive' globalizers and non-globalizers (173). Analysis by an author from the Middle East, Ali Abdel Gadir Ali, confirms that the Arab poor stand to benefit from trade-induced economic growth, even though they can benefit only by 50 per cent of the increase in per capita income – contrary to the celebrated result of Dollar and Kraay (2001, 2002) that promises the poor a one-to-one increase (52).

Third, the view of globalization as a beacon of stability also has supporters equipped with both compelling arguments and evidence. For example, Lawrence Summers argues that although economic growth in itself does not necessarily imply stability, 'economic integration engenders greater political stability and reduced potential for conflict' (Summers 1999). He cites Japan's dramatic post-war development and the more recent expansion of other economies of East Asia as the examples of mutually beneficial openness and peaceful integration into the global economy.

GLOBALIZATION'S FAULTS

Although the critics of globalization often equate this phenomenon with the rise in international trade and rarely dispute its ability to accelerate economic growth in select countries (the first of the above-discussed impacts), they perceive an outcome of global integration as fundamentally vicious, involving an increase in inequality and vulnerability. Curiously, the accounts of the detractors of globalization that are exactly opposite to those of its champions, are also promptly supported by evidence.

The negative impact of globalization is often illustrated by the example of China's entry into the global economy, which has coincided with an unparalleled rise in the country's within-country inequality. Similarly, regional Gini indices for Central and Eastern Europe and the CIS surged from 0.256 in 1988 to 0.464, in 1993, as these regions opened their economies (Milanovic 1999, 19). As shown by Grzegorz Kolodko in this volume, transition economies of Central and Eastern Europe and the CIS experienced a dramatic increase in inequality between the late 1980s (when it was lower than in Western Europe) and the early 2000s (when it became comparable with inequality in the rest of the world); the income distribution in Central and Eastern Europe and the CIS still remains in flux (203).

Finally, there are data consistent with the proposition that globalization raises the vulnerability of countries and individuals. Integration with international financial markets increases the propensity of a country to develop economic crises, which are in turn associated with enormous economic and psychological costs (World Bank 2000, p. 7). Nancy Birdsall (2001) argues that volatility, including some spells of negative growth, is more likely in more open economies. Bill Easterly et al. have advanced the same argument (2001). As acknowledged by Siow Yue Chia, a contributor to this volume from Singapore, the general perception of globalization's positive role in generating growth and employment in East Asia as well as in bolstering the sustainability of that region's economic miracle has been questioned in the aftermath of the 1997 financial crisis (98).

'TRUST BUT CLARIFY'

As is evident from our summary of the views on globalization, they range from very positive to exceedingly negative, and what is particularly surprising, every one of the opposing views can be corroborated by facts. This latter observation raises a series of questions: Why and how does globalization provoke such contradictory interpretations? Do the opposite interpretations hold any validity? Given the existing controversy, is it possible to arrive at a reasoned judgment on the merits of globalization and develop the means to cope with this phenomenon?

Offering some clues for unraveling these puzzles, one of the contributors to this volume, Ali, acknowledges that the term '"globalization" means different things to different people' (37). Other contributors, Roberto Bouzas and Ricardo Ffrench-Davis point to the different 'faces' of globalization,'which they interpret both as a market phenomenon and as a policy agenda that asymmetrically reflects preferences and vested interests. They distinguish between the 'positive' face of globalization – one that refers to structural trends in technology and their effects on economic distance – and the 'normative' face, which takes the shape of policy recommendations (217).

Learning from these insights by researchers from the developing world, the editors of this book have endeavored to help the reader 'cut through the confusion' by exploring in the opening chapter the extent to which the various interpretations of globalization are determined by the phenomenon's definition and measurement and/or by the reliance on specific examples to draw general conclusions. Thus, if perspectives on globalization are indeed closely tied to the specific understanding of globalization or the way in which it is measured, then it may be possible to reconcile the seemingly conflicting views of different authors. Similarly, since the impact of global integration is highly context-specific, the phenomenon provides an endless supply of fuel for the differing interpretations arrived at by different observers. To reduce misunderstandings arising from the reliance on individual country cases, the opening chapter considers aggregate data across various regions of the developing world. As a result, it paints a 'big picture,' distinguishing between regions-globalizers and non-globalizers. It also explores the consistency of general observations with specific evidence from various parts of the developing world and thus serves as a preview to the subsequent chapters.

DIVERSITY AND THE CAIRO CONSENSUS

The views of the contributors to this book reflect the disparate experiences of various regions and therefore inevitably diverge. Nevertheless, one should note that while Cairo conference participants often disagreed in their assessment of the present-day reality of globalization, they were mostly positive and constructive in their approach to the future. They highlighted the potential of globalization to improve the human condition and attempted to define the paths toward a more equitable world (Dinello 2003, 9–10).

As a result of this common view of the future, a surprising general consensus emerged at the conference. This 'Cairo Consensus' signifies a broad agreement on two key points. First, to escape the fate of marginalized pariahs, states should actively involve themselves in the global economy and society. Second, to maximally benefit from globalization, they must fully consider local circumstances and vigorously address the undesirable side effects of the phenomenon.

Within this fledgling consensus – with its dual welcome of the developing world's entry into a global universe and of its prudent adjustment to the perils of this endeavor – there are enthusiasts and skeptics among the contributors to this book. For example, S. Ibi Ajayi, author of Chapter 3 on Sub-Saharan Africa, reveals himself as an ardent proponent of globalization when he expresses his conviction that 'embracing globalization has been, is and still will be a key ingredient for Africa's successful economic growth and development' (90). On the other side of the spectrum, Bouzas and Ffrench-Davis, researchers from Latin America, doubt the researchers' ability to secure solid evidence on the relationship between globalization and equity and to offer credible advice to policy-makers on this subject (230).

Nevertheless, both Ajayi and the co-authors Bouzas and Ffrench-Davis believe that deeper integration into the world economy raises the potential for economic growth and for improved well-being, even though the recent experience of their respective regions suggests that such potential may not always materialize. In general, the authors of the subsequent chapters tend to largely support the view that globalization gives the developing world an opportunity – though not a guarantee – to accelerate economic growth and to eventually close the gap with the developed world. Regions reluctant to globalize risk falling behind, with implications for worldwide equity and vulnerability. To translate the globalization-linked opportunity into reality, effective home-grown policies to cope with the phenomenon are essential.

CONSENSUS: THESIS ONE

The contributors to this book generally endorse the thesis that full participation in the world economy is imperative for preventing marginalization of countries and regions and for mitigating inequity among them. In his discussion of South Asia, a newcomer to the global economy, Sisira Jayasuriya welcomes the vigorous 'opening up' of this region in recent decades, which represents an almost complete reversal of the protectionist policies of the 1970s, which were marked by pervasive state intervention in the domestic economies (137). Jayasuriya indicates that India has demonstrated unprecedented growth momentum and has achieved an impressive decline in absolute poverty (157).

Writing about East Asia – the region with a long and largely successful history of economic integration, Chia confirms that countries in the region are 'among the major beneficiaries of the global open trading system'. Furthermore, she argues, 'East Asian countries are among the major beneficiaries of the global open trading system… enabl[ing the region] to achieve economic progress beyond that achievable with the limited domestic resources and markets of individual economies' (99). In respect to China, whose pattern of inequality is dominated by regional disparities and the rural–urban gap, Chia agrees with the view that rising inequality is a result of differing regional degrees of participation in globalization, with globalized regions fairing better (123).

Consistent with his support for globalization, Ajayi notes that 'there are no successful cases of fast-growing countries that followed inward-looking policies' (90). He views the failures of Sub-Saharan Africa as the result of the lack of its 'meaningful integration' in the global economy. Even though there are external causes behind Africa's marginalization – the unfavorable terms of trade, the developed countries' trade restrictions on goods from Africa, and their subsidies for domestic agriculture – according to Ajayi, these factors do not fully explain the region's internal fiascos.

CONSENSUS: THESIS TWO

The general endorsement of globalization is, however, insufficient unless it is accompanied by explicit efforts to offset the negative side effects of globalization, considering specific local conditions and needs. Many contributors to this book link the success of these efforts to the quality of national institutions. Using evidence from the CIS, Yudaeva contends that strong institutions, together with a strong government commitment to secure a favorable investment climate, are essential for successful globalization – one that would positively affect the development of transition economies (187). While insisting on achieving equitable income distribution through smart indigenous policies, Ali cites Dani Rodrik, 'Policy makers need to forge a domestic growth strategy, relying on domestic investors and domestic institutions' (Rodrik 2001, 2).

Sharing the optimistic view that the negative effects of globalization can be counterbalanced by sound social policies and will be eventually more than compensated by faster economic growth, Ajayi emphasizes that the benefits of global integration for Africa are contingent on the continent's ability to improve institutions and initiate policy changes. His list of recommendations includes an improvement of macroeconomic fundamentals and the acceleration of structural reforms, adjustments in trade and combating capital flight, the development of the human capital and private sector development and the improvement of infrastructure and governance (88).

On a more pessimistic note, Bouzas and Ffrench-Davis signal the greatest frustration with the failure of Latin America to improve its income distribution, which remains the most unequal in the world, but also argue, 'Domestic institutions and policies are critical [for] reap[ing] the benefits of deeper integration into the world economy' (216). Even though they acknowledge that 'Globalization restricts the range of policy choice at the disposal of public sector officials,' they observe that the 'reduction in policy discretion has been uneven across countries,' thus indicating that globalization cannot be an excuse for the lack of will on the part of national governments to act (233).

The program of necessary government actions endorsed by Chia includes improvement of efficiency and cost competitiveness as well as innovation in both the national and regional contexts, while making a special provision for groups at the greatest risk of distress (133). Her proposal reflects the experience of the 1997 East Asian financial crisis, which disproportionately hit low-income groups. On his part, Jayasuriya echoes support for safety nets for the most vulnerable groups raised by Chia, Kolodko and other contributors to this book. He argues that in the context of South Asia, which is comparable only to Sub-Saharan Africa in its concentration of the poor, economic growth is sustainable only under conditions of public action intended to decrease inequality. He therefore encourages 'public action to provide less privileged households, communities and regions with broader access to resources such as education and skills, transport and communications infrastructure' as a means to control both economic and political volatility (158) .

INVOLVEMENT PLUS ADJUSTMENT

In summary, all contributors to this book, including the editors, share a belief that globalization helps (or may help) rather than hurts equity in the world. This consensus is very important, considering that it is endorsed by researchers from the developing world, the alleged victim of globalization.

It is also important that even the negative experience with globalization in some countries has not managed to invalidate the vital message reinforced in Cairo: To survive and prosper in the contemporary world, countries should involve in the process of globalization, while safeguards for the vulnerable groups and compensation for losers from globalization should be a part of the adjustment to the new global reality. The promise, if not yet the reality, of the positive impact of globalization on equity is thus predicated on the national governments' ability to handle this phenomenon to best effect.

By sponsoring this publication, GDN hopes to promote analysis by scholars from the developing world on the process of globalization and to share the convergence of their views, despite their disparate regional experiences, towards the Cairo consensus. By generally supporting social science research in the developing world, it also nurtures the reliable basis of this dialogue. GDN's capacity-building efforts would be rewarded if this book in any way contributes to clarifying and advancing the debate on globalization and equity. Its efforts in applying research to policy would be also rewarded if this book effectively adds the voices of researchers from the developing world to this debate and reaches the research community and policy-makers worldwide.

REFERENCES

Bhagwati, Jagdish (2004), *In Defense of Globalization*, New York: Oxford University Press.

Bhagwati, Jagdish and Anne Krueger (1973), 'Exchange control, liberalization and economic development', *American Economic Review*, **63** (2), 419–27.

Bhagwati, Jagdish and T.N. Srinivasan (2002), 'Trade and poverty in the poor countries', *American Economic Review*, **92** (2), 180–83.

Birdsall, Nancy (2001), 'New Findings in Economics and Demography: Implications for Policies to Reduce Poverty', in Nancy Birdsall, Allen C. Kelley and Duke Steven Sinding (eds.), *Population Matters – Demographic Change, Economic Growth and Poverty in the Developing World*, New York: Oxford University Press.

Dinello, Natalia (2004), 'Cairo consensus: reforms as a path to equitable globalization', *Globalism and Social Policy Programme: Policy Brief*, **4** (1), 9–26.

Dollar, David and Aart Kraay (2001), 'Globalization, Inequality and Poverty Since 1980,' World Bank: Washington, DC, www.worldbank.org/research/global.

Dollar, David and Aart Kraay (2002), 'Growth is good for the poor', *Journal of Economic Growth*, **7** (3), 195–225.

Dollar, David and Aart Kraay (2004), 'Trade, growth and poverty', *Economic Journal*, **114** (493), F22–F49.

Ebeid, Atef (2003), 'Egypt in a Globalizing World', speech delivered at the GDN Fourth Annual Conference, Cairo, Egypt, 19–21 2003 available at www.gdnet.org/pdf/Fourth_Annual_Conference/Plenary1/Ebeid_speech.pdf.

Easterly, Bill, Roumeen Islam and Joseph Stiglitz (2001), 'Volatility and Macroeconomic Paradigms for Rich and Poor Countries', in Jacques Dreze (ed), *Advances in Macroeconomic Theory*, New York: Palgrave.

Friedman, Thomas L. (1999), *The Lexus and the Olive Tree*, New York: Farrar, Straus & Giroux.

Little, Ian, Tibor Scitovsky and Maurice Scott (1970), *Industry and Trade in Some Developing Countries*, New York: Oxford University Press.

Milanovic, Branko (1999), 'True World Income Distribution, 1988 and 1993: First Calculations Based on Household Surveys Alone', Washington, DC, World Bank Working Paper No. 2244.

Mubarak, Suzanne (2003), 'Globalization, Gender and Development', speech delivered at the GDN Fourth Annual Conference, Cairo, Egypt, 19–21 2003, available at

www.gdnet.org/pdf/Fourth_Annual_Conference/WelcomingDinner/Suzanne_
Mubarak_speech.pdf.

Olson, Mancur with Martin C. McGuire (1996), 'The economics of autocracy and
majority rule: the invisible hand and the use of force', *Journal of Economic
Literature*, **34** (1), 72–96.

Rodrik, Dani (2001), 'Trading in illusions', *Foreign Policy*, **123** (2), 54–62.

Soros, George (2002), *George Soros on Globalization*, New York: Public Affairs.

Srinivasan, T.N. and Jagdish Bhagwati (1999), 'Outward Orientation and Development:
Are Revisionists Right?' festschrift for Anne Krueger, Columbia University,
New York, 19 September 1999, available at http://www.columbia.edu/~jb38/
Krueger.pdf.

Stiglitz, Joseph E. (2002), *Globalization and Its Discontents*, New York: W.W.
Norton.

Summers, Lawrence H. (1999), 'Distinguished lecture on economics in government:
reflections on managing global integration', *Journal of Economic Perspectives*, **13**
(2), 6–8.

World Bank (2002), *Globalization, Growth and Poverty: Building an Inclusive World
Economy*, New York: Oxford University Press.

World Bank (2000), 'Poverty in an Age of Globalization', World Bank Globalization
Briefing Paper, October.

1. Globalization and Equity: Cutting Through the Confusion

Natalia Dinello and Lyn Squire

As shown in the Introduction to this book, the views on globalization range from very positive to exceedingly negative. Moreover, the evidence supports the claims of benefits of globalization coexists with credible corroboration of its faults. This chapter explores two reasons for the variety of perspectives on globalization: the tendency of different observers to focus on particular aspects of the larger phenomenon; and their propensity to rely on specific examples to support more general propositions.

The first task of this chapter is to clarify the terms used in the ongoing debate on the impact of globalization on equity by reviewing the existing definitions of these phenomena, selecting their particular dimensions and measurements and analyzing their relationship using data across various regions of the developing world. To cut through the confusion caused by the proliferation of various conceptions of both 'globalization' and 'equity', we inquire into their numerous meanings and ask whether globalization in one dimension entails globalization in another. We suspect that the interpretation of globalization and its impact largely depends on its definition and on the choice of corresponding dimensions and measurement.

The chapter's second task is to shed light on the reasons why the drastically contrasting views on this matter can all be supported by evidence. To this end, we draw on aggregate global data in addition to individual countries. The methodology of complementing evidence from case studies with data from cross-national studies is consistent with a consensus that has emerged within the social sciences as to the value of both types of investigations (Laitin 2000). Overall, it is our belief that individual case studies, no matter how compelling, cannot substantiate a general conclusion. For generalizations to be truly convincing, global data are imperative.

If the views of the impact of globalization on equity were indeed determined by their attributed meanings, this finding would underpin the importance of careful definitions and explicit operationalization of concepts. If broad generalizations were not necessarily consistent with lessons from country cases, this would also rationalize contradictory beliefs, rather than questioning their validity. As a result, such an exploration would help remove the seeming disagreements on globalization and highlight the points of accord.

The essence of this chapter is captured in its structure, which includes four sections: definitions, conceptualization, evidence and consensus. The first two sections – on definitions and conceptualization – help to explain the diversity of views regarding the impact of globalization. Neither 'globalization' nor 'equity' is uniformly defined, especially when these concepts are interpreted to embrace not only economic dimensions but also political, social and cultural aspects. It should not be surprising that various authors arrive at different conclusions when they differ on basic concepts. Accordingly, Section 1 reviews the existing definitions of globalization and equity and chooses which operational definitions will be used in this chapter. Section 2 completes the argument by conducting an empirical analysis of the correlation between regional and country rankings, where each ranking reflects a different dimension and measurement of globalization. It demonstrates that some common measures of globalization in the economic and political sphere are not, in fact, positively related.

Next we consider evidence. Commentators often use specific examples to make their point. Predictably the coexistence of both positive and negative examples allows for the proliferation of different conclusions. For general inferences to have any value, however, it is important that the vivid but often context-specific examples that have inflamed the globalization debate be counterbalanced by global data. With this in mind, Section 3 examines the cross-regional and cross-country evidence on the relationship between measures of globalization in its two dimensions – economic and political – and two aspects of inequity: that *among* regions and countries, and that *within* regions and countries.

The evidence indicates changes in inequity *among* regions and countries as non-globalizers become marginalized, while some globalizers from the developing world manage to catch up with their more developed counterparts. This dynamic, in turn, exposes the dangers of the reluctance or inability to globalize as well as the benefits of global integration. The evidence also reveals the increasing inequity *within* some countries, especially those undergoing transition. This finding suggests that the transformation from centrally planned to market-based economic systems – a phenomenon associated with but not confined to globalization – may be the major cause of this unfortunate outcome.

Finally, we explore the consistency between our observations and the points of agreement among the authors of the subsequent chapters, that is the 'Cairo Consensus' outlined in the Introduction to this book. In particular, we highlight the common outlook on how to cope with globalization that emerges from the chapters despite the inevitable disagreements on specific issues. Readers dismayed by the wide range of conflicting contemporary views on globalization may see a ray of hope in the fledgling consensus on how to manage globalization to best effect.

DEFINITIONS

Globalization

Despite the large stock of literature on globalization, there is no single widely accepted definition of the phenomenon. Existing definitions range from those exclusively focused on economics – the level of integration of national economies into expanding international markets, particularly in terms of trade and capital investment – to broader descriptions of the interdependence of countries and regions of the world in economic, political, social, and cultural terms. Branko Milanovic identifies the 'Freedom and ability of individuals and firms to initiate voluntary economic transactions with residents of other countries' as a definition commonly used by World Bank researchers (Milanovic 2003, 6). However, not all World Bank researchers consistently follow this definition. For example, the report 'Poverty in an Age of Globalization' states, 'Globalization can be summarized as the global circulation of goods, services and capital, but also of information, ideas and people' (2000, 1). The report thus identifies several factors that mutually reinforce each other in promoting the integration of societies around the world.

Most of the contributors to this book emphasize the economic aspect in their definition of globalization. For example, Ali indicates that the term globalization 'refers to the observed process of increased international economic integration driven largely by technological advances in transport and communications.' Similarly, Sisira Jayasuriya conceives globalization as the 'opening up' of domestic economies to the global economy through the liberalization of trade and investment regimes, deregulation of domestic markets' and other processes.

Nevertheless, it must be recognized that the trend toward economic openness is occurring at the same time as increases in political, social, and cultural openness, which manifest themselves in the open flow of information, easily crossed borders, intensified cultural exchange and the development of global consciousness. While trade and financial liberalization stimulate economic integration, the democratization of societies nurtures political and socio-cultural integration, through a process that favors freedom of speech, travel and association. In an increasingly interdependent world, nations experience pressure from their neighbors and international organizations to 'open up' to a global society, meet globalization's challenges and devise means of adjustment to the inevitable social and cultural changes.

To reflect this broader conceptualization of globalization, this chapter explores both its political and economic dimensions. In addition to measures of economic integration (the shares of trade and foreign direct investment (FDI) in gross domestic product (GDP)), we consider measures of economic liberalization and political openness. At the same time, reflecting the dominance of the economic definition in the worldwide debate, we choose indicators of economic integration as the basis for comparison with other globalization measures, for distinguishing between regions, globalizers and non-globalizers and for analyzing the relationship between globalization and equity. These operational choices of basic indicators are driven by conventionalities as well as by data availability.

Equity

Similar to 'globalization', the term 'equity' is also defined in many different ways. The *Merriam-Webster Dictionary* describes it in the most general sense as 'justice according to natural law or right; specifically: freedom from bias or favoritism'. *Roget's Thesaurus* offers several definitions: impartiality, disinterestedness, even-handedness, fair play, fairness, integrity and justice. Equity is thus broader than income equality. The concept addresses both the equality of opportunity (the 'Fair Play' perspective) and the equality of condition (the 'Fair Shares' perspective) (Ryan 1981). The Fair Play perspective considers inequalities of income to be justified if they arise as a result of merit-based competition. In contrast, the equality of condition presupposes the rights of an individual to a reasonable share of societal resources or to a decent standard of living, connoting redistributive egalitarianism.

In the best-known conceptualization of equity, John Rawls (1971, 100) proposed corrective measures designed to ensure a fair system of equality of opportunity and a just system of end results. Calling it 'the principle of redress,' Rawls maintained that the social conditions necessary for true equality of opportunity have to be preserved within a framework of regulation by political and legal institutions, which may include the prevention of the excessive accumulation of property and wealth (73). In particular, Rawls (96) argued that social and economic inequalities are acceptable if they are arranged to improve the position of the least advantaged. This perspective places the focus squarely on the poorest of the poor.

When thought of in connection to globalization, equity certainly refers to both opportunities and end results. But in this case the term also captures the opportunities and equality of condition linked to the characteristics of a 'borderless' world, such as freedom of communication, travel and having a voice within the structures of international governance. This is consistent with a broader definition of globalization that encompasses the free movement of ideas and people as much as it does the free movement of goods and capital.

Similar to the basic operational definition of globalization as economic integration in this chapter, we rely on the narrow definition of inequity as the inequality of income. Its other aspects are intentionally left outside the scope of our analysis here, although we recognize their relevance and would welcome their exploration in reference to globalization.

CONCEPTUALIZING GLOBALIZATION: DIMENSIONS AND MEASURES

This section focuses on the relationships between various measures of three basic dimensions of globalization: economic integration, economic liberalization and political openness. We rely on data reported for the seven developing regions, with information on the high-income countries of the Organization for Economic Co-operation and Development (OECD) (excluding Eastern Europe, Turkey and Mexico) included as reference points. The use of aggregate data conceals significant within-region variation (a point to be explored later), but it has the advantage of providing a direct link to the subsequent chapters focused on particular regional contexts.

Economic Integration

The most commonly used measures of economic integration are the shares of combined exports and imports and gross FDI in GDP. As shown in Table 1.1, which contains data on both indicators for 2000, the rankings consistently highlight East Asia as the prime globalizer. This region is rated at the very top on both indicators. In 2000, combined exports and imports of this region amounted to 111 per cent of GDP, and its share of gross FDI in GDP (11.5 per cent) exceeded that of high-income OECD countries (10 per cent).

Table 1.1 Measures of Economic Integration: Trade and FDI

Region	Trade as share of GDP 2000 (%)	Rank	FDI as share of GDP 2000 (%)	Rank
Globalizers				
East Asia	110.99	1	11.50	1
Central/Eastern Europe	100.30	2	6.49	2
Commonwealth of Independent States	78.54	3	2.58	4
Non-globalizers				
Sub-Saharan Africa	63.54	4	1.91	6
Middle East/North Africa	63.36	5	1.96	5
Latin America/Caribbean	41.81	6	4.86	3
South Asia	33.95	7	0.63	7
High-income OECD	46.29		10.03	

The pattern, however, becomes more nuanced once we look beyond the leading globalizer. The transition economies of Central and Eastern Europe and the Commonwealth of Independent States (CIS) appear to have achieved stunning progress in joining the global economy in both dimensions, particularly in view of their prolonged isolation from the major markets until the late 1980s. Sub-Saharan Africa emerges as a surprising fourth-ranked region in terms of trade share. Much of African trade, however, reflects the continued reliance on traditional primary products rather than the penetration of new markets. The figures on FDI and the consequent ranking of Sub-Saharan Africa as the sixth region are more in line with the predominant understanding of this region as largely marginalized. Data for Latin America and the Caribbean demonstrate the reverse combination of characteristics: It is well integrated with respect to FDI but much less so with respect to trade. The Middle East and North Africa as well as South Asia are positioned near the bottom in both dimensions.

The two economic measures included in Table 1.1 do not fully reflect all dimensions of economic integration. Moreover, the regional aggregation hides sharp variations across countries and within regions. While the Pearson correlation coefficient between regional rankings by the two criteria of economic integration is 0.75, it is weaker between similar rankings of individual countries (0.45). Nevertheless, in order to draw the broad picture

Table 1.2 Measures of Economic Liberalization

Region	Integration Rank	Heritage Index Measure	Rank	Fraser Index Measure	Rank
Globalizers					
East Asia	1	3.50	3	5.58	5
Central/Eastern Europe	2	2.96	1	5.74	3
CIS	3	3.64	7	4.49	7
Non-globalizers					
Latin America/Caribbean	4	3.30	2	6.09	1
Middle East/North Africa	5–6	3.55	4	5.71	4
Africa	5–6	3.57	5–6	5.47	6
South Asia	7	3.57	5–6	5.96	2
High-income OECD		2.13	–	7.80	–

Note: Ranks in the first column reflect the averages of the two ratings in Table 1.1. In the Heritage Foundation index, 1 stands for the freest economies and 5 indicates the most economically repressed economy. In the Fraser Institute index, 0 indicates no economic freedom, and 10 stands for greatest economic freedom. Regional indexes are computed as the sum of country ratings weighted by population.

of global integration based on commodities and capital, we intentionally disregard variations and simplify the distinction between globalizers and non-globalizers by setting arbitrary benchmarks. For the purpose of this chapter, we describe regions as globalizers if their volume of trade exceeds 75 per cent of their GDP and their volume of FDI exceeds 2.5 per cent of their GDP. These dual criteria place East Asia, Central and Eastern Europe, and the Commonwealth of Independent States among the globalizers and Sub-Saharan Africa, Middle East and North Africa, Latin America and the Caribbean, and South Asia among the non-globalizers. We will use this categorization as the starting point for our comparison with other dimensions of globalization— those reflecting government policies and the legal structures that determine formal arrangements for economic and political openness.

Economic Liberalization

Measures of economic integration depend on a range of factors, including the size of the domestic economy, the availability of natural resources and the economic policies of the country. Therefore, measures of globalization based on policy and legal arrangements need not necessarily coincide with measures of integration. To explore the relationship between these two sets of measures, we draw on the Heritage Foundation/Wall Street Journal *Index of Economic Freedom* (Miles et al. 2004)[1] and the Fraser Institute *Economic Freedom of the World* Index (Gwartney et al. 2003).[2]   Table 1.2 allows for comparison of the regional rankings based on data for trade and FDI (Table 1.1) with those reflecting indexes of economic freedom and liberalization. (Appendix includes detailed data on these indexes.)

Table 1.2 reveals a high correlation between the regional rankings (0.68) in the Heritage and Fraser indexes. There is an even higher correlation between the country rankings (0.85), suggesting that notwithstanding the regional aggregation, the two indicators of economic liberalization paint a similar picture. At the same time, the table demonstrates the complexity of the globalization phenomenon. The data suggest that formal economic freedom – as determined by government policies and legal structures – does not always translate into actual economic integration, and that, vice versa, some markets manage to 'open up' against the backdrop of state regulation. At the country level, the Pearson correlation coefficients between the rankings for economic integration (trade shares) and for economic liberalization, as measured by the Heritage and Fraser Indexes, tend toward zero.

As seen from Table 1.2, the selection of a particular measure of globalization largely determines conclusions about its extent. Thus, based on the measures of economic liberalization, the Commonwealth of Independent States can be categorized as a non-globalizer and the Latin America and Caribbean region as a globalizer. This finding is the exact reverse of the result emerging from the analysis of measures of economic integration. As suspected, the definition of globalization and the choice of measurement determine the interpretation of this phenomenon and the ensuing classification of regions.

Political Openness

To address the broader conceptualization of globalization as a phenomenon going beyond economics, we must, at a minimum, capture the characteristics of political openness. Therefore, we rely on the following measures. First, ratings compiled on the basis of the *Freedom in the World* surveys conducted

Table 1.3 Political Openness and Democracy

Region	Integration Rank	Freedom Rank	*Dem* Rank	*Parcomp* Rank	*EIEC* Rank	*LIEC* Rank
Globalizers						
East Asia	1	5	7	7	7	7
Central/Eastern Europe	2	3	1	1	2	1
CIS	3	7	4	4	4	5
Non-globalizers						
Latin America/Caribbean	4	1	2	2	1	2
Middle East/North						
Africa	5–6	4	6	5	6	6
Africa	5–6	6	5	6	3	4
South Asia	7	2	3	3	5	3

by Freedom House.[3] Second, two variables – extent of democracy (DEM) and openness of the political system or party competitiveness (PARCOMP) – from the Polity IV data series assembled by the Center for International Development and Conflict Management (CIDCM) of the University of Maryland.[4] Third, the Executive Index of Electoral Competitiveness (EIEC) and the Legislative Index of Electoral Competitiveness (LIEC) from the Database of Political Institutions compiled by the Development Research Group of the World Bank.[5] (The Appendix to this chapter includes detailed data on these measures.)

The literature on globalization suggests that economic integration and political democracy may reinforce each other. Globalization imposes pressures on countries to democratize – a phenomenon labeled as the 'diffusion' or 'political contagion' of democracy (Diamond 2000; Coppedge 1999). Apart from driving democratization through forces outside country borders, globalization may influence it indirectly domestically. Several studies have shown that advances in standards of living and wealth produce a measurable positive effect on democracy (Barro 1999; Burkhart and Lewis-Beck 1994; Pei 1999). When international trade and injections of foreign capital improve economic indicators, they can also make society more politically open. In turn, democratization can make the free movement of capital, ideas and people both possible and customary, further promoting globalization.

In this respect, the evidence reveals a high degree of consistency among measures of political freedom, in that the high-income OECD countries (not shown in Table 1.3) are the most politically open societies, followed in the developing world by Central and Eastern Europe, Latin America and the Caribbean, and South Asia, in that order (see Table 1.3). Regional rankings reflecting various measures of political openness are highly correlated, in some cases exceeding the value of 0.9 for the correlation coefficient. There is also consistency between the indicators of political openness of these regions and their economic liberalization ratings, which highlight the OECD countries as the freest economies and Central and Eastern Europe, Latin America and the Caribbean, and South Asia as the least repressed regions in the developing world. At the country level, the Pearson correlation coefficient of rankings based on political freedom (Freedom House ratings) and economic liberalization (Heritage index) is 0.72.

However, the relationship between either political freedom or economic liberalization and the degree of economic integration is far from clear-cut. This is best illustrated by the example of the leading regional globalizer as measured by economic integration: East Asia. Almost consistently ranked as the least politically free and economically somewhat repressed region in 2000, East Asia nevertheless achieved high levels of international trade and FDI. On a more general note, country-level rankings on political freedom do not correlate with rankings based on economic integration. This is similar to the lack of relationship between economic integration and economic liberalization.

Corroborating our earlier observation, Table 1.3 shows that the meaning we attribute to globalization largely determines our perception of the participation of various regions in the process. In particular, it demonstrates that global integration in its economic dimension does not necessarily entail globalization in terms of political openness and vice versa. The close correlation between measures of economic liberalization and political freedom suggests that a common set of institutional factors influences both. Meanwhile, the lack of correlation of either of these measures with economic integration implies that the latter may be largely determined by other factors, such as the size of the domestic economy and the natural resource base.

General Trends and Variations

Our exploration of economic and political openness in the developing world largely confirms the views of the contributors to this book. According to Chia, East Asia is fully involved in the global economy, although the public sentiment about this involvement is mixed, demonstrating temporal ups and downs. As argued by Kolodko, Central and Eastern Europe aggressively pursues acceptance by global players, but the combination of globalization and transition has led to painful shifts in society. The Commonwealth of Independent States countries display signs of being integrated into the global economy and society, but this process has been slow and hesitant (Yudaeva). According to Bouzas and Ffrench-Davis, Latin America continues to experience enormous struggles with globalization. Ali's and Ajayi's respective presentations of Middle East and North Africa and Sub-Saharan Africa paint a picture of those regions as being mostly marginalized. Finally, according to Jayasuriya, South Asia has only recently embarked on the path of globalization and is yet to reap the benefits of its global engagement.

The general trends highlighted in Tables 1.1–1.3 conceal, however, significant variations among the countries within each region. For instance, within East Asia, Singapore and Hong Kong were rated as the freest economies in the world – even more free than high-income OECD countries. At the same time, Singapore and Hong Kong demonstrated the greatest integration in the global economy – unmatched by any other country in the world, at least in terms of trade. In 2000 their shares of trade in GDP amounted to 339.6 and 295.4 per cent, and shares of FDI in GDP were 11.2 and 85.4 per cent, respectively. Similarly, in Central and Eastern Europe, Estonia and the Czech Republic were rated as the most economically free countries in their region, on par with high-income OECD countries. These countries also achieved high economic openness in terms of trade and FDI.

Yet, this country-level consistency between economic freedom and integration does not occur for every country, which explains contradictory cumulative indicators for the regions. Thus, the largest East Asian country, China, with its political suppression and insufficient economic liberties, influences the overall picture of high economic integration in the region combined with the lack of economic and political freedom. In Central and Eastern Europe, there is a gap between the most successful reforming countries that serve as the vehicles of globalization (such as Estonia, Slovakia and the Czech Republic) and the weaker reformers, which lag behind in terms of economic integration (such as Albania and Romania).

The evidence confirms that while a combination of economic and political freedom can create a favorable climate for integration into world markets (as indicated by the cases of the OECD and Central and Eastern Europe countries), the actual degree of integration depends on other factors as well; reality does not always match theoretical expectations. As shown in Tables 1.2 and 1.3, formal arrangements of economic and political openness cannot serve as predictors of actual globalization as measured by economic integration. Regimes lacking in civil liberties and political competitiveness (such as many countries of East Asia) can still be economic globalizers, while societies with flourishing democracies (such as India) lag far behind in terms of economic integration. It requires time and the confluence of several factors to create the incentives and opportunities for a country to be fully incorporated in the global economy.

The intricate interaction between economic and sociopolitical factors can be demonstrated by referring to the cumulative A.T. Kearney/Foreign Policy Magazine Globalization Index, which is based on the broad assessment of information technology, finance, trade, personal communication, politics and travel.[6] Consistent with some of our previous observations, high-income OECD countries emerged in the 2002 Globalization Index (2000 data) as unambiguous globalizers, ranked as a group higher than countries in any region of the developing world: among the top 15 countries, 14 were OECD countries, with Ireland occupying first place. In East Asia, tiny Singapore was ranked as the third most globalized country of the world, while the populous states of China and Indonesia were located close to the bottom—as 53rd and 59th respectively; their relatively low rankings are due not only to economic indicators, such as trade and FDI, but also to the underdevelopment of international tourism and Internet usage and to rather weak political engagement. The variation among countries in the Central and Eastern Europe region is less stunning: most of them ranked immediately after the OECD countries. The leaders in terms of globalization were the Czech Republic and Slovakia. Of the 62 countries included in the Globalization Index, Iran was at the very bottom (using both 2000 and 2002 data), immediately preceded by Peru and Colombia in 2000 and by India and Egypt in 2002.

EVIDENCE ON GLOBALIZATION AND EQUITY

While the authors of the subsequent chapters discuss the relationship between globalization and equity in intricate detail based on data from various regions, we focus here on the extent to which two widely held views on the issue are supported by the available evidence. These common views may be summarized as follows:

- Globalization is associated with increasing inequity *among* regions and countries.
- Globalization is associated with increasing inequity *within* regions and countries.

These two propositions constitute the heart of the critics' concern about the impact of globalization. As indicated above, for the purpose of distinguishing between globalizers and non-globalizers, we use an operational definition of globalization as economic integration. However, to test the two propositions, we explore both economic integration as measured by trade and FDI as shares of GDP (Table 1.1) and political openness as measured by Freedom House ratings. The previous section on 'Conceptualizing Globalization' has shown that Freedom ratings are highly correlated with measures of economic liberalization (Table 1.2) and with other indicators of political freedom and democracy (Table 1.3). As another reminder, inequity is operationally defined as the inequality of income.

Inequity among Regions and Countries

While disparity among countries is a fact of life, it is not cast in stone. Between-country inequalities – differences in the average incomes of national populations – change depending on the countries' relative economic performance. In a situation where low-income countries are able to accelerate their rate of growth beyond that achieved by rich countries, inequality between nations will decline. However, if low-income countries see their growth rates plummet, then differences between countries will inevitably widen. Considering the importance of economic growth for the relative well-being of regions and countries, we will explore whether growth and globalization go together. If indeed economic and political openness are consistent with growth, it is reasonable to assume that participation in the globalization process can decrease inequities among regions and countries.

Economic integration and growth
It is widely believed that international trade constitutes an 'engine of growth'. Reinforcing the argument in favor of international trade, practically no country applying autarkic policies has managed to sustain a high growth performance over a prolonged period (Bhagwati and Srinivasan 2002). A combination of the failure to take advantage of free trade opportunities and other ineffective domestic policies leads to marginalization, as shown in this volume by Ali and Ajayi with respect to Middle East and North Africa and Sub-Saharan Africa, respectively. But even if we disregard the impact of other domestic policies, the resistance to integrate into the global economy under conditions when one's neighbors 'open up' decreases market shares of exports and doubly disadvantages non-globalizers. A recent study suggests that Middle East and North Africa countries have experienced serious challenges from the open trade policies introduced by their key competitors in global markets (Esfahani and Squire 2004). Whenever countries try to remain outside the process of globalization, they run the risk of declining export shares as their competitors adopt more effective trade policies. This finding helps us to understand why

Table 1.4 Economic Integration and Growth

Region	Integration Rank	Net Growth Rank	Net growth per capita, 1980– 2000 (%)	GDP per capita, 1980*	GDP per capita, 2000*
Globalizers					
East Asia	1	1	202.8	376.5	1139.8
Central/ Eastern Europe	2	3	22.4	2751.6	3368.6
CIS	3	7	–44.9	3055.1	1683.1
Non-globalizers					
Latin America/ Caribbean	4	4	12.5	3626.5	4079.3
Middle East/ North Africa	5–6	5	7.6	2353.6	2533.2
Sub-Saharan Africa	5–6	6	–25.5	789.2	588.1
South Asia	7	2	99.8	240.2	479.9
High-income OECD	–	–	53.3	19735.8	30259.1

Notes: Net growth is computed as the difference between GDP per capita for 2000 and 1980, divided by GDP per capita for 1980.
*In constant 1995 US$.

many non-globalizers have been marginalized as a result of their resistance to global integration.

Largely confirming the benefits of economic integration for economic growth, Table 1.4 distinguishes East Asia as the most dynamically developing region, with its 2000 GDP per capita exceeding the 1980 level by a factor of three. At the other extreme, one of the non-globalizers – Sub-Saharan Africa – saw its GDP per capita plummet by a quarter during the same period. The implications for individual well-being are enormous. According to Table 1.4, the average person from Sub-Saharan Africa had twice as much income as the average East Asian in 1980, but only one-half 20 years later. While GDP per capita in high-income OECD countries exceeded the same indicator in Sub-

Saharan Africa 25 times in 1980, this differential increased to almost 52 times in 2000. This last observation, more than any other, has led to the common view that inequity is increasing in the world. While East Asian and Central and Eastern Europe countries have reduced their gap with the high-income OECD countries, many non-globalizers, in particular most countries of the Middle East and North Africa and Latin America and the Caribbean, have seen their relative positions worsen, while Sub-Saharan Africa has clearly been marginalized.

Yet, the experience of globalizers and non-globalizers is far from uniform. South Asia has achieved much better economic performance in 1980–2000 than could be predicted based on the degree of its economic integration, while the CIS, due to continuing political and economic turmoil since the late 1980s, has experienced an even greater decline than Sub-Saharan Africa. The following chapters on various regions of the world help to explain the varied outcomes. Our task at this point is merely to highlight the apparent broad relationship between globalization and economic performance. In this respect, we note a modest correlation (the Pearson correlation coefficient is 0.43) between regions' ranks determined by one indicator of economic integration – the share of FDI in GDP – and by the net growth in their per capita income, even though regional aggregation hides significant variations among countries (the Pearson correlation coefficient between the same country-level rankings is lower at 0.22).

A review of Table 1.4 suggests, however, that there are two obvious outliers among the regions in terms of their growth record as related to their globalization characteristics. One of them is the CIS, where a painful transformation of its socioeconomic system caused a protracted economic crisis, from which this region is still recovering. Another outlier is South Asia, whose impressive net growth in the 1980s and 1990s happened against the backdrop of considerable political openness but weak economic integration into the global world. Excluding these two regions from the calculation of the correlation between the regional integration and net growth ranks yields a very strong Pearson correlation coefficient of 0.98. On the country level, if we exclude the CIS countries and South Asia, the Pearson correlation coefficient between rankings based on international trade and net growth amounts to 0.36, while the same coefficient between rankings based on FDI and net growth is 0.34.

Similar to Central and Eastern Europe, the globalizing countries within the CIS have already accelerated their growth. It remains to be seen whether such economic performance will be sustainable in the long run. It also remains to be seen whether South Asia could continue on the path of relatively fast growth if it fails to better integrate in the global economy. In any case, the above-noted correlation coefficients as well as the experiences of individual regions and countries – both successful globalizers and failing non-globalizers – provide some support for the proposition that participation in the global economy brings benefits in the form of higher growth. But because many other factors are also at play there is no systematic or automatic relationship between integration in the world economy and economic performance.

Political openness and growth
It was shown above that measures of economic integration and political openness are not closely correlated. Nevertheless, it is widely believed that political openness has value in its own right and leads to a higher quality of life. In addition to providing opportunities to engage in economic activities with foreign partners, the politically globalized world offers international travel and the exchange of information without any restrictions. It also supports at least minimum guarantees of human rights and security, through media-enforced transparency and pressure from international institutions. Some studies suggest that democracy is a prerequisite for sustained growth (Olson 1996), that economic development fosters democratic performance (Burkhart and Lewis-Beck 1994) and that democracy improves growth by reinforcing progress in economic liberalization (Fidrmuc 2003). Although tensions between political democratization and economic adjustment are recognized – as shown by the analysis of African societies struggling to achieve economic equity and to consolidate fragile democracy – it is considered possible to reconcile the political and economic processes (Sandbrook 1997).

Even among many of the studies doubting the existence of a relationship between democracy and economic growth, there is evidence that democratic regimes produce stable, not high or low, growth in national income (Quinn and Wooley 2001), and that democratization has, at least, not undermined economic performance (Fish 1999). The reverse effects of income on democracy – via investment in physical and human capital – have been found to be robust and positive (Helliwell 1994).

Consistent with these observations on the link between political freedom and economic growth, Table 1.5 highlights the correspondence between Freedom and Net Growth ranks of all regions, with the exception of East Asia and Latin America and the Caribbean. South Asia – the second fastest growing area of the world, where GDP per capita doubled from 1980 to 2000 – has enjoyed considerable political openness (ranking second in terms of political freedom), while the region's economies have benefited from the recent wave of liberalization in the 1990s, as indicated by Jayasuriya in this book. Overall, there is a substantial correlation (the Pearson correlation coefficient is 0.54) between regions' Freedom and Net Growth ranks and a modest correlation

Table 1.5 Political Openness and Economic Growth

Region	Freedom Rank	Net Growth Rank	Net Growth per capita, 1980–2000 (%)
Globalizers			
East Asia	5	1	202.8
Central/Eastern Europe	3	3	22.4
CIS	7	7	−44.9
Non-globalizers			
Latin America/ Caribbean	1	4	12.5
Middle East/North Africa	4	5	7.6
Sub-Saharan Africa	6	6	−25.5
South Asia	2	2	99.8

Note: The Freedom rank reflects the ratings of the Freedom House surveys. It is highly correlated with other ranks of political openness in Table 1.3. The net growth is computed as the difference between GDP per capita for 2000 and 1980, divided by GDP per capita for 1980.

between the same country-level rankings (the Pearson correlation coefficient is 0.36).

In the same vein, Central and Eastern Europe — the region ranked third on Net Growth – has achieved high levels of economic liberalization and political freedom as well as economic integration (see Tables 1.2–1.4). Note that contrary to Central and Eastern Europe, the CIS – another economically integrated globalizer – ranks last among the developing/transition regions on both net growth and political freedom. As suggested by Table 1.5, this contrast between the CIS's sharp net decline and Central and Eastern Europe's moderate growth can be linked to the more effective political transformation of the latter region. Indeed, Central and Eastern Europe launched and implemented both political and economic reforms earlier and more consistently than the CIS during the tumultuous 1980s and 1990s. While both South Asia and Central and Eastern Europe are in the process of catching up with more prosperous countries, the Middle East and North Africa and Sub-Saharan Africa are lagging even further behind due to low economic growth in the former and net decline in the latter region. The dismal economic performance of both regions matches their lack of political freedom.

To summarize the findings from both Tables 1.4 and 1.5, the regions' Net Growth ranks are consistent with either their indicators of economic integration or with characteristics of political openness at a regional level, but not necessarily with both of these measures of globalization on a systematic basis at the country level. As we have shown, globalization has many facets, and one facet does not automatically predicate the presence of another in a given country. As a result, we observe that economic growth goes together with at least some measures of globalization and can be reinforced by their combination, with important implications for inequality among regions and countries. Those developing countries involved in globalization in at least some of its aspects have a greater chance of eventually catching up with their more developed counterparts. The drastically divergent rates of integration can, however, lead to a widening gap among countries.

Inequity within Regions and Countries

While differences between average income levels across countries are a matter of concern to all throughout the world, each country is particularly preoccupied with its own internal disparities. In this context, the critics of globalization have blamed the phenomenon for rising inequality and specifically for hurting the poor. To explore the alleged link between globalization and within-country inequities, we first examine whether economic integration goes together with economic inequality as measured by the Gini coefficient. We then focus on the most vulnerable group, the poor, to examine whether the evidence is consistent with the claim that globalization increases misery, as argued by the detractors of globalization, or whether it actually reduces poverty, as the proponents of global integration believe. Finally, we address an issue of political openness and probe the link between political freedom and inequality as measured by the Gini coefficient.

Economic integration and income inequality

The 2002 World Bank report *Globalization, Growth and Poverty* concludes that within countries, globalization has not, on average, affected inequality, and that growth in the new globalizers can be a political opportunity for redistribution policies that favor the poor (p. 2). As discussed in the Introduction to this book, the studies of Dollar and Kraay (2001, 2002, 2004) present impressive evidence on the positive relationship between globalization, general well-being and poverty reduction, which is corroborated by the findings of other researchers.

Yet, the analysis of globalization and income distribution offered by Milanovic portrays a more complicated picture: The effect of openness on income distribution depends on a country's average income level, and openness makes income distribution worse before making it better. Specifically, in

Table 1.6 Economic Integration and Income Inequality

Region	Integration Rank	Inequality Reduction Rank	Mean Gini 1981	Mean Gini 2001	Annual Change in Inequality 1981–2001 (%)
Globalizers					
East Asia	1	4	0.3673	0.4001	0.45
Central/Eastern Europe and CIS	2–3	6–7	0.2358	0.3739	2.93
Non-globalizers					
Latin America/ Caribbean	4	5	0.4656	0.5157	0.55
Middle East/North Africa	5–6	1	0.4318	0.3687	−0.73
Sub-Saharan Africa	5–6	3	0.4816	0.4614	−0.21
South Asia	7	2	0.3340	0.3162	−0.27
High-income OECD	–	–	0.3505	0.3746	0.34

Note: The country-level data on the Gini coefficients were aggregated to the regional level by calculating simple, not population-weighted, averages.

countries with low average income levels, the rich initially benefit from openness. But as income rises, that is around the income level of $5,000–$7,000 per capita at international prices, the situation changes and the relative income of the poor and the middle class rises compared to the rich (Milanovic 2003). The complexity of the relationship has been also revealed by another study by Milanovic and Squire (2003). The authors explore the impact of trade openness on the labor market, focusing on the area that is most immediately affected by globalization. The results of their study suggest that trade reforms tend to increase inter-occupational wage inequality and skill premiums, while reducing wage inequality between industries.

In our analysis of the economic aspects of globalization and within-country inequality, we rely on the expanded Deininger and Squire dataset on income inequality, initially published in 1996 (Deininger and Squire 1996), to determine regional achievements in reducing inequality. The regions' Inequality Reduction ranks are based on the annual percentage change in the Gini coefficient between 1981 and 2001, and are compared with the regions'

Integration ranks based on their international trade and FDI. In addition, we consider the results of country-level least-squares regressions using Gini data for the pre-globalization era and the period of global integration (after 1989).[7]

Table 1.6 reveals two points. First, with one important exception – that is in the combined rank for Central and Eastern Europe/CIS – annual changes in inequality have been relatively small. For example, the Gini index for Sub-Saharan Africa has barely moved in 20 years. As we shall see, the implication of this finding is that growth in average income is usually the critical factor in determining the outcome for the most vulnerable group, the poor. A further implication is that cross-country empirical analyses cannot easily isolate the impact of global integration – for example, that of trade openness – on inequality, precisely because changes in inequality tend to be small. As a result, even minor changes in the sample of countries or time periods can lead to different results in cross-country econometric analysis, as the literature reveals.

The second implication is central for the debate on globalization and equity. Table 1.6 shows that the only regions to experience a reduction in inequality– the Middle East and North Africa, South Asia and Sub-Saharan Africa – are all in the category of non-globalizers, according to their degree of integration in the world economy. At the same time, the regions characterized as globalizers – East Asia and Central and Eastern Europe/CIS – saw inequality worsen. This appears to provide evidence in support of the argument that integration in the global economy increases inequality within regions and countries, even though the changes themselves may be small.

Before unequivocally endorsing this argument, however, we should explore an alternative explanation. Consider the results of the country-level linear models using Gini data (minimum three observations since 1989) for 50 countries worldwide (Deininger and Squire 2004). The period covered by these data thus corresponds to the era usually associated with the phenomenon of globalization. A statistical test of regression coefficients failed to prove significance of any trend in 35 of the 50 countries, thereby confirming the relative stability of income distribution, even through the period of most intensive global integration. In 13 countries, however, an upward trend is clearly detectable. Of these, ten, including China, are countries undergoing transition from centrally planned economic systems to market-based ones. The effect of transition is also apparent from a comparison of transition economies and other countries in the entire sample of 50 countries. Of the 17 transition countries, ten, or almost 60 per cent, saw inequality rise. In the remainder of the sample, only 3, or less than 10 per cent out of 33 countries, experienced an increase in inequality. The upsurge of the Gini coefficients in transition economies is both obvious and logical, considering their historical shift from politically enforced income leveling to the triumph of market forces in determining the labor costs.

When we consider the region most integrated in the world economy, East Asia, we arrive at similar conclusions. Of the six East Asian counties with sufficient Gini observations after 1989, only two – China and Singapore – experienced a rise in inequality, one (Thailand) saw inequality decline and the remaining three exhibited no trend either way. Thus, if we exclude the one transition economy (China), inequality increased only in one country out of five globalizers. Contributing to the Cairo Consensus on the positive impact of globalization, these findings suggest that while some countries may have experienced an upsurge in inequality, and while some groups may have suffered income losses attributable to globalization, there is no compelling evidence that globalization systematically increases inequality within countries. If anything, the evidence points to the dominant role of the transition from centrally planned to market-based economies as the explanatory factor behind the upsurge in inequality within these countries.

To summarize our discussions of inequity *among* and *within* regions and countries, we have observed significant differences in terms of the growth of national economies and of their involvement in the globalization process, with serious implications for further expansion of between-country inequality, while annual changes in within-country inequality have proven to be relatively small and largely unaffected by the process of globalization. These findings echo Milanovic's calculations of the distribution of world income inequality based on household surveys, which peculiarly capture changes in inequality both among and within countries. Milanovic demonstrates that world income inequality increased from 1988 to 1993 and that between-country inequalities are the most important factor behind world inequality, with differences between countries' mean incomes explaining 75–88 per cent of overall inequality (Milanovic 1999, 51). This evidence reinforces the argument that the impact of globalization on worldwide equity has mostly manifested itself in the decline in the income of marginalized countries, relative to globalizing nations, rather than in increases in within-country inequality.

Economic integration, growth and poverty reduction

Given two of our preceding observations – that the regions and countries integrated into the world economy tend to grow faster than others and that income distribution within countries is relatively stable – it should come as no surprise that globalizing countries have often enjoyed significant reductions in poverty. Indeed, it is now well established that economic growth usually reduces poverty. It has been shown, for example, that aggregate economic growth is highly correlated with growth in the incomes of the poor and that

Table 1.7 Economic Integration, Growth and Poverty Reduction

Region	Integration Rank	Net Growth Rank	Poverty Reduction Rank	Population living below $1 per day 1981 (%)	Population living below $1 per day 2001 (%)
Globalizers					
East Asia	1	1	1	57.7	15.6
Central/Eastern Europe	2	3	6	0.3	1.4
CIS	3	7	7	0.3	6.4
Non-globalizers					
Latin America/ Caribbean	4	4	4	9.7	9.5
Middle East/North Africa	5–6	5	3	5.1	2.4
Sub-Saharan Africa	5–6	6	5	41.6	46.4
South Asia	7	2	2	51.5	31.3

Note: The source of most figures in the last two columns is Chen and Ravallion (2004, Table 1). The 2001 figures for Central and Eastern Europe and the CIS are calculated using PovcalNet, an interactive electronic tool that allows replicating calculations by World Bank's researchers. No distinction is made between the 1981 figures for Central and Eastern Europe and the CIS because information on PovcalNet is insufficient for this purpose.

countries that have been successful in terms of economic growth are also very likely to have been successful in reducing poverty (Bigsten and Levin 2001). On average across countries, an increase of 1 per cent in average income corresponds to an increase of 1 per cent in the income of the poor (Gallup et al. 1998). Chia's review in this book of the studies on globalization in East Asia highlights research by Barry Eichengreen, which demonstrates that poverty in East Asia declined sharply between 1975 and 1995 (Eichengreen 2002). Another study, by Yunling Zhang and coauthors, shows China's great benefits from opening up to the outside world, including pronounced poverty reduction (Yunling et al. 2002).

Table 1.7 explores whether the benefits of globalization and growth do indeed translate into poverty reduction. As seen from the table, the fastest growing regions – East Asia and South Asia – have been the most successful in decreasing the percentage of their population living in abject poverty. There is perfect consistency between their highest Net Growth and Poverty Reduction ranks. On the other side of the spectrum, the regions that experienced net economic decline in 1980–2000, the CIS and Sub-Saharan Africa, simultaneously saw an upsurge in the population living below $1 per day. However, as already shown above, the CIS and Central and Eastern Europe represent special cases, as regions that have recently rejected an egalitarian ideology, with inevitable implications for their policies and ensuing increases in inequality.

The country-level analysis confirms regional observations. The leading fast-growing globalizers in the developing world, such as Hong Kong and Singapore, have achieved high standards of living, comparable to those of the OECD countries, and alleviated abject poverty. The Central and Eastern Europe countries and successful country outliers in the less integrated regions (such as Chile) have also attained higher rates of well–being and relatively low poverty. At the same time, many countries of Latin America and the Caribbean, the Middle East and North Africa and Sub-Saharan Africa cannot escape the vicious cycle of resistance to globalization, autarky, low or negative economic growth and continuous misery. The favorable impact of economic integration on the standards of living in general, and poverty reduction in particular, is another critical ingredient of the Cairo Consensus.

Political openness and income inequality
The relationship between political openness and within-country inequality is, meanwhile, more complicated than the link between economic openness and inequality. Contrary to the theoretical expectation that democracy should lead to a more equal income distribution, most empirical studies have failed to prove this relationship. Seeking to understand this enigma, Mark Gradstein, Branko Milanovic and Yvonne Ying have argued that the democratization effect works through ideology. In societies where equality is highly valued (Confucian and communist societies), there is less of a distributional conflict across income groups hence democratization may have only a negligible effect on inequality. On the other hand, in societies where equality is not valued as much (Protestant/mixed Christian societies and societies without a dominant religion), democratization reduces inequality through redistribution, as the poor outvote the rich (Milanovic et al. 2001). However, regardless of ideology, and contradicting earlier research that failed to detect the effect of democracy on inequality, the most recent study by Milanovic has found that democracy has a positive effect on the income shares of the middle classes, while leaving unchanged those at the top and the bottom (Milanovic 2003, 23–24).

Table 1.8 Political Openness and Income Inequality

Region	Freedom Rank	Least Inequality Rank, 2001	Mean Gini 2001
Globalizers			
East Asia	5	5	0.4001
Central/Eastern Europe	3	3–4	0.3739
CIS	7	3–4	0.3739
Non-globalizers			
Latin America/ Caribbean	1	7	0.5157
Middle East/North Africa	4	2	0.3687
Sub-Saharan Africa	6	6	0.4614
South Asia	2	1	0.3162
High-income OECD			0.3746

Note: The country-level data on the Gini coefficients were aggregated to the regional level by calculating simple, not population-weighted, averages.

At the same time, some studies offer evidence of the relationship between economic development (in particular, the standard of living), and a gradual rise in democracy (Barro 2000, 42). Moreover, the relationship between the level of economic development and the level of democracy found in most quantitative cross-national research implies that the largest gains in democracy are experienced by countries at intermediate levels of development, which in turn are associated with the highest levels of income inequality (Muller 1995).

To explore the link between political openness and income distribution, Table 1.8 draws on the inequality data presented in Table 1.6. It ranks regions by their degree of inequality and compares the outcome with ranking according to the Freedom Index. A comparison of these ranks produces a contradictory picture. On the one hand, it suggests that political openness – under which the public has a voice – may matter for limiting inequality. South Asia, which ranks second on freedom, has the lowest mean Gini coefficient in the world and has managed to reduce inequality since 1981. In contrast, East Asia experiences both the lack of freedom and high and increasing income inequality. However, the persistence of drastic inequality in the freest region, Latin America and the

Caribbean, and much lesser inequality in the largely authoritarian Middle East and North Africa leads us to question the existence of a link between political freedom and income distribution. This skepticism is curiously consistent with the failure of many previous studies to empirically prove the direct association between political openness and within-country inequality.

THE CAIRO CONSENSUS

As shown above, we have made clear-cut choices in this chapter with respect to conceptualization and operationalization of globalization and equity. This selectivity is motivated by the intention to limit expectations and to emphasize that our observations can be replicated only if the same definitions and measures are used. The explicitness also serves as a reminder to the scholarly community that the starting point of research often determines its outcome, and that research findings are inseparable from initial assumptions and concept interpretations. We hope that the recognition of this reality will cut through both the confusion and inflammatory debate about globalization and equity. Indeed, such a debate could often be avoided if the conflicting sides plainly stated their terms of reference. Although this mostly genuine confusion loses its innocence when 'vested interests', referred to in this book by Bouzas and Ffrench-Davis (218) become actively involved, clarification of the concepts and their measures can pave the way for reconciling many of the existing perspectives on globalization and equity.

Having taken precautions against misunderstanding, we have arrived at several observations suggesting that globalization can be good for the developing world. First, the top globalizers in terms of economic integration, East Asia and Central and Eastern Europe, demonstrated high growth rates during the globalization era of 1980–2000; so did one of the most politically open regions in the world, South Asia. On the other side of the spectrum, one of the non-globalizers, Sub-Saharan Africa, experienced a serious decline and has been marginalized, resulting in a drastic income decline for the average African. As a result, among-country inequality increased. Second, although inequality has also increased since 1981 in several countries of the world, annual changes have been relatively small. Moreover, in this respect there is no compelling evidence that globalization systematically increases inequality within countries, except where it is inextricably bound to the process of transition to a market-style economy. Third, there is evidence that globalization and growth eventually translate into poverty reduction in most regions and countries. In particular, the fastest growing regions – economically well-integrated East Asia and politically open South Asia – have been the most successful in decreasing the percentage of their population living in abject poverty.

Our observations should certainly be viewed with caution. They represent the results of a very rough, sketchy worldwide analysis, which has involved much simplification. As a result, regional aggregation hides significant variations among countries. Sharing our own cautious approach, several of the other contributors to this book recognize that the causal links between globalization and equity are far from straightforward. In particular, Bouzas and Ffrench-Davis complete their analysis with a frank acknowledgment that 'there are no obvious or universal conclusions that can be offered as ready-to-use policy recipes' (236). On his part, Ali labels his results as 'tentative' and endorses them as a 'calling for increased research efforts that need to be made to ascertain the possible effects of "globalization" ' (60).

Regardless of this general cautiousness, our observations are consistent with the views of other contributors to this book in their corroboration of the two theses constituting the so-called Cairo Consensus. Our key findings – association of globalization with higher growth rates and poverty reduction, with no compelling evidence of its association with the rise in income inequality within countries independent of the transition process – confirm the first thesis of the Consensus: Involvement in global economy and society is important for preventing marginalization of countries and regions and for mitigating inequity among them.

Reiterating our observations, Chia confirms both the positive relationship between globalization and economic growth and the link between economic growth and poverty reduction (114). Similarly, Ali writes about the positive spill-over effect of trade-induced economic growth for the poor (60), while Jayasuriya states with the reference to the overall Asian experience that 'more, rather than less, openness may be pro-poor' and that 'the evidence from South Asia favors the view that growth associated with liberalization has been poverty-reducing' (152).

At the same time, our findings resulting from the probing of specific issues are often mixed, including deviations from the general conclusion about the benefits of globalization. For example, of the two globalizers (Central and Eastern Europe and the CIS) the former region has achieved moderate net growth in 1980–2000, while the latter has experienced a sharp decline. As another example, despite its qualification as a non-globalizer, South Asia recorded impressive economic growth in the 1980s and 1990s. Moreover, the rate of poverty reduction in South Asia is on a par with that in the leading globalizer, East Asia, and the decline in income inequality has been greater than in East Asia, signaling that global integration may not necessarily be the only means of achieving the goals of economic development and well–being.

These 'irregular' inferences from our analysis highlight a fundamental fact that globalization provides no guarantee of better economic performance and greater equity. It rather offers an opportunity for achievement, which is contingent on effective domestic policies. These findings are therefore consistent with the second thesis of the Cairo Consensus, which emphasizes the importance of adjustment based on local conditions and needs.

Similar to our suggestion that the difference in economic performance between Central and Eastern Europe and the CIS is due to the more effective and more rapid economic and political transformation of the former region, Yudaeva faults weak institutions for the CIS's pains during its transition. Meanwhile, the improvements in equity in South Asia have occurred against the backdrop of slow globalization. Possibly, they can be attributed to the deliberate efforts to 'balance economic growth with domestic policies and institutions [intended] ... to minimize any negative impacts on vulnerable groups and individuals' (100). This strategy is emphatically endorsed by Chia with respect to East Asia, but it is applicable to other regions of the world. Chia's view is seconded by a researcher of South Asia, Jayasuriya, who calls for full attention to the distribution of income in this politically volatile region (152). Other authors, including Kolodko and Ali, also follow this approach.

The Cairo Consensus is certainly not cast in stone. It is open to further development and enrichment through research and outreach to policymakers. Indeed, as noted by Ali, the research community should go beyond general advocacy messages on globalization by articulating context-specific strategies to help policymakers tackle distributional conflicts (60). By building on this yet fledgling consensus, researchers from the developing world can, however, consolidate their forces and increase their joint contribution to addressing the ills associated with globalization, taking advantage of its benefits and steering this phenomenon toward a most equitable path.

NOTES

Data collection and analysis for the opening chapter was conducted with the assistance of Jim Bang, University of Illinois at Urbana-Champaign; Shaymal Chowdhury, International Food Policy Research Institute; Hadi Salehi Esfahani, University of Illinois at Urbana-Champaign; Klaus Deininger, World Bank; Branko Milanovic, Carnegie Endowment for International Peace; Irina Papkov, GDN Secretariat; Martin Ravallion, World Bank; Kristina Mihailova, GDN Secretariat, and Kareff May Rafisura, GDN Secretariat.

1. The Heritage Foundation index is based on 50 variables grouped in ten categories, including a specific category for 'capital flows and foreign investment'. To obtain a final *Index of Economic Freedom* score, each country is given a score ranging from 1 to 5 for each of ten categories, and these scores are then averaged (using equal weights). Countries with a score between 1 and 2 have the freest economies; those with a score around 3 are less free; those with a score near 4 are excessively regulated; and those with a score of 5 are the most economically repressed. Scores refer to 161 countries (2001 data) and are based on various sources, including World Bank, *World Development Indicators*; U.S. Central Intelligence Agency, *The World Factbook*; Economic Intelligence Unit, *Country Reports* and *Country Profiles*, and International Monetary Fund, *World Economic Outlook* (Miles et al. 2004, 71–72). Scores included in Table 1.2 are based on the 2000 data from the 2003 *Index of Economic Freedom*.

2. The Fraser Institute index consists of 21 components within the 5 major areas; one of these areas is titled 'freedom to exchange with foreigners'. Each of 21 components and their subcomponents are placed on a scale of 0 to 10 that reflects the distribution of the underlying data. (0 stands for no economic freedom and 10 stands for greatest economic freedom.) The component ratings within each of five areas are averaged to derive ratings for each of the five areas. In turn, the summary rating is the average of the five area ratings (Gwartney et al. 2003, 6). Ratings refer to more than 100 countries and are based on 38 distinct pieces of data from various sources, including World Bank, *World Development Indicators*; International Monetary Fund, *International Financial Statistics*; and World Economic Forum, *Global Competitiveness Report* (Gwartney et al. 2003, 24–32). Ratings included in Table 1.2 are based on the 2000 data from *Economic Freedom of the World: 2002 Annual Report*.

3. *The Freedom in the World* survey monitors the progress and decline of political rights and civil liberties in 192 nations and 18 related and disputed territories (2003). The Freedom House survey team assigns ratings based on a wide range of sources, including fact-finding missions around the world and a vast array of published materials (*Freedom in the World* 2003). A country or territory is assigned a numerical rating on a scale of 1 to 7 based on the total number of raw points awarded to the political rights and civil liberties checklist questions. For both checklists, 1 represents the most free and 7 the least free. Each pair of political rights and civil liberties is then averaged to determine an overall status of 'Free', 'Partly Free' and 'Not Free'. Those whose ratings average 1–2.5 are considered Free, 3–5.5 Partly Free and 5.5–7 Not Free. The dividing line between Partly Free and Not Free falls at 5.5. The total number of raw points is the definitive factor that determines the final status: countries and territories with combined points of 0–33 are Not Free, 34–67 points are Partly Free and 68–100 are Free.

4. Polity IV contains coded annual information on regime and authority characteristics for all independent states with population exceeding 500,000 and covers the years 1800–2002. DEM is defined as 'general openness of political institutions' and is assigned scores by the managers of Polity IV based on a number of checkpoints. The scores range from 0 to 10. PARCOMP defined as 'extent to which non-elites are able to access institutional structures for political

expression' is assigned scores ranging from 0 to 5. Values of both variables increase as the levels of democracy and political openness increase (Marshall and Jaggers 2002).

5. The Database of Political Institutions contains 113 variables for 177 countries (sovereign states with populations exceeding 100,000) since 1975. The mostly objective and disaggregated variables provide details about elections, electoral rules, type of political system, party composition of the opposition and government coalitions, the extent of military influence on government, checks and balances and political stability. The two main sources of data are *Europa Year Book* and *Political Handbook of the World*. The Executive Index of Electoral Competitiveness (EIEC), which ranges from 1 to 7, indicates whether the leader of a country (president, prime minister or other) is elected and if so, whether s/he is elected by small groups (a junta or an electoral colleges) or by the general public, and whether one or many parties with multiple candidates participate in elections. The highest scores stand for competitively elected executives. Similarly, the Legislative Index of Electoral Competitiveness (LIEC), which also ranges from 1 to 7 (the highest scores stand for competitively elected legislatures), highlights whether legislature is elected and, if so, under which conditions it is elected (with single or multiple parties competing for seats, and with single or multiple candidates representing a party) (Beck et al. 2000, 2, 11–12, 30).

6. The A.T. Kearney/Foreign Policy Globalization Index, which has been available since 2002 (using 2000 data), tracks and assesses changes in four key components of global integration: economic integration; personal contact; technological connectivity and political engagement. The data for each given variable within these four components are normalized through a process that assigns values to data points for each year relative to the highest data point that year. For simplicity the base year is assigned a value of 100. The given variable's scale factor for each subsequent year is the percentage growth or decline in the normalized score of the highest data point, relative to 100. Country index scores are then derived by summing all the indicator scores, with double weighting of FDI due to its particular importance in the ebb and flow of globalization. Technological variables and political variables are each collapsed into single indicators, with equal weightings for the component variables. The 62 countries ranked in the 2004 Globalization Index account for 96 per cent of the world's GDP and 84 per cent of the world's population ('Measuring Globalization: Who's Up, Who's Down?', 2003).

7. These regressions have been conducted by Klaus Deininger and Lyn Squire for their paper 'Revisiting Inequality: New Data, New Results,' a work in progress.

REFERENCES

Barro, Robert J. (1999), 'Determinants of democracy', *Journal of Political Economy*, **107** (6), 158–83.

Barro, Robert J. (2000), 'Rule of Law, Democracy, and Economic Performance', in Gerald P. O'Driscoll, Jr., Kim R. Holmes and Melanie Kirkpatrick (eds), *2000 Index of Economic Freedom*, Washington, DC: Heritage Foundation.

Beck, Thorsten, George Clark, Alberto Groff, Philip Keefer and Patrick Walsh (2000), 'New Tools and New Tests in Comparative Political Economy: The Database of Political Institutions', Washingon, DC, Policy Research Working Paper No. 2283.

Bhagwati, Jagdish (2004), *In Defense of Globalization*, New York: Oxford University Press.

Bhagwati, Jagdish and T.N. Srinivasan (2002), 'Trade and poverty in the poor countries', *American Economic Review*, **92** (2), 180–83.

Bigsten, Arne and Jorgen Levin (2001), 'Growth, Income Distribution and Poverty: A Review', Helsinki, United Nations University, World Institute for Development Economics Research (WIDER) Working Paper No. 129.

Burkhart, Ross E. and Michael S. Lewis-Beck (1994), 'Comparative democracy: the economic development thesis', *American Political Science Review*, **88** (4), 903–10.

Chen, Shaohua and Martin Ravallion (2004), 'How Have the World's Poorest Fared Since the Early 1980s?' Washington, DC, World Bank Policy Research Working Paper No. 3341.

Coppedge, Michael John (1999), 'Patterns of Diffusion in the Third Wave of Democracy', World Society Foundation project report, available at www.unizh.ch.

Deininger, Klaus and Lyn Squire (1996), 'Measuring inequality: a new data-base', *World Bank Economic Review*, **10** (3), 565–91.

Deininger, Klaus and Lyn Squire (2004), 'Revisiting inequality: new data, new results', Cairo, Egypt, Egyptian Center for Economic Studies Distinguished Lecture Series No. 18.

Diamond, Larry (2000), 'The global state of democracy', *Current History* (December), 413–18.

Dollar, David and Aart Kraay (2001), 'Globalization, Inequality and Poverty Since 1980', World Bank: Washington, DC, available at www.worldbank.org/research/global.

Dollar, David and Aart Kraay (2002), 'Growth is good for the poor', *Journal of Economic Growth*, **7** (3), 195–225.

Dollar, David and Aart Kraay (2004), 'Trade, growth and poverty', *The Economic Journal*, **114** (493), F22–F49.

Eichengreen, Barry (2002), 'Capitalizing on Globalization', Manila, Philippines, Asian Development Bank, ERD Working Paper No. 1.

Esfahani, Hadi Salehi and Lyn Squire (2004), 'Explaining Trade Policy in the Middle East and North Africa', in Hadi Salehi Esfahani, Ebrahim Elbadawi, Hanaa Kheir El-Din and Mohamed Lahouel (eds), *Essays in Honor of Heba Handoussa*, forthcoming.

Fidrmuc, Jan (2003), 'Economic reform, democracy and growth during post-communist transition', *European Journal of Political Economy*, **19** (3), 583–604.

Fish, M. Steven (1999), 'Post-communist subversion: social science and democratization in East Europe and Eurasia', *Slavic Review*, **58** (4), 794-823.

Freedom House (2002), *Freedom in the World 2001–2002*, New York: Freedom House, available at www.freedomhouse.org.

Freedom House (2003), *Freedom in the World 2003*, New York: Freedom House, available at www.freedomhouse.org.

Freedom House (2004), *Freedom in the World 2004: Gains for Freedom amid Terror and Uncertainty*, New York: Freedom House, available at www.freedomhouse.org.

Gallup, John Luke, Steven Radelet and Andrew Warner (1998), 'Economic Growth and the Income of the Poor', Cambridge, MA, Harvard University Institute for International Development, CAER II Discussion Paper No. 36.

Gradstein, Mark, Branko Milanovic and Yvonne Ying (2001), 'Democracy and Income Inequality: An Empirical Analysis,' Washington, DC, World Bank Policy Research Working Paper No. 2561.

Gwartney, James and Robert Lawson with Neil Emerick (2003), *Economic Freedom of the World: 2003 Annual Report*, Vancouver, BC: Fraser Institute.

Helliwell, John F. (1994), 'Empirical linkages between democracy and economic growth', *British Journal of Political Science*, **24** (2), 225–48.

Kearney, A.T. and Foreign Policy Magazine (2003), 'Measuring Globalization: Who's Up, Who's Down?', dataset available at www.foreignpolicy.com/wwwboard/g-index.php.

Laitin, David (2002), 'Comparative Politics: The State of the Subdiscipline', in Ira Katznelson and Helen Milner (eds), *Political Science: The State of the Discipline*, New York: W.W. Norton, pp. 630–59.

Marshall, Monty G. and Keith Jaggers (2002), 'Polity IV Project: Political Regime Characteristics and Transitions, 1800–2002', College Park, MD, University of Maryland, Center for International Development and Conflict Management, dataset available at www.cidcm.umd.edu/inscr/polity.

Milanovic, Branko (1999), 'True World Income Distribution, 1988 and 1993: First Calculations Based on Household Surveys Alone', Washington, DC, World Bank Policy Research Working Paper No. 2244.

Milanovic, Branko (2003), 'Can We Discern the Effect of Globalization on Income Distribution? Evidence from Household Surveys', Washington, DC, World Bank Policy Research Paper No. 2875.

Milanovic, Branko and Lyn Squire (2003), 'Do Pro-openness Policy Reforms Increase Wage Inequality? Some Empirical Evidence', manuscript.

Miles, Marc A., Edwin J. Feulner, Jr., Mary Anastasia O'Grady and Ana I. Eiras (eds) (2004), *2004 Index of Economic Freedom*, Washington, DC: The Heritage Foundation.

Muller, Edward (1995) 'Economic determinants of democracy', *American Sociological Review*, **60** (6), 966–82.

Olson, Mancur with Martin C. McGuire (1996), 'The economics of autocracy and majority rule: the invisible hand and the use of force', *Journal of Economic Literature*, **34** (1), 72–96.

Pei, Minxin (1999), 'Economic Institutions, Democracy, and Development', Washington, DC, Carnegie Endowment for International Peace, Carnegie Economic Reference Network Web Note No. 5, available at www.ceip.org.

Quinn, Dennis P. and John T. Woolley (2001), 'Democracy and national economic performance: the preference for stability', *American Journal of Political Science*, **45** (3), 634–57.

Rawls, John (1971), *A Theory of Justice*, Cambridge, MA: Harvard University Press.

Ryan, William (1981), *Equality*, New York: Pantheon Books.

Sandbrook, Richard (1997), 'Economic liberalization versus political democratization: a social-democratic resolution?' *Canadian Journal of African Studies*, **31** (3), 482–516.

Srinivasan, T.N. and Jagdish Bhagwati (2001), 'Trade and Poverty in the Poor Countries,' Department of Economics, Yale University, manuscript, available at www.econ.yale.edu/srinivas/trade_poverty.pdf.

World Bank (2002), *Globalization, Growth and Poverty: Building an Inclusive World Economy*, New York: Oxford University Press.

World Bank (2000), 'Poverty in an Age of Globalization', World Bank Globalization Briefing Paper, October.

Zhang Yunling, Shao Zhiqing and Su Zuegong (2002), *Impact of Globalization on Economic Disparity: Comparing Southeast Asia and China*, Beijing: Institute of Asia Pacific Studies, Chinese Academy of Social Sciences.

APPENDIX

Table 1.A1 Measures of Economic Freedom

	Heritage Foundation Index of Economic Freedom 2000 data		Fraser Institute Economic Freedom of the World index 2000 data	
	Summary scores	Capital flows and foreign investment	Summary ratings	Freedom to exchange with foreigners
Globalizers				
CE Europe	2.96	2.82	5.74	6.93
CIS	3.64	3.48	4.49	6.83
East Asia	3.50	3.93	5.58	6.77
Non-globalizers				
Latin America	3.03	2.97	6.09	6.65
Middle East/ North Africa	3.55	3.20	5.71	5.87
South Asia	3.57	3.02	5.96	5.31
Sub-Saharan Africa	3.57	3.06	5.47	6.17
High-income OECD	2.13	2.05	7.80	7.95

Note: In the Heritage Foundation index, 1 and 2 stand for the freest economies, and 5 indicates the most economically repressed economy. In the Fraser Institute index, 0 notifies no economic freedom, and 10 stands for greatest economic freedom.

Table 1.A2 Freedom in the World Ratings (Freedom House, 2000 data)

	PR	CL	Combined average ratings
Globalizers			
Central/Eastern Europe	1.77	2.41	2.09
CIS	5.12	4.96	5.04
Non-globalizers			
East Asia	6.11	5.55	5.83
Latin America/Caribbean	2.73	3.16	2.95
Middle East/North Africa	5.62	5.55	5.58
South Asia	2.73	3.47	3.10
Sub-Saharan Africa	4.52	4.38	4.45
High-income OECD	1.05	1.56	1.31

Note: Ratings included in this table are taken from the *Freedom in the World 2000–2001* report, which is based primarily on the 2000 data. Rating 1 represents 'the most free' and 7 'the least free' entities. Regional ratings are computed as the sum of country ratings weighted by population.

Table 1.A3 Scores on Democracy (Dem) and Party Competitiveness (Parcomp) from Polity IV database

	1980		1990		2000	
	Dem	Parcomp	Dem	Parcomp	Dem	Parcomp
Globalizers						
Central/Eastern Europe	0.02	1.00	4.67	3.00	8.71	4.14
CIS	0.00	1.00	1.58	1.53	5.16	3.44
Non-globalizers						
East Asia	0.19	1.21	0.58	1.30	1.60	1.61
Latin America/ Caribbean	2.77	2.50	6.72	3.72	7.57	3.78
Middle East/ North Africa	2.01	2.00	2.35	2.88	2.81	2.73
South Asia	6.32	2.68	7.08	2.89	7.50	3.63
Sub-Saharan Africa	2.38	1.65	0.58	1.45	3.48	2.41
High-income OECD	9.70	4.73	9.74	4.94	9.81	4.94

Note: The scores range from 0 to 10 for Dem and from 0 to 5 for Parcomp. Higher values represent higher levels of democracy and party competitiveness (political openness). Regional scores are computed as the sum of country scores weighted by population.

Table 1.A4 Scores in the Database of Political Institutions: Executive Index of Political Competitiveness (EIEC) and Legislative Index of Political Competitiveness (LIEC)

	1980		1990		2000	
	EIEC	LIEC	EIEC	LIEC	EIEC	LIEC
Globalizers						
Central/Eastern Europe	3.00	3.94	2.81	4.89	6.88	7.00
CIS	—	—	—	—	6.32	6.09
Non-globalizers						
East Asia	3.06	3.73	3.22	3.68	3.77	3.88
Latin America/ Caribbean	5.51	5.66	6.81	6.81	6.98	6.78
Middle East/ North Africa	3.94	4.33	4.65	5.29	5.92	6.02
South Asia	6.35	6.37	6.85	6.75	6.17	6.29
Sub-Saharan Africa	3.92	4.01	2.99	3.28	6.35	6.23
High-income OECD	6.97	7.00	7.00	7.00	7.00	7.00

Note: The scores range from 1 to 7, with the highest scores standing for competitively elected executives and legislatures. Regional scores are computed as the sum of country scores weighted by population.

2. Globalization and Inequality in the Arab Region

Ali Abdel Gadir Ali

The term 'globalization' means different things to different people. However, there seems to be general agreement that the term refers to the process of increased international economic integration driven largely by technological advances in transport and communications. George Soros, an active participant in the process, writes that the term means the 'development of global financial markets, the growth of transnational corporations and their increasing domination over national economies' (Soros 2002, 1). In the succinct words of the World Bank's Joseph Stiglitz, globalization means 'the removal of barriers to free trade and the closer integration of national economies' (2002, ix).[1]

In 2002 the World Bank (2002a, 23–51) summarized the history and economic effects of globalization. It is noted that globalization occurs through trade (measured relative to world income), migration (proxied by the number of immigrants to the United States) and capital flows (proxied by the stock of foreign capital in developing countries relative to their gross domestic product (GDP)). The study identified three waves of globalization: 1870–1914, 1945–80 and 1980 to the present. Reduced transportation costs were central to all identified globalization waves. Strictly speaking, only the second and third waves reached the developing countries, including those of the Arab region.[2]

According to the World Bank's analysis, during the second wave of globalization trade in manufacturing between advanced countries was substantially freed of restrictions and transport costs fell by one-third between 1950 and 1970. The developing countries, however, did not participate in, or benefit from, the second wave. For developing countries, while:

> . . . per capita income growth recovered from inter-war slowdown, it was substantially slower than in the rich economies. The number of poor people continued to rise, but non-income dimensions of poverty improved – notably rising

life expectancy and rising school enrollments. In terms of equity, within developing countries in aggregate there was little change either between countries or within them. As a group, developing countries were left behind by developed countries (World Bank 2002a, 31).

The third wave of globalization has three characteristics. First, a large group of developing countries broke into global markets. Second, other developing countries became increasingly marginalized in the world economy and suffered declining incomes and rising poverty. Third, international migration and capital movements became substantial. The World Bank identified 24 developing countries as having globalized during this third wave. The measure used to identify the countries that have globalized is the increase in the trade (exports and imports) to GDP ratio over the period 1970–97. Jordan is the only Arab country on this list. Thus, most of the Arab region has been left out of the third wave of globalization.[3]

The literature provides a number of alternative measures of inequality in the distribution of consumption expenditure or income, as appropriate proxies for the standard of living and hence the welfare of individuals. The most widely used measure of inequality in the distribution of income is the Gini coefficient.[4] This statistic varies from zero (where every person in the society has the same income, indicating the absence of inequality and representing conditions of perfect equality) to one (where one person gets all the income and the rest receive nothing, indicating the presence of complete inequality).[5] Thus, higher Gini coefficient values indicate higher degrees of inequality in the distribution of the relevant attribute.

The World Bank study notes five ways globalization affects inequality (World Bank 2002a, 46–51). First, globalization has been equalizing in OECD countries, 'as inequality between countries has radically decreased', but there was increased inequality in some countries possibly due to domestic policies.[6] Second, overall inequality has also declined for both the OECD countries and the new globalizers. Third, within-country inequality has increased in the new globalizers, due to the increased inequality in China, which accounts for one-third of the population of this group of countries. Fourth, a sample of 137 countries found that there exists 'no relationship between changes in openness and changes in inequality, whether openness is measured by the share of trade in income, the Sachs–Warner measure of openness, average tariff rates or capital controls'.[7] Finally, although on average openness does not affect inequality, in low-income countries it is associated with greater inequality.[8] In addition to these World Bank results, a recent, and rather influential, empirical finding purported to establish an indirect link between globalization and the average income of the bottom 20 per cent of the population. According to

Dollar and Kraay, increased trade volumes, under globalization, increase the rate of growth of per capita income and that the average income of the poor increases one-for-one as per capita income (2001a, 2001b).

This chapter analyzes the Arab region in order to contribute to the current debate on the possible effects of globalization on inequality.[9] The chapter begins by looking at the current levels of globalization in Arab countries. Three World Bank globalization measures are used: (1) the annual rate of increase of the trade/GDP ratio over the period 1980–2000; (2) the stock of foreign direct investment (FDI) to GDP in 1999; and (3) the number of Arab immigrants to the United States between 1990 and 2000. Next, the chapter presents evidence on unequal income distribution in the Arab countries. This section notes the constraints imposed by limited data but nonetheless reports available results on the state and time trend of inequality in the region. The chapter then offers results on the indirect and direct effects of globalization on inequality in the region. The chapter closes with a summary and some concluding remarks.

GLOBALIZATION IN THE ARAB COUNTRIES

Despite their common cultural and historical heritage, the Arab countries vary greatly in their economic structures, level of development, geographic location and type of governance and institutions. To highlight the economic diversity of the region, the Economic Research Forum (ERF 1998) grouped the countries of the region into four broad categories:[10] (1) mixed-oil economies (Algeria and Iraq); (2) oil economies (Bahrain, Kuwait, Oman, Qatar, Saudi Arabia and the United Arab Emirates); (3) diversified economies (Egypt, Jordan, Lebanon, Morocco, Syria and Tunisia); and (4) primary-export economies (Djibouti, Mauritania, Sudan and Yemen). The 1996 distribution of population and GDP over these country groups was such that diversified economies accounted for 48 per cent of population and 28 per cent of GDP; mixed-oil economies accounted for 21 per cent of population and 24 per cent of GDP; primary-export economies accounted for 20 per cent of population and only 3 per cent of GDP; while oil economies accounted for only 11 per cent of population and 46 per cent of GDP. Intra-Arab diversity is also captured by differences in per capita GDP. Not surprisingly, oil economies top this scale with a per capita GDP of about $9,000 in 1996, followed by mixed-oil economies ($2,400). Diversified economies rank third with a per capita GDP of $1,300 while primary-export economies' per capita GDP amounted to only $300.

The production structures of the four groups differ as well. Thus, in 1996 the agricultural sector accounted for 24 per cent and 23 per cent of GDP in primary-export economies and mixed-oil economies, respectively, and for 16 per cent in diversified economies while it accounts for only 2.4 per cent of GDP in oil economies. The manufacturing sector accounted for 14.4 per cent of GDP in diversified economies, 11 per cent in mixed-oil economies and oil economies, and 9 per cent in primary-export economies. Thus, none of the country groups of the region could be considered as industrialized (defined as having a manufacturing sector contribution of 20 per cent of GDP). Extractive industry, however, contributed fairly large shares in oil economies (35 per cent of GDP) and mixed-oil economies (27 per cent of GDP).[11]

This diversity will affect, among other things, the speed with which countries can integrate in the world economy and the current level of globalization of each country.[12] To ascertain globalization levels the World Bank indicators can be used to calculate the rate of growth of the trade/GDP ratio over the period 1980–2000 for each country for which relevant information is available. The World Bank uses trade intensity, FDI and immigration to the United States to evaluate globalization levels.

Trade Intensity

Judging Arab countries by the level of their trade-intensity ratio in the year 2000 the evidence shows that three countries score above 100 per cent (Bahrain 145 per cent, Jordan 111 per cent and UAE 114 per cent). Another three countries have ratios in excess of 90 per cent (Tunisia and Yemen 92 per cent and Mauritania 98 per cent). Seven countries have ratios in excess of 60 per cent (Algeria 64 per cent, Kuwait 88 per cent, Morocco 69 per cent, Oman 81 per cent, Qatar 78 per cent, Saudi Arabia 75 per cent and Syria 73 per cent).[13] The remaining five Arab countries have ratios less than 60 per cent (Egypt 39 per cent, Lebanon 51 per cent, Libya 42 per cent, Comoros 58 per cent and Sudan 33 per cent). The evidence also shows that the trade–intensity ratio fluctuated in most of the Arab countries during the period under consideration. The time trend, and its statistical significance, is reported in Table 2.1.

Table 2.1 shows that, using the World Bank's trade measure of globalization, five of the eighteen Arab countries for which data are available can be considered as having globalized during the current phase of globalization: Morocco, Syria, Tunisia, UAE and Yemen. Jordan, which was identified by the World Bank as the only globalized Arab country, does not make it to the list of globalizers if the period is extended to the year 2000. Of the Arab globalizers identified in Table 2.1, two countries are perhaps surprising: Syria and Yemen. The other three are obvious candidates for globalization status, given their trade liberalization policies during the past two decades.

Table 2.1 Globalization in the Arab Countries: Annual Growth Rates of Trade/GDP Ratios for a Sample of Arab Countries 1980–2000

Country	Estimated Coefficient	Absolute t-value	Growth Rate (%)	Status
Algeria	−0.0004	0.0558	−0.04	Not Globalized
Bahrain	−0.0257	9.2969	−2.57	Not Globalized
Comoros	−0.0045	1.5574	−0.45	Not Globalized
Egypt	−0.0232	3.7271	−2.32	Not Globalized
Jordan	−0.0013	0.2559	−0.13	Not Globalized
Kuwait	−0.0083	2.2644	−0.83	Not Globalized
Lebanon	−0.0436	7.8787	−8.18	Not Globalized
Libya	−0.0265	2.3233	−2.65	Not Globalized
Mauritania	−0.0165	4.6795	−1.65	Not Globalized
Morocco	0.0109	4.7619	1.09	Globalized
Oman	−0.0103	3.9650	−1.03	Not Globalized
Qatar	−0.0040	0.7121	−0.40	Not Globalized
Saudi Arabia	−0.0176	5.9724	−1.76	Not Globalized
Sudan	−0.0078	0.4909	−0.78	Not Globalized
Syria	0.0314	5.3579	3.14	Globalized
Tunisia	0.0074	2.2993	0.74	Globalized
UAE	0.0190	5.0617	1.90	Globalized
Yemen	0.0293	3.1703	2.93	Globalized

Source: Author's estimation of a trend equation of the form [Ln x = α + βT] where x is the trade/GDP ratio and T is time.

FDI

A second World Bank measure of globalization is the country's level of FDI. This measure can be looked at in terms of the flow of FDI as a ratio of GDP or as the stock of the accumulated flows as a percentage of GDP. However, neither formula offers a reasonable threshold beyond which a country would be considered as having globalized. According to Milanovic (2002) the ratio based of the flows of FDI does not seem to be a significant explanatory variable of inequality. Instead, this study uses the weighted average ratio of the stock of FDI to GDP for the 24 countries identified as globalizers by the World Bank (2002a) as the benchmark for identifying the status of Arab countries. The ratio of the stock of FDI to GDP in 1999 is provided in UNCTAD (2001) and the purchasing power parity (PPP) gross national income for 2000 are used as

Table 2.2 FDI Stocks/GDP Ratios in the Arab Countries: 1980–99

Country	1980	1985	1990	1995	1999	Status
Algeria	3.1	2.2	2.1	3.3	3.0	Not Globalized
Bahrain	2.0	10.8	13.8	43.8	100.0	Globalized
Comoros	–	–	–	–	–	–
Djibouti	1.0	1.0	1.3	2.8	6.9	Not Globalized
Egypt	9.9	16.4	25.6	23.9	19.1	Not Globalized
Iraq	–	–	–	–	–	–
Jordan	4.0	9.6	15.3	9.5	19.3	Not Globalized
Kuwait	0.1	0.2	0.1	-	1.7	Not Globalized
Lebanon	0.5	0.9	1.9	1.2	5.5	Not Globalized
Libya	–	–	–	–	–	–
Mauritania	–	5.7	5.6	8.6	10.7	Not Globalized
Morocco	1.0	3.4	3.5	9.2	16.0	Not Globalized
Oman	8.1	12.0	16.3	16.1	15.7	Not Globalized
Qatar	1.1	1.3	0.8	5.7	16.9	Not Globalized
Saudi Arabia	–	25.2	21.5	17.8	20.0	Not Gloablized
Somalia	4.8	0.5	–	–	4.3	Not Globalized
Sudan	0.4	0.6	0.4	0.7	9.7	Not Globalized
Syria	–	0.2	1.6	1.8	6.5	Not Globalized
Tunisia	66.7	83.0	59.0	61.2	57.0	Globalized
UAE	1.4	1.8	2.2	4.4	5.3	Not Globalized
Yemen	3.7	4.5	3.8	51.0	16.1	Not Globalized

Source: UNCTAD (2001, 325 Annex Table B6).

weights. For the 24 globalizers, the ratio varied from a high of 65.3 per cent for Malaysia to a low of 1.5 per cent for Bangladesh. The simple average ratio is 22.96 per cent with a standard deviation of 16.23 percentage points, while the weighted average is 21.7 per cent.

Using the weighted average ratio of FDI stock/GDP among the World Bank-designated globalizers as the benchmark for classifying countries, it can easily be seen from Table 2.2 that only Bahrain (with a ratio of FDI stock/GDP of 100 per cent) and Tunisia (with a ratio of 57 per cent) can be considered as having 'globalized' by the end of 1999. The ratio for the rest of the Arab countries is less than 21.7 per cent of GDP, the World Bank benchmark. Saudi Arabia (with a ratio of 20 per cent), Jordan (19.3 per cent) and Egypt (19.1 per cent) are borderline cases.

Table 2.3 Immigrants to the United States by Region of Birth: 1990–2000

Year	Arab Countries	Av. per Arab Country	Globalizers	Av. per Globalizer	All Countries
1990	23,033	1,097	965,035	40,210	1,536,483
1991	27,070	1,289	1280,801	53,367	1,827,167
1992	27,884	1,329	475,101	19,796	973,977
1993	28,577	1,361	417,103	17,379	904,292
1994	27,244	1,297	374,246	15,594	804,416
1995	32,837	1,564	321,674	13,403	720,461
1996	36,374	1,732	436,369	18,182	915,900
1997	31,630	1,506	382,459	15,936	798,378
1998	27,677	1,318	329,464	13,728	654,451
1999	26,556	1,265	334,698	13,946	646,568
2000	33,242	1,583	428,955	17,873	849,807

Source: Compiled from USINS (2000, 11–14 Table 3). For country details see Ali (2003, Annex Tables A2 and A3).

Immigration to the United States

The third World Bank measure of globalization is the number of immigrants to the United States.[14] The World Bank (2002a, 23) looks at immigrants to the United States by decade from 1870 to 2000. The measure is defined in flow terms and, again, the World Bank does not establish a threshold beyond which a country would be considered globalized. One possible comparative benchmark would be the average number of immigrants sent by the group of states identified as globalizers.

Detailed information on immigration to the United States is provided in the U.S. Immigration and Naturalization Service (USINS) annual reports. The fiscal year 2000 USNIS report (2000, 11–14 Table 3) provides relevant country information for the period 1990–2000. For 1990 and 1991 the United States admitted about 1.5 and 1.8 million immigrants, respectively.[15] The number of immigrants up to the year 2000 fluctuated with an overall declining trend where by 2000 about 850,000 immigrants were admitted to the United States. Using the detailed country information, Table 2.3 provides a comparison between Arab immigrants; those from the group of globalizers and those from other developing regions.

Table 2.3 clearly shows that immigrants from Arab countries do not constitute a significant flow in absolute numbers. However, the total number of Arab immigrants does show an increasing trend. This trend could best be looked at in terms of the share of Arab immigrants in the combined totals from all countries. The table shows that this share has increased from about 2.9 per cent in 1992 to about 4.1 per cent in 1999 and 3.9 per cent in 2000. But using the average number of immigrants from the World Bank group of globalizers shows that no Arab country sent more than 6,186 immigrants (Egypt's level in 1996) during any single year over the period under consideration. This is obviously lower than the lowest recorded average number of immigrants (13,403 in 1995) sent by the average country from the group of globalizers. Thus, according to this particular measure, none of the Arab countries could be considered as having 'globalized' during the period 1990–2000.

Only Tunisia appears in both the set of Arab globalizers defined by the rate of growth of the trade/GDP ratio and the set of Arab globalizers defined by the stock of FDI to GDP ratio. This narrow finding confirms the World Bank's result, noted above, that the Arab region, through the year 2000, seems to have been left out of the current wave of globalization.

INEQUALITY IN THE ARAB COUNTRIES

Based on the Gini coefficient and the most recent high-quality data available, Table 2.4 compares inequality among world regions.[16] The table, adapted from Deininger and Olinto (2002), adopts the standard World Bank classification of world regions. The Middle East and North Africa region of the World Bank is represented in the Deininger and Squire (1996) high-quality data set by six Arab countries. Table 2.4 summarizes the degree of inequality for various regions over five five-year periods (1966–90), and provides a highly aggregated picture. Nonetheless, it will be helpful to compare the Arab region with other regions in terms of income inequality levels and trends.

Table 2.4 shows that the Arab countries, as a group, ranked second behind Latin America as the highest inequality region for the first two sub-periods as well as for 1981–85. During 1976–80 and 1986–90 the region ranked as the third highest inequality region. The Arab countries reported an average Gini coefficient of about 0.44, compared to an average of 0.57 for Latin America for 1976–80. For 1986–90 the Arab region's Gini coefficient (about 0.38) was the third highest behind East Asia and the Pacific (about 0.40) and Latin America (about 0.50). Importantly, all regions, except Latin America and Western Europe and North America, calculate Gini coefficients based on consumption expenditure rather than income. The distribution of expenditure

Table 2.4 Income Inequality in the Arab Countries and World Regions 1966–90 (Gini Coefficients)

Region	States	1966–70	1971–75	1976–80	1981–85	1986–90
Arab Countries	6	0.4367	0.4165	0.4190	0.4295	0.3817
East Asia/Pacific	9	0.3726	0.3889	0.3853	0.3860	0.4004
Latin America	17	0.5724	0.5093	0.4977	0.4906	0.5016
North America	2	0.3561	0.3528	0.3591	0.3512	0.3654
South Asia	4	0.3330	0.3332	0.3537	0.3668	0.3357
Sub-Saharan Africa	7	0.3900	–	0.4400	0.4121	0.3575
Western Europe	15	0.3709	0.3488	0.3082	0.2974	0.3083
Sample	60	0.4063	0.3932	0.3851	0.3691	0.3858

Source: Deininger and Olinto (2002, 23, Table 1).

is generally more equal than the distribution of income. Indeed Deininger and Squire (1996) advise researchers to adjust upward the expenditure-based Gini coefficients by adding 0.0066 to make them comparable to those based on income. Making such an adjustment, however, does not change the overall ranking of the regions. After making the adjustment, the Gini coefficient of the distribution of income in the Arab countries becomes 0.50 for the first sub-period and about 0.45 for the last, which reflect a fairly high degree of inequality in the distribution of income.[17]

In terms of inequality trends, Table 2.4 shows that inequality in the Arab region recorded a declining trend with a decrease in the Gini coefficient from about 0.44 per cent in the first sub-period to about 0.38 in the last sub-period, with a slight increase during the period 1971–85. Declining inequality trends are reported for Latin America, Sub-Saharan Africa and Western Europe, while increasing inequality trends are reported for East Asia and the Pacific and North America. Inequality in South Asia remained virtually the same. Noting that these results are based on averages over countries and that the Gini coefficient is not additively separable, the above findings should be interpreted with caution. However, the trend of declining inequality for Arab countries is confirmed by detailed official country information.

For the six Arab countries included in the Deininger and Squire database, Table 2.5 provides the Lorenz reading in terms of the share of various quintiles in consumption expenditure. For each country the information is provided for two years: a first year from the late 1980s or early 1990s and a second year from the late 1990s. Following standard practice, the first year represents the state of distribution in the early 1990s while the second year is assumed to represent the late 1990s. The underlying assumption is that the distribution of consumption expenditure over the relevant period did not change substantially, a particularly problematic assumption for the Arab countries. Table 2.5 also provides the Gini coefficients for the distribution of consumption expenditure for each country for the relevant years, as well as the annual rate of increase of the Gini coefficients.

Table 2.5 shows that inequality in the distribution of expenditure varied among Arab countries in the early 1990s. Mauritania recorded the highest degree of inequality in 1992, with an expenditure Gini of about 0.50 (corresponding to an income Gini of 0.566). Egypt in 1991 recorded the lowest degree of inequality, with an expenditure Gini of 0.32 (an income Gini of 0.386). Other high inequality Arab countries include Jordan (with an expenditure Gini of about 0.41), and Morocco and Algeria (0.39). In the early 1990s, the average Gini for the sample countries is 0.4006 with a standard deviation of 0.0487.

With the exception of Morocco, all countries in the sample show that inequality declined towards the late 1990s. The highest degree of inequality is recorded for Tunisia in 1990 (with an expenditure Gini of about 0.40, corresponding to an income Gini of 0.466) while the lowest degree of inequality is recorded for Egypt (with an expenditure Gini of about 29 per cent). High inequality countries in the late 1990s include Morocco (with an expenditure Gini of about 0.40) and Mauritania (with an expenditure Gini of about 0.39). In the late 1990s the average expenditure Gini coefficient for the sample is 0.3619 with a standard deviation of 0.0452.

In terms of time trends, Table 2.5 shows that five of the six Arab countries recorded a quantitatively important decline in expenditure-distribution inequality over relatively short periods of time. The largest decline (0.065) in the Gini coefficient is recorded for Mauritania over a period of six years. The annual rate of decline of the Gini coefficient for Mauritania is 0.028. The second largest absolute decline is recorded for Egypt (0.0301 percentage points). Morocco is the only country that recorded an increase in inequality of 0.0062 percentage points, but the increase is not quantitatively significant, being at an annual rate of 0.0022.

Thus, contrary to the results by Li, Squire and Zou (1998) the distribution of expenditure in the Arab region tends to show quantitatively significant changes over fairly short periods of time. This declining trend conforms to the results of Deininger and Olinto (2002) summarized in Table 2.4. However, this recorded trend does not seem to accord with an intuitive understanding of the economic and social changes occurring in most of the Arab countries in the sample. Given the short periods of time over which the above changes

Table 2.5 Changes in the Distribution of Consumption Expenditure for a Sample of Arab Countries

Country	Poorest 20%	2nd poorest 20%	3rd poorest 20%	4th poorest 20%	Richest 20%	Expenditure Gini	Annual Gini Change (%)
Algeria:							
1988	6.86	10.97	14.94	20.74	46.55	0.3873	
1995	7.00	11.60	16.10	22.70	42.60	0.3553	−1.22
Egypt:							
1991	8.71	12.49	16.27	21.44	41.09	0.3200	
1995	9.50	13.20	16.60	21.4	39.00	0.2899	−2.44
Jordan:							
1991	6.47	10.29	14.61	20.94	47.69	0.4066	
1997	7.60	11.40	15.50	21.10	44.40	0.3635	−1.85
Mauritania:							
1992	3.60	10.30	16.20	23.00	46.20	0.4632	
1998	6.20	10.80	16.40	22.00	45.60	0.3914	−2.77
Morocco:							
1991	6.57	10.45	14.97	21.71	46.30	0.3920	
1998	6.50	10.60	14.80	21.30	46.60	0.3982	0.20
Tunisia:							
1985	5.54	9.63	12.24	21.02	49.57	0.4343	
1990	5.86	10.41	15.27	22.13	46.33	0.4024	−1.54

Source: Deininger and Squire database.

in the expenditure distribution have occurred, and given the fact that the underlying structural factors affecting inequality are not likely to have undergone drastic changes over the same period, the causal factors remain open to empirical investigation. Perhaps changes in macroeconomic policy explain the change. Almost all of these countries experienced macroeconomic policy changes during the indicated time periods. However, the precise ways in which macro policy changes affect income inequality are not theoretically well known, though the design and content of most policy packages suggest that they would worsen the expenditure-distribution levels. Importantly, these macroeconomic policy packages included trade policies designed to further open these countries to the global market.[18]

An alternative hypothesis would be that the household surveys used to calculate these Gini coefficients somehow fail to capture the top expenditure groups which emerged following the implementation of the policy packages. A case in point is Egypt. For example, Datt, Jolliffe and Sharma (1998, 16, Table 3) report a Gini coefficient of 0.35 for 1997. Their result is based on the Egypt Integrated Household Survey, a nationally representative survey which collects information on household composition, income, consumption and several other characteristics. Based on these results, income inequality in Egypt could be seen to have increased by an annual rate of 0.099 since 1995 or 0.015 since 1991. This result would conform to casual observations of distribution levels in Egypt.

To properly assess the effect of globalization on inequality in the Arab region, an income-distribution profile for the region as a whole can be generated utilizing the income distribution information available at the country level (i.e. Milanovic 2002; Sala-i-Martin 2002). As noted earlier, constructing a regional distribution based on country information attempts to assign per capita incomes to the various income classes while assuming that there is an even distribution within each income class. Using the standard Lorenz curve relationship between the share of the bottom p^{th} percent of the population and the overall average income in a given country, such assignment of incomes can be undertaken. Recall that the share of the bottom p^{th} percent of the population, $L(p)$, is given by the Lorenz relationship:

$$L(p) = p \ [\mu_p/\mu] \qquad (2.1)$$

where μ is the overall mean income and μ_p is the mean income of the bottom p^{th} percentage of the population and p varies from zero to one. The results for all countries can then be arrayed in terms of per capita incomes in an ascending order.

Table 2.6 Distribution of Income in the Arab Region: High-quality Data

Quintile	Expenditure Share Early 1990s (%)	Expenditure Share Late 1990s (%)
First	5.8	6.1
Second	11.2	11.7
Third	18.6	18.7
Fourth	27.0	26.7
Fifth	37.3	36.8
Gini Coefficient	.3274	.3177

Source: Author's calculations based on Table 2.5.

The above approach was applied to the six high-quality data samples plus Yemen. The resulting group of countries represented about 57 per cent of the population of the Arab region in 1998. For the early 1990s and late 1990s, 35 per capita income groups were generated. The early 1990s' per capita incomes in the sample of Arab countries ranged from a low per capita income of $94 to a high of $4,769 with a mean of $1,981; while for the late 1990s' period the range is from $218 to $4,797with a mean of $1,917. On the basis of these groups, quintile distributions of income were generated and the Gini coefficients were calculated. The results are reported in Table 2.6.

As expected from the preceding discussion of inequality levels in various Arab countries, where countries posted a decline in the Gini coefficient between the first and second years, Table 2.6 shows that for the high-quality sample of Arab countries, inequality in the distribution of consumption expenditures declined during the 1990s. The Gini coefficient dropped from 0.327 in the early 1990s to 0.318 in the late 1990s. Of the seven Arab countries used in Table 2.6, Tunisia, Morocco and Yemen have been globalized according to the World Bank's trade measure.

To better capture the diversity of the Arab countries mentioned above, the high-quality sample was augmented with two countries for which distribution data is available, although its quality has not been assessed. These countries are Kuwait, for which data is available for 1987 and 1996 (Kuwait Ministry of Planning 2001), and Sudan, with data available for 1987 and 1999. For the early 1990s' period, 66 per capita consumption groups were generated, which ranged from a low of $37 to a high of $21,682 with an overall mean of $2,110. For the late 1990s' period 63 per capita consumption groups were generated

Table 2.7 Distribution of Income in the Arab Region: Expanded Sample

Quintile	Expenditure Share Early 1990s (%)	Expenditure Share Late 1990s (%)
First	5.12	4.47
Second	12.27	10.65
Third	17.58	16.08
Fourth	23.96	22.95
Fifth	41.08	45.85
Gini Coefficient	.3343	.3802

Source: Author's calculations.

which ranged from a low of $71 to a high of $18,535 with an overall mean of $2,237. The resulting distributions are reported in Table 2.7.

The results of the expanded sample show that inequality in the Arab region increased during the 1990s as reflected in an increase in the Gini coefficient from 0.3343 in the early 1990s to about 0.40 in the late 1990s. Expanding the sample does not increase the number of Arab globalizers, but their share in total population and income has declined. Comparing the results of Tables 2.6 and 2.7 indicates the sensitivity of the results to the sample composition and does not provide conclusive evidence about the effect of globalization on inequality in the region.

THE EFFECT OF GLOBALIZATION ON INEQUALITY

The most celebrated empirical study on the effect of globalization on inequality is by Dollar and Kraay (2001a; 2001b).[19] They indirectly find the link between globalization and inequality by first establishing that the mean income of the poorest 20 per cent of the population has a unitary elasticity with respect to the overall mean income (a relationship which is true by definition) and then by noting that trade intensity is positively associated with growth in per capita income in the empirical growth literature. Dollar and Kraay conclude, 'We have found little evidence of a systematic effect of trade volumes on income inequality. Combining this observation with the results on the growth benefits of greater trade, we conclude that the balance of the evidence suggests that, on average, greater globalization is a force for poverty reduction'. In the context of the Dollar–Kraay definition of the poor, their conclusion tells policymakers, 'On average, greater globalization is a force for reducing inequality' (2001a, 33).

Indirect Effect

Ali and Elbadawi (2001) presented an alternative set of results on the relationship between the mean income of the poor and overall mean income, where the poor are properly defined as those falling below an appropriately defined poverty line instead of the bottom 20 per cent of the population. (The mean income of the poor could also be derived from the relationship between the headcount measure and the poverty-gap measure).[20] On the basis of this definition it can be shown that the elasticity of the mean income of the poor with respect to overall mean income is not, in general, equal to one. The elasticity in question depends on three components: the income elasticity of the headcount ratio (call it E_H); the income elasticity of the poverty-gap ratio (call it E_{PG}); and the income elasticity of the poverty line (call it E_z). Indeed Ali and Elbadawi show that the elasticity of the mean income of the poor with respect to overall mean income (call E_{yp}) is given by:

$$E_{yp} = E_z + (1 - E_z)(1 - E_H/E_{PG}) \qquad (2.2)$$

If the poverty line is assumed constant across countries, and possibly over time as is the World Bank convention, E_z will be zero and the elasticity of the mean income of the poor with respect to overall mean income will depend on the magnitude of the income elasticities of the poverty measures and that generally it is not equal to one.[21] For a sample of 48 developing countries, including the six Arab countries for which high-quality data are available, the elasticity of the mean income of the poor with respect to mean income is calculated in a direct fashion in Ali and Elbadawi (2001). According to the results the highest response is recorded for Latin America where a 1 per cent increase in the overall mean income will be expected to increase the mean income of the poor by 0.51 percentage points. The lowest response is reported for the Asian group of countries where the mean income of the poor increases by 0.43 of the percentage increase in the mean income of society. For the whole sample the increase in mean income of the poor is slightly lower than half, 0.47, of the percentage increase in the mean income of society. At this

Table 2.8 The Elasticity of the Mean Income of the Poor with Respect to Mean Income in a Sample of Arab Countries

Region	Income Elasticity of Headcount Ratio (E_H)	Income Elasticity of Poverty-gap Ratio (E_{PG})	Ratio of Elasticities (E_H/E_{PG})	Income Elasticity of the Poverty Line (E_z)	Income Elasticity of the Average Income of the Poor (E_{yp})
Algeria	−2.67	−3.00	0.89	0.305	0.38
Egypt	−3.54	−5.67	0.62	0.239	0.53
Jordan	−2.28	−3.51	0.65	0.348	0.58
Mauritania	−1.26	−1.13	1.11	0. 145	0.05
Morocco	−2.13	−3.29	0.65	0.289	0.54
Tunisia	−1.86	−2.60	0.72	0.430	0.59
Mean	−2.29	−3.20	0.77	0.290	0.45
S.D.	0.77	1.48	0.19	0.100	0.21

Source: Ali and Elbadawi (2001, 15, Appendix Table A2).

level of analysis, therefore, there is no evidence to support a strict one-to-one proportionality, given the proper definition of the average income of the poor.[22] These results align better with an intuitive understanding of what was happening to the poor during economic growth episodes than does the claim that the 'income of the poor rises one-for-one with overall growth'.[23] The results for the six Arab countries are reported in Table 2.8.

Table 2.8 shows that among the Arab countries, Tunisia recorded the highest response of the mean income of the poor to an increase in overall mean income, followed by Jordan, Morocco and Egypt. The lowest response is recorded for Mauritania. The overall mean elasticity for the Arab countries is 0.45, which is not statistically different from 0.5. Thus in the Arab countries the positive growth effect of trade does not increase the poor's mean income one-for-one, as claimed by Dollar and Kraay, but rather by only 50 per cent of the increase in per capita income.

In addition to the above direct calculations of the elasticity of the average income of the poor with respect to overall mean income, Ali and Elbadawi (2001) also conducted a regression test for the proportionality hypothesis.

Table 2.9 Regression Results: Dependent Variable Logarithm of Mean Income of the Poor

Independent Variables	Original Dollar–Kraay Specification	Dollar–Kraay Specification	Quadratic in Levels	Quadratic in Logs
Av. Income			0.0073	
			(0.0014)	
(Av. Income)^2			−0.000007	
			(0.000004)	
Ln Av. Income	0.6937	0.6929		−0.892
	(0.0937)	(0.0955)		(0.467)
(Ln)^2 Av. Income				0.1633
				(0.059)
SSA Dummy		−0.0058	−0.1644	−0.1453
		(0.1858)	(0.058)	(0.059)
Constant	1.342	1.3472	2.749	4.07
	(0.368)	(0.4127)	(0.1005)	(1.069)
R^2	0.5354	0.5354	0.899	0.901
Adjusted R^2	0.5253	0.51477	0.892	0.894

Source: Ali and Elbadawi (2001, 10, Table 6).

In addition to the original Dollar and Kraay (2001b) specification, where the logarithm of the mean income of the poor is regressed against the logarithm of the overall mean income, quadratic formats in the level and log of overall mean income were run to allow the elasticity in question to vary according to the level of development, as reflected by the overall mean income. In view of the observed significant difference of Sub-Saharan Africa, a dummy variable was introduced for this region. The results are summarized in Table 2.9, where bracketed values are adjusted White's heteroskedasticity consistent standard errors.[24]

Table 2.9 reports a set of interesting results. The first column corresponds to Dollar and Kraay and provides a direct estimate of the elasticity of the mean income of the poor with respect to mean income of society. According to the results, the elasticity of the mean income of the poor is about 0.69, and, with a t-value of 3.27, it is significantly different from one. The results for the quadratic in levels and in logs show that the curvature term in mean income is highly significant (at better than 5 per cent level of significance), which

Table 2.10 Income Elasticity of the Mean Income of the Poor in Arab Countries

Country	Quadratic in Levels	Quadratic in Logs
Algeria	0.67	0.67
Egypt	0.54	0.57
Jordan	0.75	0.72
Mauritania	0.34	0.39
Morocco	0.64	0.65
Tunisia	0.87	0.81
Mean (S.D.)	0.63 (0.18)	0.63 (0.14)

Source: Ali and Elbadawi (2001, 16, Appendix Table A3).

suggests that, in general, the income elasticity of the mean income of the poor should be expected to vary between countries depending on the state of development as captured by overall average income.

On the basis of the results for the quadratic specifications, the income elasticity of the mean income of the poor with respect to overall mean income can be calculated for various countries and groups of countries. The calculations show that, for the whole sample, the mean income elasticity of the average income of the poor is 0.58 (with a standard deviation of 0.25) for the quadratic in levels and 0.59 (with a standard deviation of 0.23) for the quadratic in logs. For the quadratic in levels, the mean elasticity varied from a low of 0.40 for Sub-Saharan Africa to a high of 0.76 for Latin America and for the quadratic in logs the range of the mean elasticity is from a low of 0.43 for Sub-Saharan Africa to a high of 0.76 for Latin America. Results for the six Arab countries are reported in Table 2.10.

The results for the Arab countries are similar to those for other regions and the whole sample in the sense that the mean elasticity is identical under the two specifications. For the Arab countries, and from the information provided in the table, it is easy to show that the regional elasticities are significantly different from one. For the elasticity based on the quadratic in levels the t-value is 5.04, while for the quadratic in logs the t-value is 6.47. Tunisia recorded the highest response of the mean income of the poor to changes in overall mean income, followed by Jordan, Algeria, Egypt, Morocco and Mauritania. These findings confirm the earlier results based on direct calculations and, more importantly, caution against using constant elasticities in general. Thus, on average, the growth effects of 'globalization', in the sense of possible increases in per

Table 2.11 Openness and the Average Income of the Poor (dependent variable is the logarithm of the average income of the poor)

Independent Variables	I	II	III	IV	V	VI	VII	VIII
Ln Av. Income	0.6525 (14.65)	0.6389 (13.16)	0.6562 (14.71)	0.6529 (16.40)	-2.9354 (3.96)	-2.8554 (3.84)	-2.7626 (3.76)	-2.4565 (4.03)
(Ln Av.Income)^2					0.2518 (4.91)	0.2459 (4.80)	0.2407 (4.72)	0.2174 (5.15)
OPNAV	-0.0193 (0.09)				0.1459 (0.80)			
OPENADJAV		0.1800 (0.78)				0.1859 (0.95)		
SWAV			0.0112 (0.13)				0.0024 (0.04)	
WTOAV				0.0887 (1.13)				0.0798 (1.12)
Constant	1.2043 (3.95)	1.3138 (3.80)	1.1765 (3.89)	1.1404 (1.68)	13.5834 (5.22)	13.1772 (5.09)	12.1302 (5.04)	13.79 (5.61)
No. of Observations	49	49	47	51	49	49	47	51
Adjusted R^2	0.8084	0.8116	0.8173	0.8289	0.8784	0.8802	0.8823	0.8872

Note: The income elasticity of the average income of the poor is less than one, as Ali and Elbadawi (2001) have argued.

capita income, will be expected to benefit the Arab poor only to the extent of about 63 per cent of the percentage increase in per capita income, rather than the claimed one-to-one effect.

Direct Effects

The direct effects of globalization on inequality can be captured by regressing various inequality measures as dependent variables on measures of globalization or measures of openness as proxy for 'globalization'. The Dollar and Kraay (2001b) data set produces a sample of 51 countries for which the mean income can be calculated, as was done by Ali and Elbadawi (2001). In their data set, Dollar and Kraay provide four measures of openness: (1) exports plus imports as a share of GDP in PPP. The variable is taken as a five-year average up to and including the year of the survey. This variable is denoted as OPENAV; (2) adjusted OPENADJAV which is based on the residuals from pooled ordinary least squares regression of OPENAV on the Frankel–Romer instrument and the logarithm of population in 1990;[25] (3) the Sachs and Warner openness dummy, denoted SWAV, and defined as a five-year average up to and including the year of the survey;[26] and (4) a dummy variable for membership (=1) in WTO or GATT, denoted as WTOAV, and defined as a five-year average up to and including the year of the survey.[27] The results are reported in Table 2.11 where figures in brackets are White heteroskedastic consistent t-values.

Columns I–IV in Table 2.11 report results on the basis of the original Dollar and Kraay specification for the various measures of openness. As for the effect of openness on the mean income of the poor, it is clear that none of the openness indicators has a statistically significant effect. The trade intensity measure has a negative effect in the sense that, controlling for the overall income level, it is expected that an increase in trade volumes as a ratio of GDP will reduce the average income of the poor. For the other three measures there is a positive relationship which must be appropriately interpreted.

Columns V–VIII in Table 2.11 report the results of the effect-of-openness measures on the mean income of the poor for the quadratic format, which allows the elasticity of the mean income of the poor with respect to overall mean income to vary with the level of development, as captured by per capita GDP. Interestingly, a Kuznet's process seems to exist, in the sense that at early stages of development the average income of the poor seems to decline before it increases. This is captured by both the negative and significant coefficient of the logarithm of overall mean income and by the positive and significant coefficient of its squared logarithm. This means that as per capita income increases, the mean income of the poor tends to decline first before it increases. As for the effect of the various measures of openness on the mean income of the poor, the results for the original Dollar and Kraay specification obtain for the quadratic form. None of the measures is significantly related to the average income of the poor.

The above two sets of results confirm the results reported by Dollar and Kraay regarding the effect of openness on the mean income of the poor where the poor are defined as the poorest 20 per cent of the population. To the extent that these various measures of openness can be taken to reflect the globalization levels of countries, then it can be concluded that perhaps the poor will not be affected by globalization. More direct results, however, would require the use of a more direct measure of globalization.

To apply the direct measures of globalization, a new sample of 58 countries for which Gini coefficients are available for the 1990s was chosen from Dollar and Kraay's data set. A test of the effect of globalization on inequality was performed by regressing the Gini coefficient on the World Bank's measures of globalization, namely the rate of increase of the trade intensity ratio over the period 1980–2000 (TGR); the stock of FDI as a ratio of GDP in 1999 (FDI); and the logarithm of the average annual number of immigrants to the United States, where the average is taken over the period 1990–2000 (LIM). In all regressions a dummy (DUM) for Arab countries is introduced. The Arab countries in the sample are Algeria (for which the Gini coefficient is reported for 1995), Egypt (1991), Jordan (1997), Mauritania (1993), Morocco (1990), Tunisia (1990) and Yemen (1992). The test follows the convention that one Gini observation from the 1990s is taken to represent inequality during the entire decade. The Gini coefficient and its logarithm are used as dependent variables. The qualitative results, as well as the explanatory powers, of the two formats are similar and as such only the results for the Gini logarithm are reported in Table 2.12, where the absolute values of the White heteroskedastic consistent t-values are between brackets.

Table 2.12 shows the expected direction of qualitative effect of each globalization measure on its own as well when all measures are considered together. In all the results the dummy for Arab countries is negative and significant, indicating that in the 1990s income inequality in the Arab countries was on average lower than prevailing levels in the developing countries of the sample. The results show that increased participation in world trade as reflected by the growth rate of the trade intensity measure is likely to reduce inequality in developing countries in a statistically significant fashion. A 1 per cent increase in the rate of growth of trade intensity is expected to reduce the Gini index by 0.01 per cent. On its own increased trade explains about 9 per cent of the observed variation in inequality in developing countries. Globalization as captured by immigration to the United States is also expected

Table 2.12 Globalization and Inequality in Developing Countries (dependent variable = logarithm of the Gini coefficient)

Model	TGR (growth rate of Trade/GDP)	FDI Stock/GDP	LIM	DUM (logarithm of annual immigrants to United States)	Constant (Arab dummy)	Adjusted R^2 (%)
I	-0.0109 (1.81)*			-0.1997 (3.60)**	3.8850 (125.2)***	9.19
II		0.0011 (2.98)***		0.1531 (2.75)***	3.8198 (122.3)***	9.17
III			-0.0249 (2.54)**	-0.1753 (3.97)***	4.0311 (55.53)***	15.16
IV	-0.0096 (1.46)	0.001 (2.49)**		-0.1848 (3.27)**	3.8506 (103.9)***	11.1
V	-0.0030 (0.39)		-0.0224 (2.04)**	-0.1837 (3.81)***	4.0222 (53.33)***	13.8
VI		0.0008 (1.95)*	-0.0225 (2.24)**	-0.1654 (3.61)***	3.9887 (49.79)***	16.1
VII	-0.0025 (0.31)	0.0008 (1.89)*	-0.0205 (1.85)*	-0.1727 (3.42)***	3.9816 (49.05)***	14.7

Note: *, **, and *** indicate significance at the usual 10, 5 and 1 per cent levels.

to reduce inequality in the developing countries in a statistically significant fashion. A 1 per cent increase in the average number of emigrants per country per year is expected to reduce the Gini coefficient by 0.03 per cent. On its own immigration to the United States explains about 9 per cent of the observed variation in inequality. In contrast to the effect of these two globalization measures, an increase in the ratio of the stock of FDI to GDP is expected to increase inequality in a statistically significant fashion, but the effect is rather small. A percentage point increase in the FDI/GDP ratio increases the Gini coefficient by 0.001 per cent. On its own the FDI variable explains 15 per cent of the variation in inequality.

In all the remaining results the trade intensity variable loses its statistical significance. The two other globalization measures keep their significance as well as the qualitative direction and the quantitative magnitude of their effect. The FDI and immigration variables together explain about 16 per cent of the variation in inequality in developing countries, while the three globalization measures explain about 15 per cent. Either way these seem to be reasonable results in view of the known structural and policy variables affecting inequality in various economies.

CONCLUSION

This study has produced four important results. First, the Arab region, diverse and oil rich as it may be, has so far been left out of the third globalization wave of globalization. At best, using the growth rate of trade/GDP ratio over the period 1980 to the present as the indicator of globalization, only five Arab countries could be considered as having globalized: Morocco, Syria, Tunisia, United Arab Emirates and Yemen. The only Arab country identified by the World Bank as having globalized, Jordan, does not belong to this set of Arab globalizers. This suggests that the identification of countries on the globalization scale is sensitive to the period over which globalization measures are constructed. Using the FDI stock as a ratio of GDP as a measure of globalization, only two Arab countries can be considered as having globalized by the end of 1999: Bahrain and Tunisia. At the other extreme, using the immigration to the United States measure of globalization, albeit in a heuristic fashion, none of the Arab countries could be considered as having globalized as yet.

Second, despite the problems involved in getting high-quality data on income or expenditure distribution, there is evidence to show that the Arab region boasts a fairly high degree of income inequality. The time trend of the degree of inequality, however, is subject to debate. Official data show inequality to have declined during the 1990s. Given the fact that the Arab region has so far been left out of the third globalization wave, it is not clear whether globalization is responsible for this declining trend.

Third, as in many other developing countries, the Arab poor, appropriately defined, stand to benefit from trade-induced economic growth by about 50 per cent of the increase in per capita income. This is contrary to the celebrated result that purports to promise the poor a one-to-one increase in their incomes as a result of a globalization-induced increase in per capita incomes.

Finally, preliminary evidence suggests a direct causal link between globalization as measured by FDI/GDP ratio and immigration to the United States in such a way that FDI increases inequality while immigration reduces it.

These tentative results should be considered as calling for increased research to ascertain the possible effects of globalization on various social dimensions in developing countries. Inequality in the distribution of the fruits of economic growth is an important aggregator of the social consequences which are likely to have serious implications for political stability with an obvious corollary for macroeconomic stability. In this respect, strong policy advocacy messages in the form of claims that globalization-induced economic 'growth is good for the poor' are not likely to help policymakers in developing countries, including the Arab states.[28] As rightly noted by Rodrik (2001, 2), world 'markets are a source of technology and capital; it would be silly for the developing world not to exploit these opportunities. But globalization is not a short cut to development. Policymakers need to forge a domestic growth strategy, relying on domestic investors and domestic institutions'. Such growth and development strategies can resolve the conflicts that may arise from deeper integration in world markets.

NOTES

I am grateful to Ahmed Al-Kawaz, Khalid Affan, Gary McMahon, an anonymous referee and the editors of this book for comments on an earlier draft and to Jamal Hamid for research assistance. I am also grateful to Professor Eltahir M. Nur, of the University of Khartoum, Sudan, for presenting the paper on my behalf at the GDN conference in Cairo.

1. For a similar definition see Rodrik (1999, vii), who defines it as 'the whirlwind of technological change and liberalized trade and investment that is bringing huge gains in communications and efficiency, and effecting huge shifts in production and wealth'. From a political-economy perspective, Gray (2002, 55) notes that one possible definition of globalization is the

'worldwide spread of modern technologies of industrial production and communication of all kinds across frontiers – in trade, capital, production and information'.

2. The World Bank's report draws on the recent work of Williamson (1997) and Lindert and Williamson (2001) on the history of globalization and inequality.

3. The other 23 globalized developing countries are: Argentina, Bangladesh, Brazil, China, Colombia, Costa Rica, Côte d'Ivoire, Dominican Republic, Haiti, Hungary, India, Jamaica, Malaysia, Mali, Mexico, Nepal, Nicaragua, Paraguay, Philippines, Rwanda, Thailand, Uruguay and Zimbabwe.

4. The Gini coefficient is based on the Lorenz curve. The Lorenz curve is drawn on the basis of the cumulative percentage shares of the population (on the horizontal axis) against their corresponding cumulative percentage share of income (on the vertical axis), where the population groups are arrayed from poorest to richest. The curve joining the plotted points is the Lorenz curve. If income is equally distributed such that every person gets the mean income, then the Lorenz curve coincides with the diagonal joining the point zero on the horizontal axis to the point 100 per cent on the vertical axis; otherwise, the curve traces points that lie below the diagonal. The ratio of the area between the diagonal and the Lorenz curve to the area of the unit triangle defines the Gini coefficient.

5. For other measures of inequality see Sen (1997, 24–46) and Kakwani (1980, 63–95). In Sen's notation let n be the number of people in the population and y_i, and x_i be the income and the share of income of person i and let μ be the average level of income. The statistical measures of inequality include the following: (a) the range: $E = [\max_i y_i - \min_i y_i]/\mu$; (b) the relative mean deviation: $M = \Sigma \mid \mu - y_i \mid / n\mu$; (c) the variance: $V = \Sigma (\mu - y_i)^2/ n$; (d) the coefficient of variation: $C = V^{0.5}/\mu$; and, (e) the standard deviation of the logarithms of income: $SL = [\Sigma (\log\mu - \log y_i)^2/ n] 0.5$. Another famous measure of inequality is known as Theil's measure, which is based on the idea of entropy and is defined as $T = \Sigma x_i \log nx_i$. The most famous welfare-based measure of inequality is Atkinson's measure which relies on the idea of the equally distributed equivalent income, y_e, defined as that level of per capita income which if enjoyed by everybody would make total welfare exactly equal to the total welfare generated by the actual distribution of income. Atkinson's measure is given by $A = 1 - (y_e/ \mu)$.

6. See Atkinson (1999) for an alternative view of the time trend on inequality and causal factors in OECD countries.

7. This result is based on the work of Dollar and Kraay (2001a). The investigation involved regressing the income share of the poorest 20 per cent of the population on various measures of openness.

8. This result is due to Ravallion (2001), who applied the concept of convergence used in the empirical growth literature which requires regressing the observed change in inequality between two dates on the initial level of inequality in a test equation of the form $\Delta G_i = a + b G_{i0}+ e_i$; where G is the Gini coefficient or any other inequality measure and the subscript i denotes the country. There will be inequality convergence if b is negative and significantly different from zero. Using 86 inequality spells for 21 countries, Ravallion (2001, 13)

concludes that evidence is found of inequality convergence, with a tendency for within-country inequality to fall (rise) in countries with initially high (low) inequality. 'It seems that countries are tending to become more equally unequal, heading toward a Gini index of around 40 per cent'.

9. According to GDN regional perspectives the coverage of this chapter should have been the Middle East and North Africa (MENA) region, which includes Iran and Turkey. Confining the analysis to the Arab region is deliberate in view of the fact that in most of the analysis dealing with inequality and poverty issues the MENA region is usually represented by six Arab countries: Egypt, Jordan, Tunisia, Morocco, Algeria and Yemen (see, for example, Chen and Ravallion 2000). The reason for this practice in the relevant literature is the unavailability of high-quality distribution data for the other countries in the MENA region. On the other hand some of the countries that belong to the Arab region but do not belong to MENA are usually classified as Sub-Saharan Arab countries: Djibouti, Mauritania, Somalia and Sudan. For regional coverage similar to ours see Page and van Gelder (2002, 2n2) who confine MENA to the six Arab countries noted above in addition to Iraq.

10. Due to a lack of adequate data, Libya, Palestinian territories, Somalia and Comoros were not included in the classification. Such a classification scheme remains arbitrary but can be useful for the purposes of the analysis.

11. It is worth noting that most of the Arab countries (except Bahrain, Kuwait, Oman, Syria, Qatar, Saudi Arabia and the United Arab Emirates) have implemented structural adjustment programs since the 1980s with the objective of enhancing their production efficiency through various liberalization measures, including trade liberalization and privatization. Moreover, under the auspices of the League of Arab States an attempt has been made to liberalize trade between Arab countries within the context of WTO rules. The process to create an Arab Free Trade Area is still under way.

12. Despite the fact that WTO membership is not used as a measure of globalization, it should be noted as of 23 April 2004, the World Trade Organization had 147 members, including 11 Arab countries: Bahrain, Djibouti, Egypt, Jordan, Kuwait, Mauritania, Morocco, Oman, Qatar, Tunisia and UAE. Another five Arab countries are observers: Algeria, Lebanon, Saudi Arabia, Sudan and Yemen.

13. Readers interested in the details of the trade ratios in the Arab region may wish to consult the earlier expanded version of this chapter, which appeared as Ali (2003). The time series on the trade ratios is compiled from the World Bank (2002b), Arab Monetary Fund (2002; 1985) and the League of Arab States et al. (2000; 1995).

14. While it can be argued that for the Arab region migration to Europe, and possibly to the oil-rich Middle East countries, is important, it should be noted that the World Bank used migration to the United States in view of the availability of detailed data. Migration to the New World defined the very first wave of globalization, when the United States was an important destination. Moreover, it is not clear in what sense migration of Arabs to the Arab region would constitute integration into world markets. Therefore, the use of immigration

to the United States is consistent with both the practice of the World Bank as well as the historical evidence.

15. The figures for 1990 and 1991 are considered exceptionally high due to the legalization of illegal immigrants (mainly Mexicans) and to the special provisions for the Chinese after the Tiananmen Square incident in 1989. I am grateful to an anonymous referee for pointing this out to me.

16. High-quality data on income inequality are required to (1) be based on household surveys; (2) be based on comprehensive coverage of all sources of income or uses of expenditure; and (3) be representative of the population at the national level, that is, not confined to sectors or groups of population (Deininger and Squire 1996).

17. Such average comparisons are sensitive to the countries included in the sample and they should only be used as indications. Moreover, due to the fact that the Gini coefficient is not additively separable it is very difficult to compare their averages over countries. Alternative methodologies compute inequality measures from decile observations from various countries of a given region, as will be noted below.

18. For a possible explanation of the declining trend see Page and van Gelder (2002).

19. The *Economist* (2000a, 2000b, 2001) celebrated the result three times while Moore (2001) used the result to preach to Arab delegates on the importance of working for the success of the Doha WTO meetings.

20. Note that the headcount measure of poverty is given by $H = q/n$, where q is the number of people with incomes below the poverty line, z. The poverty gap measure of poverty $PG = H (1 - y_p/z)$, where y_p is the average income of the poor. Therefore, the average income of the poor, $y_p = z (1 - PG/H)$. Thus the average income of the poor can be calculated once information on the headcount, the poverty gap and the poverty line is available. This, of course, requires calculating the poverty measures.

21. Note that a necessary and sufficient condition for E_{yp} to equal one is that E_z is equal to one, which will obtain if the poverty line is assumed to be a constant proportion of overall average income. If such an assumption is made it can be shown that all poverty measures that are homogeneous of degree zero in mean income and the poverty line will be functions of the degree of inequality in the distribution of income. This automatically implies that E_H will be zero. Moreover, note that if E_z is assumed to be zero, equation 1.2 in the text collapses to that equation derived by Kakwani (1980).

22. On the basis of detailed country calculations, a t-test was performed on these results for regions and for the whole sample, where it is found that for all regions except Sub-Saharan Africa the income elasticity of the average income of the poor is not significantly different from 0.5. The income elasticity of the poor in Sub-Saharan is significantly lower than 0.5.

23. For similar results see Foster and Székely (2001) who use the concept of general means to track low incomes. The authors specifically acknowledge that it is the difficulty of computing appropriately defined average income of the poor, using poverty lines for a large number of countries, and the arbitrariness of poverty lines, that prompted them to use the concept of general means to track low incomes. Their overall conclusion is, 'living standards at the

bottom of the distribution improve with growth, but that the poor gain proportionately much less than the average individual' (Foster and Székely 2001, 17).

24. Dollar and Kraay (2002) argue that simple OLS could result in inconsistent parameter estimates for at least three reasons: measurement errors, omitted variables bias or endogeneity due to feedback from mean income of the poor to society's mean income. These econometric issues can be investigated further, but for our purposes the results should be taken as possible confirmation to the direct calculations reported above.

25. Frankel and Romer (1999), in the context of exploring the role of trade in explaining growth, regressed bilateral trade flows as a share of GDP on measures of country mass (area and population), distance between trade partners, and other geographical variables and then constructed a predicted aggregate trade share for each country using the estimated coefficients.

26. Sachs and Warner (1995) define a country as closed if it had any of the following: non-tariff barriers covering 40 per cent or more of trade; average tariff rates of 40 per cent or more; a black market premium of 20 per cent or more; a socialist government; or a state monopoly on major exports.

27. Other measures of openness in the Dollar and Kraay data set include: capital account restriction, denoted KARESTAV; and import taxes as a share of imports, denoted IMPTAXAV. These were not used because they will reduce the size of the sample for which we can calculate poverty measures and hence the average income of the poor.

28. One possible use of the results of the chapter for policy advocacy purposes is to say that Arab countries need to make more efforts to participate in global markets. For such policy message to be convincing for policy-makers the advocates need to be more specific on what these additional efforts are supposed to be.

SELECTED BIBLIOGRAPHY

Ali, Ali Abdel Gadir (2003), 'Globalization and Inequality in the Arab Region', Kuwait, Arab Planning Institute, Working Paper No. API/WPS 0307.

Ali, Ali Abdel Gadir and Ibrahim Elbadawi, (2001), 'Growth Could Be Good for the Poor', unpublished paper.

Arab Monetary Fund (1985), 'National Accounts', www.amf.org.ae.

Arab Monetary Fund (2002), 'National Accounts', www.amf.org.ae.

Atkinson, Anthony B. (1999), 'Is Rising Inequality Inevitable? A Critique of the Transatlantic Consensus', Helsinki, United Nations University, World Institute for Development Research (UNU/WIDER), Annual Lecture No. 3.

Chen, Shaohua and Martin Ravallion (2000), 'How Did the World's Poorest Fare in the 1990s', World Bank, Policy Research Department Working Paper No. 2409.

Datt, Gaurav, Dean Jolliffe and Manohar Sharma (1998), 'A Profile of Poverty in Egypt: 1997', Washington, DC, International Food Policy Research Institute, Food Consumption and Nutrition Division, FCND Discussion Paper No. 49.

Deininger, Karl and Pedro Olinto (2002), 'Asset Distribution, Inequality and Growth', Washington, DC, World Bank, Working Paper No. 2375.

Deininger, Karl and Lyn Squire (1996), 'Measuring inequality: a new data-base', *World Bank Economic Review*, **10** (3), 565–91.

Dollar, David and Aart Kraay (2001a), 'Trade, Growth and Poverty', World Bank, Policy Research Department Working Paper No. 2615.

Dollar, David and Aart Kraay (2001b), 'Growth is Good for the Poor', World Bank, Policy Research Department Working Paper No. 2587.

Dollar, David and Aart Kraay (2002), 'Data Set for Growth is Good for the Poor', World Bank, www.worldbank.org.

Economist (2000a), 'Quantity and quality', 30 September.

Economist (2000b), 'Growth is good', 27 May.

Economist (2001), 'Globalization and its critics: a survey of globalization', 29 September.

Economic Research Forum of Arab Countries, Iran and Turkey (ERF) (1998), Economic Trends in the MENA Region; Cairo, Egypt.

Foster, James and Miguel Székely (2001), 'Is Economic Growth Good for the Poor? Tracking Low Incomes Using General Means'. Paper presented at UNU/WIDER Development conference 'Growth and Poverty', Helsinki.

Frankel, Jeffrey and David Romer (1999), 'Does Trade Cause Growth?', *American Economic Review*, **89** (3), 379–99.

Gray, John (2002), *False Dawn: The Delusions of Global Capitalism*, London: Granta Books.

Kakwani, Nanak (1980), *Income Inequality and Poverty: Methods of Estimation and Policy Applications,* Oxford: Oxford University Press.

Kuwait Ministry of Planning, (2001), 'Household Income and Expenditure Survey 1999–2000: Preliminary Results', Kuwait: Central Statistical Department.

League of Arab States, Arab Fund for Economic and Social Development, Arab Monetary Fund and OAPEC (1995), *Unified Arab Economic Report 1995,* Cairo, Egypt (in Arabic).

League of Arab States, Arab Fund for Economic and Social Development, Arab Monetary Fund and OAPEC (2000), *Unified Arab Economic Report 2001*, Cairo, Egypt (in Arabic).

Li, Hongyi, Lyn Squire and Henfou Zou (1998), 'Explaining international and intertemporal variations in income inequality', *Economic Journal*, **108**, 26–43.

Lindert, Peter and Jeffrey Williamson (2001), 'Globalization and Inequality: A Long History'; address to the World Bank Annual Bank Conference on Development Economics – Europe, www.worldbank.org.

Milanovic, Branko (2002), 'Can We Discern the Effects of Globalization on Income Distribution? Evidence from Household Budget Surveys', Washington, DC, World Bank, Policy Research Working Paper No. 2876.

Moore, Mike (2001), 'The WTO and the Arab World: Preparation for Doha', address to UNCTAD's High-Level Meeting for Arab Countries, 20-21 June; www.unctad.org.

Page, John and Linda van Gelder (2002), 'Globalization, Growth, and Poverty Reduction in the Middle East and North Africa, 1970–1999'. Paper presented to Mediterranean Development Forum conference MDF-4, Amman, Jordan; www.worldbank.org/mdf.

Ravallion, Martin (2001), 'Inequality Convergence', Washington, DC, World Bank Working Paper, 23 January.

Rodrik, Dani (1999), 'The New Global Economy and the Developing Countries: Making Openness Work', Washington, DC, Overseas Development Council, Policy Essay No. 24.

Rodrik, Dani (2001), 'The Developing Countries' Hazardous Obsession with Global Integration'. Speech at John F. Kennedy School of Government, Harvard University, Cambridge, MA, 8 January; www.southcentre.org/papers/nonsouthwestcenter/ toc.htm.

Sachs, Jeffrey and Andrew Warner (1995), 'Economic Reform and the Process of Global Integration', Washington, DC, Brookings Institution, Papers on Economic Activity, No.1.

Sala-i-Martin, Xavier (2002), 'The Disturbing Rise in Global Income Inequality', Cambridge, MA, National Bureau for Economic Research, Working Paper No. W8904.

Sen, Amartya (1997), *On Economic Inequality*, Oxford: Clarendon Press.

Soros, George (2002), *On Globalization*, Oxford: Public Affairs Ltd.

Stiglitz, Joseph (2002) *Globalization and Its Discontents*, London: Allen Lane, Penguin Press.

United Nations Committee on Trade and Development (2001), *World Investment Report 2001: Promoting Linkages*, Geneva: UNCTAD.

U.S. Immigration and Naturalization Service (2000), *Fiscal Year 2000 Statistical Yearbook*, www.ins.usdoj.gov.

Williamson, Jeffrey (1997), 'Globalization and inequality: past and present', *World Bank Research Observer*, **12** (2), 117–38.

World Bank (2002a), *Globalization, Growth and Poverty: Building an Inclusive World Economy*, Oxford and New York: Oxford University Press.

World Bank (2002b), *World Development Indicators 2001*, Washington, DC, CD-ROM.

3. Sub-Saharan Africa: The Myth and the Reality

S. Ibi Ajayi

'Globalization' is not a new phenomenon. It can be loosely defined as 'the increasing interaction among, and integration of, the activities, especially economic activities, of human societies around the world' (Mussa 2000). More concretely, however, it 'refers to the growing economic interdependence of countries worldwide through the increasing volume and variety of cross-border transactions in goods and services and of international capital flows and also through the more rapid and widespread diffusion of technology' (International Monetary Fund 1997c, 45). Globalization encompasses both a description and a prescription (United Nations Development Programme 1997). The description lies in widening international flows of trade, finance and information into a single, integrated global market, while the prescription lies in liberalizing national and global markets in the belief that free flows of trade, finance and information will produce the best outcome for both growth and human welfare. The most important aspects of economic globalization are the breaking down of national economic barriers, the international spread of trade, financial and production activities and the growing power of transnational corporations and international financial institutions in these processes (Khor 2000).

This chapter analyzes the issues of globalization and equity with specific reference to Sub-Saharan Africa. It does not deal with globalization and equity within individual African countries. Specifically, it analyzes the issues connected with Africa's integration into the global economy using different indicators. It discusses Africa's poor macroeconomic performance relative to the rest of the world. It also discusses how Africa can be integrated into the global economy, taking maximum advantage of the opportunities while minimizing associated risks. In the process, Africa may bridge the global inequality gap.

The chapter begins by sketching the parameters of globalization and equity and their relevance to Africa. Next it discusses the benefits and risks of globalization and how globalization would help Africa advance economically. Channels of global interaction are discussed to establish how well Africa is currently integrated into the global economy. The chapter next focuses on how Africa can better operate in the global economy and increase its income relative to the rest of the world. However, integration alone will not make a country grow. African states must also adopt policies that will enhance its growth prospects. Although external factors may complicate Africa's growth in trade and investment, the situation is not hopeless.

THE BENEFITS AND RISKS OF GLOBALIZATION

Globalization has many positive, innovative and dynamic aspects. These include greater market access, as well as increased access to capital, information and technology. Even though globalization has brought opportunities for growth and development for both the rich and the poor countries, not all countries have been able to take advantage of the new opportunities. Globalization worldwide has brought about a quantum leap in trade, capital flows and movement of people. Trade flows increased by sixteen-fold in the last fifty years as a result of removing trade barriers. Opening up to international trade has helped many countries grow far more quickly than they would have otherwise. World exports of goods and services almost tripled in real terms between 1970 and 2000. Capital flows expanded even faster, with total foreign direct investment (FDI) soaring from $160 billion in 1991 to $1.1 trillion in 2000. FDI to developing countries increased from $24 billion in 1990 to $178 billion in 2000. The whole world has become more prosperous and healthier as a result. In some countries, per capita income tripled, child mortality rates halved and life expectancy climbed.

The benefits of globalization are similar to those of specialization and market expansion through trade as emphasized by the classical economists. The simple argument for free trade is that it allows countries to concentrate on activities in which they have a comparative advantage, and it subjects firms to the healthy discipline of foreign competition. Specialization and competition yield higher productivity and increased living standards. Consumers can enjoy a wider constellation of goods and services at lower costs. With globalization, a country can access larger and more diversified sources of finance. FDI brings cheap technology and other forms of intellectual capital to countries, saving them the cost of reinventing the wheel. Despite tremendous poverty, Africans can still benefit from globalization. Given Africa's comparative advantage in abundant, low-cost unskilled labor, it should concentrate on producing simple, labor-intensive goods. By increasing output and exports of this kind, Africa will see an increasing demand for unskilled labor and an increase in local incomes.

Globalization remains a highly charged and controversial issue, because it entails many risks. Globalization can increase inequality between rich and poor countries, threaten the sovereignty of small countries, exploit workers and damage local economies by exposing them to international competition. Major cities across the globe have experienced large-scale protests connected to globalization.

Globalization also presents a number of specific concerns for developing regions, such as Sub-Saharan Africa. First, exposing domestic industries to competition from abroad threatens business owners as well as workers. If domestic industries are unable to match the productivity of their competitors, workers may see their wages drop and their jobs disappear. Second, other regions may dump their goods in Sub-Saharan Africa, which harms domestic production and hurts workers as well.

A number of developing countries, particularly in Asia, have taken advantage of globalization and made substantial progress towards closing the income gaps relative to the industrial countries. While most other regions have seen growth in trade and investment, thus fueling their structural transformation, Sub-Saharan Africa has been marginalized. In fact, its share of world trade, investment and output has declined to negligible proportions (Collier and Gunning 1995, Collier 1997). Africa has consistently lagged behind and its income gap, relative to the advanced countries and some developing countries in Asia, has widened.

WHY SHOULD AFRICA GLOBALIZE?

While Africa was shielded from the full force of the Asian economic crisis because of its slow integration into the world economy, does its isolation explain why economic prosperity has eluded much of the continent? Africa's economic marginalization has been attributed to its isolationist policy and protectionist approach to economic development (Ajayi 2000). Africa has yet to reap the real benefits of financial globalization: increased resources for productive investment (access to foreign savings which can help circumvent some of the traditional obstacles to rapid growth), efficient production using new technology and cheap access to foreign imports of investment and intermediate goods that may not be readily available at home (Ouattara 1998).

Based on an index of trade-to-GDP, Africa has been integrated into the world economy since World War II. In recent times Sub-Saharan Africa's trade, measured in goods as a percentage share of gross domestic product (GDP), rose from 42.3 per cent to 56 per cent. This ratio is comparable to East Asia and the Pacific and is higher than both the world and low-income region averages. It is also higher than Latin America and the Caribbean. This level of global integration, however, has not led to the higher growth that could lead Africa out of poverty.

There are a number of explanations for Africa's poor macroeconomic performance. These include colonial history, heavy dependence on primary products with low-income elasticity of demand, macroeconomic policy errors, extraordinarily disadvantageous geography,[1] ethnic fragmentation,[2] ineffective or non-existent institutions, civil strife, disease and inclement weather. All these factors make Africa unattractive to potential domestic and foreign investors. The rationale for opening its economy is based on a simple but powerful premise: economic integration will improve economic performance. Africa cannot and must not remain isolated; failure to open its economy will deepen its economic marginalization and further exacerbate the income disparity between it and the rest of the world. Additionally, globalization holds the promise of new opportunities for expanded markets, new technologies and ideas, heightened competition to pursue international standards of efficiency and cheaper sources of finance. Globalization promises increased productivity and, more importantly, a higher standard of living for Africa. The problem, perhaps, lies in the unusual way Africa entered the global economy.

GLOBALIZATION AND INEQUALITY: A GROWING GAP

From a political-economy point of view, it is difficult to have a widely accepted definition of equity, because the concept is rooted in the ethics of social values, and different societies have different perceptions of what is equitable.[3] Most manifestations of inequality are rooted in unequal access, capabilities or capacities. In the case of globalization, inequality can be associated with the issues of unequal access and different outcomes.[4]

Globalization has created serious debates over its effects on income inequality, average living standards and poverty. Much of the recent debate has focused primarily on Organization for Economic Co-operation and Development (OECD) countries, specifically on the claim that globalization has contributed to inequality by increasing the wage differential between skilled and unskilled workers.

Two distinguishing characteristics of contemporary globalization are its pace and its reach. As pointed out by the United Nations Development Programme (1999), the 'process is uneven and unbalanced, with uneven participation of countries and people in the expanding opportunities of globalization – in the global economy, in global technology, in the global spread of cultures and in the global governance'. The report went further to state, 'The new rules of globalization – and the players writing them – focus on integrating global markets, neglecting the needs of people that markets cannot meet'.

The unequal distribution of benefits and losses under globalization leads to the polarization between countries which gain and the other countries which either lose out or become marginalized. The uneven or unequal nature of globalization is manifested in the fast growing gap between the world's rich and poor and in the differences among countries in the distribution of gains and losses. International capital flows tend to be highly concentrated, favoring some selected countries and regions. Foreign direct investment (FDI) goes disproportionately to richer countries despite expectations that the marginal returns from investment are higher in poor countries due to the scarcity of capital. In the 1990s, 58 per cent of total FDI went to developed countries; 85 per cent of the FDI that went to developing and transition economies went to only 20 countries, and the bottom 16 combined received less than the top two together (Monsod 2000). In the 1980s and 1990s, FDI to Sub-Saharan Africa grew by 59 per cent, whereas the increases to Europe and Central Asia, East Asia and the Pacific, South Asia and Latin America and the Caribbean were 5,200 per cent, 942 per cent, 740 per cent and 455 per cent, respectively (Asiedu 2002). Africa's share of FDI dropped to 2.3 per cent in 2000 (Basu and Srinivasan 2002).

Similarly, information and technology are not disseminated evenly and freely but tend to concentrate in countries with high education levels and advanced technologies such as computers and access to the Internet. The information and communications technology revolution has created its own gap favoring the developed world. In 1998, industrial countries accounting for 15 per cent of the world population had 88 per cent of all Internet users. In contrast South Asia, with 20 per cent of the world population, had less than 1 per cent of Internet users while Sub-Saharan Africa, with 9.7 per cent of the world population, had only 0.1 per cent connected to the Internet.

The gap between the rich and the poor nations of the world is increasing. The 1999 UNDP Development Report found that, over the last ten years, the number of people earning $1 a day or less has remained static at 1.2 billion, while the number earning less than $2 a day has increased from 2.55 billion to 2.8 billion people. The gap between the top and bottom quintiles of national income has grown from 30 to 1 in 1960 to 82 to 1 in 1995. By the late 1990s,

Table 3.1 GDP Growth

Region	Average annual % growth 1990–2001	Per capita average annual % growth 1990–2001
World	2.70	1.20
Low income	3.40	1.40
East Asia and Pacific	7.50	6.20
Europe and Central Asia	−1.00	−1.10
Latin America–Caribbean	3.20	1.50
South America	5.50	3.50
Sub-Saharan Africa	2.60	0.00

Source: World Bank, World Development Indicators, CD-ROM (2003).

the 20 per cent of the world's population living in the highest-income countries had 86 per cent of world GDP, 85 per cent of world export markets, 68 per cent of FDI and 74 per cent of world telephone lines. In all categories, the bottom quintile registered barely 1 per cent.

The benefits of globalization have largely gone to the wealthiest nations. Only the rich can cross borders freely, and advanced information technology is scarce in many parts of the developing world. Africa has fared especially poorly despite its abundant resources. Africa has the worst poverty levels in the world. Compared to other regions of the world, Africa has been excluded from participation in the global economy.[5] The fastest economic growth and the fastest poverty reduction were in East Asia and the Pacific, where GDP per capita grew at a rate of 6 per cent between 1990 and 2001 and the share of people living in extreme poverty fell substantially. What, then, is the situation in Africa?

In order to understand the macroeconomic performance of Africa, it is necessary to take a long-term perspective on the issues of growth and poverty. Table 3.1 shows growth in GDP using the average annual percentage and per capita average annual growth for the period 1990–2001. During this period, Sub-Saharan Africa had an average annual growth rate of 2.6 per cent. This is in contrast to the growth rate of East Asia and the Pacific (7.5 per cent) and South America (5.5 per cent). Africa's growth rate was below both the world growth rate and the growth rate for low-income countries. While the GDP per capita of other regions grew at significant positive rates, Africa's per capita

Table 3.2 Income Inequality Measures by World Regions

Region	Gini coefficient	Share of top 20%	Share of middle class	Bottom 20%
Africa	0.51	50.6	34.4	5.2
East Asia and Pacific	0.38	44.3	37.5	6.8
South Asia	0.32	39.9	38.4	8.8
Latin America	0.49	52.9	33.8	4.5
Industrial Countries	0.34	39.8	41.8	6.3

Source: Deininger and Squire (1996), Tables 5 and 6.

growth was flat. South Asia, East Asia and the Pacific registered growth rates of 3.5 per cent and 6.2 per cent, respectively.

The figures for inequality and poverty are even more stunning. Africa has a high degree of income inequality among world regions. The high-quality data provided by Deininger and Squire (1996) can be used to compare income inequality in Africa with other regions. Table 3.2 shows that for all regions, South Asia has the most equal distribution of total expenditure (income), as well as the lowest Gini coefficient of 0.32. Also, the richest 20 per cent of the population in South Asia receive 40 per cent of total income. This is the smallest share compared to other regions of the world. Africa, as seen from the table, is the region where income is most unequal in the world, as shown by the Gini coefficient of 0.51.

Other measures confirm the high level of poverty in Africa compared to the rest of the world. Table 3.3 shows Africa fares the worst in all the different measures, implying that Africa has the highest rates of incidence, depth and severity of poverty in the world. Table 3.4 shows the share of people living on $1 per day at various periods. Africa has the greatest share of people living in poverty in all the periods shown. In 1999, about 49 per cent of Africans lived in poverty as opposed to about 16 per cent in East Asia and Pacific and 11 per cent in Latin America and the Caribbean. From these estimates, all things being equal, Africa is still expected to have the highest poverty level in the world by 2015, with 46 per cent of Africans then living on less than $1 a day.

Table 3.3 Poverty in World Regions: A Comparison

Region	Number of Countries	Per capita Expenditures (%)	Headcount ratio (%)	Poverty-gap ratio (%)	Squared poverty-gap ratio (%)
Africa	18	96	53.52 (3.60)	22.66 (1.62)	12.73 (0.93)
Asia	8	101	30.49 (5.10)	9.60 (1.51)	4.44 (1.68)
Latin America	16	241	40.60 (9.11)	18.30 (3.70)	10.43 (2.06)

Source: Ali and Elbadawi (1999).

Table 3.4 Share of People Living on Less than $1/day (%)

Region	1990	1999	2015
East Asia and Pacific	30.50	15.60	3.90
South Asia	45.00	36.60	15.70
Sub-Saharan Africa	47.40	49.00	46.00
Latin America and Caribbean	11.00	11.10	7.50
Europe and Central Asia	1.40	5.10	1.40

Source: World Bank, World Development Indicators, CD-ROM (2003).

HOW WELL IS AFRICA INTEGRATED INTO THE WORLD ECONOMY?

In order to discuss the impact of globalization on Africa and its equity implications, it is necessary to ask if Africa is fully integrated into the world economy. Some authors contend that Africa is lagging behind not just in trade, but in other areas as well. Alternative measures that attempt to capture the speed with which countries are integrating into the world economy confirm that Africa is lagging behind. Three standard indicators of global integration are international trade, capital flows and advances in communications and transport.

Trade

Trade has been a major engine of growth in the industrial countries as well as the middle-income countries. Extensive studies have consistently shown that export growth is linked to economic growth. There is also growing empirical evidence that improved trade performance is associated with increased employment opportunities and income for the poor. Dollar and Kraay (2001b) have provided clear evidence of growth among a group of developing countries which have significantly opened up to international trade.

Trade remains the principal vehicle for Africa's entry and full participation in the world economy. Trade is hardly new to Africa. Until the Atlantic slave trade began in the eighteenth century, trade between Europeans and Africans consisted of camel caravans crossing the Sahara carrying salt, fine tools and swords from Europe in exchange for gold, silver, nuts and ivory from Africa. Many African countries became European colonies responsible for supplying raw materials to factories and markets in the imperial homelands. While the volume of goods and services traded across the world has grown over the years, the volume of trade in Africa has not outpaced its GDP. In the period 1980–96, Africa was the only major region in the world to experience an absolute decline in its export earnings per person (Blooms and Sachs 1998).

Africa's trade performance over the years can be seen from its export and total trade performance. In 1980, Africa's share of world exports stood at about 5 per cent, while Asia and the Middle East shares stood at 8 per cent and about 11 per cent, respectively. Africa's share of world exports has steadily declined, while the share of other regions has increased. In the period 1980–90, Africa's share of world exports was about 3 per cent; it declined to only 1.95 per cent between 1991 and 2001. Asia, however, increased its share of world exports from 11 per cent in the period 1980–90 to about 18 per cent between 1991 and 2001 (see Table 3.5 and Figure 3.1). Based on its total export/GDP ratio, Africa has not fared too poorly (see Table 3.6). This ratio however cannot be used as an indicator of the degree of integration into the world economy, because it merely reflects the importance of primary products in trade and hence how vulnerable countries are to the vagaries of commodity prices. The ratio of trade/GDP is less important than the share of manufactured exports in total exports, which is often used as an imperfect measure of a country's ability

Table 3.5 Regional Shares in World Exports, 1980–2001

Year	Africa	Asia	Middle East	Industrial Countries	Developing Countries
1980	4.93	8.18	10.50	65.01	34.99
1981	4.12	9.02	11.01	63.80	36.20
1982	3.74	9.57	9.32	65.38	34.62
1983	3.80	10.27	7.65	66.18	33.82
1984	3.58	11.18	6.47	66.54	33.46
1985	3.47	10.91	5.43	67.91	32.09
1986	2.78	10.96	3.66	72.16	27.85
1987	2.60	12.09	3.76	71.41	28.58
1988	2.32	13.00	3.20	71.47	28.53
1989	2.31	13.35	4.11	70.36	29.63
1990	2.44	13.06	4.47	71.37	28.63
1991	2.28	14.52	3.87	70.88	29.12
1992	2.11	15.48	3.82	70.54	29.46
1993	2.00	17.04	3.58	69.01	30.99
1994	1.85	17.82	3.34	68.06	31.94
1995	1.82	18.07	3.11	67.72	32.28
1996	1.96	18.08	3.47	66.70	33.30
1997	1.94	18.62	3.40	65.88	34.12
1998	1.69	17.97	2.76	67.41	32.59
1999	1.78	18.46	3.24	66.38	33.61
2000	1.97	19.75	4.41	62.98	37.02
2001	2.02	19.25	4.33	63.17	36.84
1980–90	3.28	11.05	6.33	68.33	31.67
1991–2001	1.95	17.73	3.58	67.16	32.84

Source: Data from IMF *International Financial Statistics Yearbook* (2002).

to produce at world standards and absorb new technologies (Brahmbhatt and Dadush 1996).

Table 3.7 shows that since 1995, the share of manufactures in Africa's exports has varied between 32 per cent and 36 per cent. In contrast South Asia reported a 78–79 per cent ratio for the same period, while East Asia and the Pacific hovered between 78 and 83 per cent. With one-third of the share of exports arising from the manufacturing sector, it can roughly be said

Figure 3.1 Africa's Share in World Exports, 1980–2001

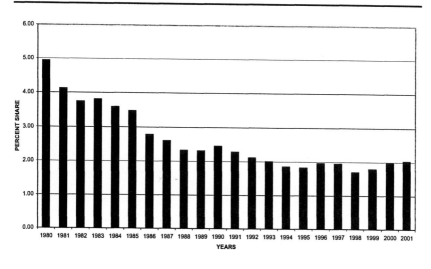

Table 3.6 Sub-Saharan Africa: Exports as a Percentage of GDP, 1980–2000

Year	Exports/GDP %	Year	Exports/GDP %
1980	32.1	1991	25.2
1981	26.9	1992	25.2
1982	25.3	1993	26.1
1983	24.1	1994	28.1
1984	25.8	1995	28.5
1985	28.7	1996	29.5
1986	27.7	1997	28.9
1987	27.1	1998	28.2
1988	26.8	1999	28.5
1989	27.3	2000	31.9
1990	27.2		

Source: World Bank, World Development Indicators (2002).

Table 3.7 Manufactures' Share in Exports of Selected Regions, 1995–2000

Year	Sub-Saharan Africa	East Asia and Pacific	South Asia
1995	34.03	78.87	76.35
1996	32.96	80.28	75.67
1997	36.99	79.66	77.49
1998	34.98	81.00	78.43

Source: World Bank: World Development Indicators (2002).

that Africa has been unable to produce at world standards and has not been absorbing technical knowledge as effectively as the other regions mentioned.

With the exception of South Africa, Mauritius, Madagascar and Angola,[6] Africa's trade has been overwhelming concentrated in a narrow range of unprocessed primary commodities. Africa's declining share in world trade is related to its skewed export profile. In general, African states have failed to diversify out of traditional primary commodity exports into more dynamic export sectors. Global demand for these commodities is nearly flat. Africa has also experienced a long-term decline in its TOT. The differing growth rates of Africa and East Asia are often explained by the difference in export structures. As primary producers, Africa has faced declining terms of trade due to the low income-elasticity of the demand for primary commodities. The impact of the terms of trade is often exaggerated unless the differential impacts of the terms of trade (TOT) on goods and the terms of trade on goods and services combined are taken into account. Figure 3.2 shows the terms of trade separated into goods and goods and services for the period 1990–2001. For TOT goods, there is an almost flat graph for most of the period. There was a noticeable decline in 1997–99, then a brief improvement until it fell again in 2000. Looking at the TOT goods and services, that measure fell throughout the period 1990–99 and rose between 1999 and 2000 and fell from thereon.

Africa has lost its global market share within its narrow range of products. For example, copper alloys were Africa's largest single export in the 1960s, with Sub-Saharan Africa supplying 32 per cent of total OECD imports. But by the early 1990s Africa's share fell to less than 10 per cent. Trade shares have declined in a number of commodities: for cocoa, trade share fell from 59 per cent in 1970–79 to 40 per cent in 1990–97; coffee fell from 28 per cent to 14 per cent and groundnuts from 40 per cent to 5 per cent.[7]

Figure 3.2a Terms of Trade: Goods (1990–2001)

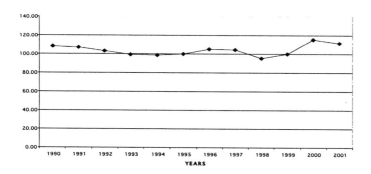

Figure 3.2b Terms of Trade: Goods and Services (1990–2001)

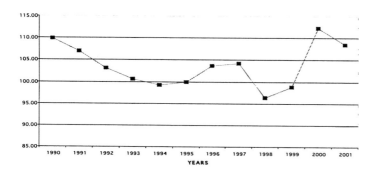

Despite substantial trade liberalization in the 1990s, Africa's trade policies remain, on the average, significantly more protectionist than those of other countries (Sharer 2001). In the United States and Canada all goods imported in 1999 attracted tariffs of 4.8 per cent and 4.6 per cent, respectively. Switzerland had a zero rate and the European Union (EU) had a rate of 5 per cent. Table 3.8 shows average tariff rates by sector for different regions of the world. As can be seen, the rates in Sub-Saharan Africa are generally higher than other regions, putting Africa at a great disadvantage compared to its trading partners and competitors.[8] Africa has therefore lost considerably from its anti-trade policies.

Other factors affecting Africa's exports include high transport costs, which influences the location of manufacturing activities, and freight rates for African exports that are sometimes 20 per cent higher than those faced by the region's

Table 3.8 Regional Tariff Rate (unweighted in per cent)

Region	Year	All Goods	Agri-culture	Manu-factures
East Asia	1994–99	9.8	13.9	9.4
South Asia	1996–99	27.7	26.3	9.4
Sub-Saharn Africa	1993–99	16.5	19.2	16.0
Middle East and North Africa	1995–98	14.4	20.8	13.2
Transition Europe	1996–99	9.6	15.7	7.8
Latin America	1995–99	10.1	13.8	9.5

Source: WTO and Trade Policy Review, various years.

competitors. For some exports in which Africa has a potential competitive advantage, transportation costs range between 15 per cent and 20 per cent. For all developing countries the net transport cost to export ratio is 5.8 per cent, compared with Africa's average of 15 per cent (Yumkella et al. 1999).

Therefore, the marginalization of Africa in world trade can be directly attributed to both external and internal causes. The external causes include the unfavorable terms of trade, agricultural subsidies in developed countries and the various institutional changes that resulted from the Uruguay Round of General Agreement on Tarrifs and Trade (GATT) trade negotiations and the subsequent creation of the World Trade Organization (WTO). The internal causes include Africa's restrictive trade and exchange-rate policies, the preponderance of primary products subject to price fluctuations and uncompetitive manufacturing production because of high transaction costs.

Capital Flows

There is a considerable amount of empirical evidence in the literature on the role of capital flows in economic growth, including strong empirical support for a positive link between capital inflows and domestic investment. Bosworth and Collins (1999) analyzed the effects of capital inflows on investment and savings for 58 developing countries in the period 1978–95 using instrumental variables to address the likely endogeneity of capital flows. They concluded that a large proportion of capital flows have been used to finance current-account deficits, and that most of the capital flow has been directed toward investment not consumption. The overriding evidence supports the fact that capital inflows contribute to growth by stimulating investment and technical progress and promoting efficient financial development. When combined with sound domestic macroeconomic policies, openness to capital flows gives a country access to a much larger pool of capital for financing development. FDI speeds up both capital accumulation and the absorption of foreign technologies. How has Africa fared relative to the rest of the world? Is Africa fully integrated into the global financial market?

While it is true that Africa has been a leading recipient of official development assistance from both bilateral and multilateral sources for many years, the continent has not received its fair share of the huge amount of other types of financial flows to developing countries over the last 30 years.

Africa integrated into the global economy in a negative sense, a large portion of Africa's wealth is held internationally in the form of capital flight (Collier 1997). Ajayi (1997) finds that capital flight varies between 24 per cent and 134 per cent of GNP. A recent study by the Economic Commission for Africa estimated that real capital flight in the period 1970–96 amounted to about $187 billion for some 30 countries in Africa. The capital flight GDP ratio has been very high. The volume of FDI totaled $160 billion in 1991 and soared to $1.1 trillion by 2000. FDI to developing countries increased from $24 billion in 1990 to $178 billion in 2000. In the 1980s and 1990s FDI to Sub-Saharan Africa grew by only 59 per cent, a fraction of the increases to Europe and Central Asia (5,200 per cent), East Asia and the Pacific (942 per cent), South Asia (740 per cent) and Latin America and the Caribbean (455 per cent) (Asiedu 2002).

FDI to Africa actually declined between the 1970s and 1980s. Over the last 20 years, FDI in the rest of the world grew much faster than in Africa (OECD 2001/2002). In 1980, Africa's share of the global stock of FDI was 5.3 per cent, compared to Asia's share of 28.1 per cent and Latin America and the Caribbean's share of 8.1 per cent. By year 2000, Africa's share of global stock of FDI dropped to 2.3 per cent as opposed to Asia and Latin America and the Caribbean, which increased their shares to 20 per cent and 9.6 per cent, respectively (see Table 3.9). Africa's FDI as a percentage of GDP has been insignificant, hovering around 1–2 per cent over the years. In year 2000, the ratio was 2 per cent.

The largest recipients of FDI in Africa are South Africa and oil-producing nations such as Nigeria and Angola. Swings in the FDI flow to these countries have major effects on the total flows to Africa. Africa attracted FDI almost entirely for raw materials extraction and did not take part in the move to

Table 3.9 Share of Global Stock of FDI (%)

	1980	1985	1990	1995	1999	2000
Developed countries[a]	58.2	60.1	73.5	69.3	63.5	65.8
Developing countries[b]	41.8	39.9	26.3	29.4	34.5	32.2
Africa	5.3	3.8	2.6	2.6	2.7	2.3
Latin America/Caribbean	8.1	8.9	6.2	6.9	10.0	9.6
Developing Europe	0.0	0.0	0.1	0.1	0.2	0.2
Asia	28.1	27.0	17.4	19.8	21.5	20.0
Pacific	0.2	0.1	0.1	0.1	0.1	0.1
Central/Eastern Europe	0.0	0.0	0.2	1.2	2.0	2.0

Notes:

a. For expositional purposes, excludes South Africa; *World Investment Report* includes South Africa in the list of developed countries.

b. For expositional purposes, includes South Africa; *World Investment Report* includes South Africa in the list of developed countries.

Source: World Investment Report (WIR).

globalization that involved a faster flow of technology and production improvements (OECD, 2001/2002).

Africa has been unable to attract adequate FDI despite the fact that the rate of return to investment in Africa has been higher than in other developing countries. Bhattacharya, Montiel and Sharma (1997) showed the net return to investment in Africa is between 20–30 per cent, as opposed to 16–18 per cent for developing countries. UNCTAD (1999) showed that in 1996, the rates of return on American FDI to Africa was 34.2 per cent, whereas the return was 19.3 per cent in Asia and the Pacific and 12.8 per cent in Latin America and the Caribbean. The low performance of Africa in attracting FDI can be directly attributed to the negative perception of the continent's political and economic activities, poor infrastructure and an inadequate legal framework for contract enforcement. Investment in Africa is seen as a high-risk activity.

Communications

The current wave of globalization is markedly different from the earlier ones not only because of easier transportation, but also due to improved communication systems around the globe. The costs of telephone calls have fallen, while the number of telephones has increased. The major distinction between earlier and later globalization lies perhaps in the connections provided by computerization and the Internet, which allows African scholars and policymakers to access the stores of knowledge in virtually all the world's computers.

While telephone costs have fallen around the world, Africa's telecommunications sector remains characterized by low network-penetration rates, outmoded equipment and long waiting lists. In many countries in Africa, people have yet to use the telephone or surf the Internet as a regular part of their everyday life. Telephone coverage in Africa is among the lowest in the world (ADB 1996). According to the ADB report, there are about 14 million telephones in Africa out of which 5 million are located in South Africa. In 1996 the average waiting time for telephone installation was 3.5 years; the highest in the world. Nine countries recorded a waiting time greater than 10 years.[9] There are also significant sub-regional differences. On average, North African countries have a greater number of telephones than do Sub-Saharan African countries. The different communication levels are associated with differences in per capita income. Countries with higher per capita income have higher telecom-penetration rates.

Complete integration into the global economy requires a well-functioning communications system readily available at affordable costs.[10] Many business transactions now are concluded on telephones and the Internet. If Africa fails to upgrade its outmoded and unreliable equipment, it will have no chance of competing in the global economy.

HOW CAN AFRICA JOIN THE GLOBAL ECONOMY AND DERIVE MAXIMUM BENEFITS?

Discussing what Africa must do in order to enter the global economy and derive maximum advantages from the process is indeed a tall order. In a way, some of the earlier discussions reveal what needs to be done.[11] Africa can benefit immensely from globalization if it positions itself appropriately. This entails a number of policy changes.

Some Stylized Facts

African leaders must appreciate several basic facts before launching reform. First, globalization is not the panacea for all of Africa's economic problems. Second, economic performance among African countries has varied considerably; Botswana, the Republic of the Congo and Equatorial Guinea have been able to attain or surpass a growth rate of 7 per cent (ECA 1999) while other countries have made substantial gains after several years of war and disturbances; others remain mired in conflict. Third, Africa must take advantage of the various dimensions of globalization: trade, FDI investment, and communications. In particular, Africa must sustain higher growth rates than recorded in the past. A liberal trading regime, by itself, is not likely to increase trade unless it is accompanied by first-rate economic growth. Fourth, different countries will reap different benefits, because existing conditions (level of education, infrastructure development, macroeconomic stability etc.) differ across Africa. Fifth, Africa currently faces few barriers to exporting its primary products. Based on present policies, Africa has little to gain from globalization. But Africa can improve its global competitiveness, diversify its exports, expand into manufacturing and attract foreign capital, which will also bring in new ideas and technology.

Yet an open trade regime, while useful, is not sufficient to propel an economy down a path of sustained growth. Policymakers must focus on the fundamentals of economic growth, namely investment, macroeconomic stability, human resources development and good governance. In *The New Global Economy and the Developing Countries*, Dani Rodrik (1999) said that the claims made by advocates of untrammeled international economic integration are frequently inflated or downright false. He argues that openness, in the sense of low barriers to trade and free capital flows, will not systematically increase growth, reduce poverty and improve the quality of life for the majority of citizens of developing nations. Evidence from the last two decades shows that the countries which have grown most rapidly since the mid-1970s are those that have not only invested a high share of their GDP, but have also maintained macroeconomic stability.

A number of African countries recording recent growth have high investment/GDP ratios (Table 3.10). Judged by international standards, the investment/GDP ratio in Africa is low. But individual countries that have grown fast, such as Botswana and Mauritius, have had much higher investment rates than such countries as Rwanda, Madagascar and Niger. Although some countries have grown more rapidly than their investment rates would indicate, for example, Zambia, these are exceptions, not the rule (Rodrik 1999).

Africa can fully realize the global economy's potential benefits only when the necessary complementary policies and institutions are in place. Africa must implement sound macroeconomic fundamentals and accelerate structural reforms to make their economies less vulnerable to swings in investor sentiments and capital flows. The requisite domestic policies address issues related to the growth of Africa in general and to specific issues related to involvement in the international economy. The domestic policies must be designed to increase Africa's participation in world trade, increase capital flows, eliminate investment risk and improve governance. While some of these

Table 3.10 Africa's FDI–GDP Ratio, Selected Years, 1980–2000

Year	FDI/GDP
1980	0.011
1981	0.671
1982	0.651
1985	1.025
1986	0.509
1994	1.229
1995	1.397
1996	1.349
1997	2.384
1998	1.989
1999	2.519
2000	2.153

Source: World Bank, World Development Indicators (2002).

goals are not strictly new, they need to be emphasized within the framework of globalization. The international aspect deals with external forces that impinge on the rate of growth of the African economy from the international sector and how removing these obstacles can promote growth through trade, investment or other mechanisms.

Trade Liberalization

Trade liberalization measures are urgently needed. These include removing trade barriers and adopting appropriate exchange-rate policies. Africa's trade is mainly in primary commodities, simply because the continent has a comparative advantage in that area. Indeed, there is considerable scope for increasing productivity in this sector. Yet the decision about which strategy Africa should adopt in the future is highly controversial. There are two lines of thinking and the two are not mutually exclusive.

The first set of arguments is that Africa's competitiveness is greatest in domestic, resource-intensive industries, which utilize local inputs and skills. Countries like Malaysia and Indonesia entered the export market with natural-resource-intensive products while India and Bangladesh are competitive in labor-intensive low-tech cotton garments and textiles. Africa, according to this argument, should therefore concentrate on unskilled labor-intensive primary-processing activities. The best short-run option appears to focus on primary products, particularly smallholder agriculture. Mauritius took a different approach and has been able to succeed in manufacturing exports by creating special export-processing zones.

The second argument is that in the long run, a more determined shift toward manufacturing and exports will be required to achieve rapid productivity growth. Industrial performance in Africa has generally been very poor. If Africa is to grow, it must not only diversify its exports into other sectors, it must also consider manufactured exports. Within this argument, the manufacturing sector should be encouraged through appropriate domestic policies and incentives. This is important because, as its proponents claim, the manufacturing sector holds the key to Africa's effective, competitive participation in the global economy. Currently, less than 3 per cent of world trade in manufactured goods and slightly less in services – approximately half of the 1980 levels – come from Africa. Creating a comparative advantage in manufacturing will generate a launching pad into the global economy.[12] Countries which strive to benefit from the global economy must give appropriate attention to the development of its manufacturing sub-sector. Therefore, it seems clear that Africa's economic development will require a major commitment to policies and institutions which promote manufactured exports. A similar approach triggered the economic growth of many countries in East and South-East Asia.

However, dealing with the manufacturing sector in Africa is not as simple as it sounds. Africa's manufacturing exports are not competitive due to inefficient production and high transaction costs. Governments have failed to promote the necessary technological capacities and training to facilitate efficient industrialization Achieving efficiency depends on policies encouraging innovation, economies of scale and availability of new goods. Existing policies have not adequately addressed Africa's unusually high transaction costs, which inhibit the development of a manufacturing sector.

Transaction costs in Africa are high for a number of reasons. First, many African countries still impose higher tariffs and non-tariff barriers than other countries. Second, international transport costs are higher in Africa than elsewhere. Manufacturers are badly handicapped by the high cost of shipping their output to foreign markets and importing the materials they need, because African road and rail networks are poorly maintained. Second, there is a lack of competition among service providers. Attempts to protect the national airlines, for example, have resulted in higher freight charges and more delivery bottlenecks than would have arisen if the system were competitive. Third, since the courts function slowly and unreliably, there are higher costs for contract enforcement. Unable to rely on the legal system, firms find themselves stuck with overpriced suppliers. Fourth, the unreliable telephone system is a direct impediment to Africa's manufacturing exports. It is more difficult to call between two cities in Africa than to call outside the continent. The exorbitant cost of international calls constitutes a de facto tax on international transactions. Fifth, electricity and water are often unreliable. Enterprises often must purchase expensive generators to guarantee a reliable source of power. In Nigeria and Uganda, for example, electricity shortages are the greatest problem facing manufacturing establishments. One-third of manufacturing equipment costs is spent on generators. These infrastructure deficiencies inhibit Africa's competitiveness in manufacturing exports and keep African firms out of the international markets. A steep reduction in transaction costs will allow private capital to flow into Africa and shift local comparative advantage toward manufacturing and higher growth (Fischer et al. 1998a). It is therefore necessary to eliminate these indirect transaction costs by adopting appropriate domestic policies.

Regional integration offers a means of overcoming the restraints imposed by the small size of African markets. Local exports could be promoted by setting up special export zones, duty-exception schemes or similar programs. Regional integration will increase long-term growth only if it is really trade-increasing, rather than an attempt to erect new protectionist barriers (Fischer 2001). For African manufacturing, increased regional trade could be a first step toward closer integration with the world economy by allowing enterprises to gain experience competing in foreign markets.

Capital Flows

Africa needs to attract substantial capital flows with a long-term commitment to the region. Most countries in Africa do not have portfolio investment flows such as bonds and equities. Given the need to have funds for development, a number of African countries have set in motion policies to attract FDI. These include liberalizing their investment laws, developing capital markets, offering fiscal incentives and easing – or eliminating – restrictions on entry and profit remittances, among others. There also is a need to strengthen the African banking and financial system in order to eliminate the weaknesses which precipitated the crisis in East Asia.

Other Policies

There are many other policies that would also smooth Africa's integration process. Although space precludes a full discussion, these steps are sketched below. African states must maintain a stable macroeconomic environment, including low inflation, manageable fiscal deficits, realistic exchange rates and appropriate interest rates. National leaders must invest in human capital to upgrade education and skills to better utilize new technologies (UNDP 1997). Intellectual capital is important in an era of globalization. Studies of the sources of growth show that rapid accumulation of human capital – and its more efficient use in key sectors – can be crucial for strengthening a nation's overall performance. Countries need to increase the quality and quantity of their infrastructure to stimulate investment and growth. Evidence suggests that infrastructure expenditure of African governments is growth enhancing. The quality of governance must be improved, since corruption and lack of transparency drive away potential investors. Finally, African states should develop the private sector and reduce state involvement in the economy. The major role of government should be to provide the necessary macroeconomic environment and infrastructural facilities for the private sector to operate. In order to increase private-sector participation, some state enterprises have been sold in the hope that the privatization process will attract foreign private capital and technology.

HOW CAN DEVELOPED COUNTRIES HELP AFRICA ENTER GLOBAL MARKETS?

Studies of Africa's levels of inequality and the region's poor macroeconomic performance must also look outside the region for causes. Many African countries are heavily indebted, although the severity of debt differs among countries. As a proportion of exports or GDP, Africa has the highest levels of external debt in the developing world (UNCTAD 1998). Debt impedes public investment in physical and human infrastructure and deters private and foreign investment (Ajayi 1999a, 1999b). There is ample evidence that Africa's external debt burden has severe consequences for investment and renewed growth (Elbadawi et al. 1997; Claessens et al. 1996).

Africa needs to develop a level playing field in the global agricultural market. Agricultural commodities have always enjoyed a special status in world trade, and industrial countries have traditionally subsidized agricultural exports. Agricultural subsidies currently amount to almost $1 billion per day, roughly six times the level of aid to developing countries. It is hypocrisy for the United States and the EU to encourage poor countries to open up their markets while imposing protectionist measures that cater to their own powerful special interests.[13] Such agricultural subsidies no doubt affect developing countries in general and Africa in particular. First, they keep world prices low so that other producers get less for their commodities. Second, as a result of the subsidies and related issues such as standards and quality, developing countries are excluded from entering the markets of wealthy countries. Third, African food producers are exposed to dumping in the form of cheap food imports. One estimate suggests that a 30 per cent reduction in agricultural subsidies by industrial countries would generate an extra $45 billion a year for developing countries (UNDP 1997). In particular, tariffs remain high on textiles and leather, key products for African producers. Countries exporting textiles and clothing are limited to specified quotas beyond which high tariffs are applicable. Removing these quotas may benefit some emerging African countries. Industrial countries have also erected non-tariff barriers in the form of price supports and special marketing arrangements, all of which exclude agricultural products from Africa.

The issues involved have been aptly summarized by Joseph Stiglitz, former principal economist for the World Bank:

> But even when not guilty of hypocrisy, the West has driven the globalization agenda, ensuring that it garners a disproportionate share of the benefits at the expense of the developing world. It was not just that the more advanced industrial countries declined to open up their markets to the goods of the developing countries – for instance, keeping their quotas on a multitude of goods from textile to sugar – while insisting that those countries open up their markets to the goods of wealthier countries; it was not just that the more advanced countries continued to subsidize agriculture making it difficult for the developing countries to compete, while insisting that developing countries eliminate their subsidies on industrial goods (2002).

Thus, trade liberalization in Africa must be supplemented by opening advanced country markets to African exports. In particular, effective protection should focus on clothing, fish, processed foods, leather products and agricultural products more generally (Fischer 2001). This will not be easy. African countries must take the initiative and claim a more active, coordinated and strategic voice in global trade negotiations (Yusuf 2000). Participating in the WTO and other rounds of negotiations can draw African countries into the mainstream of globalization. Even though tariffs have declined as a result of the Uruguay Rounds, trade in textiles and certain agricultural commodities continues to be constrained by both tariff and quota restrictions.

Having access to industrialized country markets on a permanent basis would enhance Africa's trade and eliminate some of the inequity. There are several recent developments that may improve market access to industrial countries markets. The American African Growth and Opportunity Act improves Africa's access to American markets, albeit in limited circumstances for a number of goods. Also, the European Council adopted 'Everything But

Arms' proposal for duty- and quota-free access for all products from the least developed countries from which Africa can benefit.

CONCLUSION

This chapter reflects mainly on Africa's integration into the global economy. The myth is that Africa is poor because of its marginalization in the world economy; the reality, however, is that Africa, using various indicators of global integration, is not meaningfully participating in the global economy. Yet embracing globalization has been, is and still will be a key ingredient for Africa's successful economic growth and development. With better economic policies Africa can trade more and attract more capital flows.

Globalization has brought many welcome benefits to many countries. Increased international trade and capital flows have been a major source of unprecedented economic growth and rising standards of living across the globe. There are no successful cases of fast-growing countries that followed inward-looking policies. However, developed countries, with better starting points, will see different results than poor countries with less advantageous initial conditions.

Based on any indicator, Africa has lagged behind in the global economy. Consequently, Africa's growth in GDP per capita has lagged substantially behind all other regional groups. Africa has the largest number of the world's poor. The continent has much to gain from globalization if it positions itself appropriately, but integration will not cure all of Africa's economic ailments. Growth is based on other factors including macroeconomic stability, high investment/GDP ratios, reliable accounting systems, responsible institutions and infrastructure. Africa's prospects depend on domestic policies as well as developments at the international level. Under its current course, Africa cannot benefit much. Africa must change its economic policies if it hopes to obtain the benefits offered by globalization.

NOTES

This chapter is a revised version of the paper presented at the Fourth Annual Global Development Conference on Globalization and Equity, Cairo, Egypt, January 19–21, 2003. This version has benefited from comments received from Gary McMahon; and comments from the discussant of the paper Jan Willem Gunning and other floor discussants on the day the paper was presented. Other comments were also received from reviewers at the GDN Secretariat.

1. A number of negative factors, especially disadvantageous geography, have been questioned, because many of the African countries are physically nearer to European markets than are India and Australia, both of which are performing better than many African countries.
2. For details on Africa's poor performance, see Easterly and Levine (1997), Sachs and Warner (1997) and Collier and Gunning (1998).
3. This chapter concentrates on inequality of access and outcomes rather than on equity per se.
4. Unequal access refers to inequality in the areas of trade, capital flows and technology. The outcomes are about differential GDP per capita growth and dispersion in poverty distribution.
5. There is a great diversity in Africa, which are subsumed in the aggregates used. There is evidence for example that some African countries have taken advantage of globalization. Botswana, in encouraging exports and emphasizing human development, has been able to achieve annual growth rate in GDP per capita of 6 per cent from 1980–96. Mauritius has been able to attract multinational companies by offering tax incentives.
6. A few exceptions should always be noted in the case of African trade. South Africa, Mauritius, Madagascar and Angola are exceptions to the commodity-based export profile, although Angola's primary export is unprocessed diamonds.
7. For more details see Stephen O'Brien, 'Africa in the global Economy: Issues of Trade and development for Africa', Africa Knowledge Networks Forum Preparatory Workshop, 17–18 August 2000, Addis Ababa, Ethiopia.
8. These average figures hide a great variability of rates in different African countries. For example Nigeria in 1998 had rates that were generally about 24 per cent as opposed to 22 per cent for Zambia, and 19 per cent for Mauritius.
9. These were Algeria, Eritrea, Ethiopia, Gambia, Malawi, Mozambique, Sao Tome and Principe, Sierra Leone and Tanzania.
10. While it is true that the telephone situation in Africa improved over the last ten years, the costs of telephones in Africa are higher than other regions of the world. It is known that many African countries have now embarked on the GSM telephone system. While this is good and progressive, the majority of people do not have access because of the cost.
11. This section draws heavily on my earlier work. See Ajayi (2000, 2001a).
12. From available evidence, the manufacturing and industrial sectors in Africa are not competitive. Only about five countries had a manufacturing share in excess of 20 per cent of GDP, in 1997, for example. These were Burkina Faso, Mauritius, South Africa, Zambia and Zimbabwe.
13. For more details on trade access and this assertion see *IMF Survey*, **31** (19), October 21, 2002.

REFERENCES

ADB (1996), *African Development Report* Côte d'Ivoire: African Development Bank.

ADB (1999), *African Development Report* Côte d'Ivoire: African Development Bank.

Ajayi, S. Ibi (1997), 'An Analysis of External Debt and Capital Flight in the Heavily Indebted Poor Countries of Sub-Saharan Africa,' in Zubair Iqbal and Ravi Kanbur (eds), *External Finance for Low Income Countries*, Washington, DC: International Monetary Fund.

Ajayi, S. Ibi (1999a), 'The Challenges of Financing Development in Africa'. Paper prepared on behalf of the Economic Commission for Africa for the Joint Conference of Ministers of Finance and Ministers of Economic Development and Planning, Addis Ababa, Ethiopia, 12–14 April.

Ajayi, S. Ibi (1999b), 'The Challenges of Financing Development in Africa', New York, United Nations Economic Commission for Africa, Discussion Paper Series ESPD/DPS/99/2.

Ajayi, S. Ibi (2000) 'Globalization And Africa'. Paper presented at the Biannual Research Workshop of the African Economic Research Consortium Plenary, Nairobi, Kenya, May.

Ajayi, S. Ibi (2001a) 'What Africa needs to do to benefit from globalization,' *Finance and Development*, **38** (4), 1–7.

Ajayi, S. Ibi (2001b) 'Issues of Globalization in Africa'. Paper delivered at the High-level Seminar on Globalization and Africa, Organized by the IMF and the Joint Africa Institute, Tunisia, 5–6 April.

Ajayi, S. Ibi and Mohsin Khan (eds) (2000), *External Debt and Capital Flight in Sub-Saharan Africa* Washington, DC: International Monetary Fund.

Ali, A.G. and Ibrahim Elbadawi (1999), 'Inequality and the Dynamics of Poverty and Growth'. Paper presented at the African Economic Research Consortium and the Weatherhead Center for International Affairs, Harvard University Workshop on 'Explaining African Economic Growth Performance', Cambridge, MA, 26–27.

Aninat, Eduardo (2002), 'Surmounting the challenges of globalization', *Finance and Development*, **39** (1), 4–7.

Asiedu, Elizabeth (2002), 'On the determinants of foreign direct investment in developing countries: is Africa different? *World Development*, **30** (1), 107–19.

Basu, Anupam and Krishna Srinivasan (2002), 'Foreign Direct Investment in Africa – Some Case Studies', Washington DC, International Monetary Fund, Working Paper WP/02/61.

Bhattacharya, Amar, Peter J. Montiel and Sunil Sharma (1997), 'Private Capital Flows to Sub-Saharan Africa: An Overview of Trends and Determinants', in Zubair Iqbal and Ravi Kanbur (eds), *External Finance for Low-Income Countries* Washington, DC: International Monetary Fund.

Bloom, David and Jeffrey Sachs (1998), 'Geography, demography and economic growth in Africa,' *Brookings Papers on Economic Activity 1998*, **2**, 207–73.

Bosworth, Barry and Susan M. Collins (1999), 'Capital flows to developing economies: implications for saving and investment', *Brookings Papers on Economic Activity*, **1** (spring), 143–69.

Brahmbhatt, Milan and Uri Dadush (1996), 'Disparities in global integration,' *Finance and Development*, **33** (3), 47–50.

Brautigam, Deborah (1997), 'Comments on "What Can Developing Countries Learn from East Asia's Economic Growth?" ' in proceedings of the World Bank Annual Conference on Development Economics.

Brown, Michael Barratt (1995), *Africa's Choices After Thirty Years of the World Bank* Boulder, CO: Westview.

Claessens, Stijn, Enrica Detragiachie and Ravi Kanbur,(1997), 'Analytical Aspects of the Debt Problems of Heavily Indebted poor Countries,' in Iqbal, Zubair and Ravi Kanbur (eds), *External Finance For Low-income Countries* Washington, DC: International Monetary Fund.

Collier, Paul (1997), 'Globalization: Implications for Africa' Paper presented at the International Monetary Fund–African Economic Research Consortium seminar on 'Trade Reforms and Regional Integration in Africa', Washington, DC, 1–3 December.

Collier, Paul and Jan Willem Gunning (1995), 'Trade policy and regional integration: implications for the relations between Europe and Africa', *World Economy*, **18** 387–410.

Collier, Paul and Jan Willem Gunning (1998), 'Explaining African economic performance', *Journal of Economic Literature*, **37** (March), 64–111.

Deininger, Karl and Lyn Squire (1996), 'Measuring inequality: a new data-base', *World Bank Economic Review*, **10** (3), 565–91.

Dollar, David and Aart Kraay (2001a), 'Growth is Good for the Poor', Washington, DC, World Bank Policy Research Department Working Paper No. 2587.

Dollar, David and Aart Kraay (2001b), 'Trade, Growth and Poverty,' Washington, DC, World Bank Policy Research Department Working Paper No. 2615.

Dollar, David and Aart Kraay (2001c), 'Trade, growth and poverty', *Finance and Development*, **38** (3).

Easterly, William and Ross Levine (1997), 'Africa's growth tragedy: policies and ethnic divisions', *Quarterly Journal of Economics*, **112** (4), 1203–50.

Easterly, William and Ross Levine (1998), 'The Joys and Sorrows of Openness: A Review Essay'. Paper presented at the Dutch Ministry for Development Cooperation seminar on 'Economic Growth and its Determinants', The Hague, Netherlands, 23–24 March.

Economic Commission for Africa (ECA) (1997), *Financial Sector Reforms and Debt Management in Africa*, Addis Ababa, Ethiopia.

Economic Commission for Africa (ECA) (1999), *Economic Report on Africa*, Addis Ababa, Ethiopia

Economist (1997b), 'The Asian miracle, is it over?' 1–7 March, 23–25.

Edwards, Sebastian (1993), 'Openness, trade liberalization and growth in developing countries', *Journal of Economic Literature*, **31** (3), 1358–93.

Elbadawi, Ibrahim, A., Benno J. Ndulu and Njuguna Ndung'u (1997), 'Debt Overhang and Economic Growth in Sub-Saharan Africa', in Zubair Iqbal and Ravi Kanbur (eds), *External Finance for Low-income Countries* Washington, DC: International Monetary Fund.

Fischer, Stanley (2001) 'The Challenges of Globalization in Africa'. Remarks at the France-Africa Summit, Yaounde, Cameroon, 19 January.

Fischer, Stanley, Ernesto Hernandez-Cata and Mohsin S. Khan (1998a), 'Africa: Is this the Turning Point?' Washington, DC, IMF Papers on Policy Analysis and Assessment No. 98/6.

Fischer, Stanley, Ernesto Hernandez-Cata and Mohsin S. Khan (1998b), 'The Asian Crisis and Implications for Other Economies'. Paper presented at the Internews seminar on 'The Brazilian and the World Economic Outlook', Sao Paulo, Brazil, 19 June.

Fosu, Augustin Kwasi (1990), 'Export composition and the impact of exports on economic growth of developing economies', *Economic Letters*, **34** (1), 67–71.

Fosu, Augustin Kwasi (1996), 'Primary exports and economic growth in developing countries,' *World Economy*, **19** (4), 465–75.

Fosu, Augustin Kwasi (1998), 'Joys and Sorrows of Openness: A Review Essay - Comments,' Paper presented at the Dutch Ministry for Development Cooperation seminar on 'Economic Growth and its Determinants', The Hague, Netherlands, 23–24 March.

Goldstein, Morris (1998), *The Asian Financial Crisis: Causes, Cures and Systemic Implications*, Washington, DC: Institute for International Economics.

International Monetary Fund (1997a), *IMF Survey*, 7 July.

International Monetary Fund (1997b), 'Globalization and Growth Prospects in Arab Countries', Working Paper.

International Monetary Fund (1997c), *World Economic Outlook: Globalization Opportunities and Challenges*, Washington, DC: International Monetary Fund.

International Monetary Fund (1999), *IMF Survey*, 11 October.

International Monetary Fund (2002a) *IMF Survey*, 13 May.

International Monetary Fund (2002b) *International Financial Statistics Yearbook: 2002,* Washington, DC: International Monetary Fund.

Ito, Takatoshi (1997), 'What Can Developing Countries Learn from East Asia's Economic Growth?' Paper presented at the Annual World Bank Conference on Development Economics, Washington, DC.

Kayizzi-Mugerwa, Steve (2000), 'Globalization, Growth and Income Inequality: A review of the African Experience'. Paper presented at the OECD conference on 'Globalization and Income Inequality', Paris, 30 November-1 December.

Khor, Martin (2000), 'Globalization and the South: Some Critical Issues', New York, UNCTAD Discussion Paper No. 147.

Khor, Martin (2001), *Rethinking Globalization: Critical Issues and Policy Choices*, New York: Zed Books.

Monsod, Solita (2000), 'Globalization: Challenges and Opportunities'. Paper available at www.capwip.org/resources/womparlconf2000/downloads/Monsod1.pdf.

Mussa, Michael (2000), 'Factors Driving Global Economic Integration'. Paper available at www.imf.org/external/np/speeches/2000/082500.htm.

Nzekwu, Greg (1999), 'Contemporary Experiences in Globalization'. Paper presented at the Nigerian Economic Society seminar on 'Globalization and Economic Development', Lagos, Nigeria, 11 February.

O'Brien, Stephen (2000), 'Africa in the Global Economy: Issues of Trade and Development for Africa'. Paper presented at the Africa Knowledge Networks Forum Preparatory Workshop, Addis Ababa Ethiopia, 17–18 August .

OECD (2001/2002) *African Economic Outlook: Twenty-Two Country Studies* Paris: African Development Bank and Organization for Economic Co-operation and Development.

Ouattara, Alassane (1998), 'Towards Rapid Growth in Africa'. Paper presented at the Second Tokyo International Conference on African Development, Tokyo, Japan, 19 October.

Ouattara, Alassane (1999), 'Fostering Trade and Investment – A Vehicle for Accelerating Africa's Integration into the Global Economy'. Address presented at a meeting of the Council on Foreign Relations Africa Studies Program, New York, 25 March.

Rodrik, Dani (1997), *Has Globalization Gone Too Far?* Washington, DC: Institute for International Economics.

Rodrik, Dani (1998), 'Where Did all the Growth Go? External Shocks, Social Conflict and Growth Collapses', Washington, DC, National Bureau of Economic Research Working Paper No. 6350.

Rodrik, Dani (1999), *The New Global Economy and the Developing Countries: Making Openness Work*, Baltimore, MD: Johns Hopkins University Press.

Sachs, Jeffrey and Andrew Warner (1997), 'Sources of slow growth in African economies', *Journal of African Economies*, **6** (3), 335–76.

Sala-I-Martin, Xavier (2002), 'The Disturbing "Rise" of Global Income Inequality', Washington, DC, National Bureau of Economic Research Working Paper No. 8904.

Senbet, Lemma W. (1998), 'Global Financial Crisis: Implications for Africa'. Paper presented at the African Economic Research Consortium December Workshop, Nairobi, Kenya.

Sharer, Robert (1999), 'Trade: an engine of growth for Africa', *Finance and Development*, **36** (4).

Sharer, Robert (2001), 'An agenda for trade, investment and regional integration', *Finance and Development*, **38** (4).

Stiglitz, Joseph E. (2002), *Globalization and Its Discontents*, New York: W.W. Norton.

Tsikata, Yvonne M. (2000), 'Globalization, Poverty and Inequality in Sub-Saharan Africa: A Political Appraisal'. Paper presented at the OECD Conference on Poverty and Income Inequality in Developing Countries, Paris, 30 November–1 December.

UNCTAD (1998), *World Investment Report 1998: Trends and Determinants*, New York: United Nations Committee on Trade and Development.

UNCTAD (1999), *Capital Flows and Growth in Africa*, Geneva: United Nations Committee on Trade and Development.

United Nations Development Program (UNDP) (1997), *Human Development Report 1997: Human Development to Eradicate Poverty*, New York: Oxford University Press.

United Nations Development Program (UNDP) (1999), *Human Development Report 1999: Globalization with a Human Face*, New York: Oxford University Press.

Williamson, John G. (1998), 'Globalization: The Concept, Causes and Consequences'. Keynote Address to the Congress of the Sri Lankan Association for the Advancement of Science, Colombo, Sri Lanka, 15 December.

Williamson, John G. (2002) 'Winners and Losers Over Two Centuries of Globalization'. Annual Address to the United Nations University World Institute for Development Research, Helsinki, Lecture No. 6, 5 September.

Wood, Adrian and Kersti Berge (1997), ' Exporting manufactures: human resources, natural resources and trade policy', *Journal of Development Studies*, **34** (1), 35–57.

Wood, Adrian and Trudy Owens (1997), 'Export oriented innovation through primary processing?' *World Development*, **25** (9), 1453–70.

World Bank (1997) (1998/99), *World Development Report* Washington, DC: World Bank.

World Bank (2002a), *World Development Indicators*, Washington, DC: World Bank.

World Bank (2002a), *Globalization, Growth and Poverty: A World Bank Policy Research Report*, New York: Oxford University Press.

World Bank (2003), World Development Indicators, CD-ROM.

WTO (2000), *Trade Income Disparity and Poverty*, Geneva: World Trade Organization.

Yumkella, K., T. Roepstorff, J.Vinanchiarachi and T. Hawkins (1999), 'Globalization and Structural Transformation in Sub-Saharan Africa'. Paper presented at workshop on 'Agricultural Transformation in Africa,' Nairobi, Kenya, 27–30 June.

Yusuf, Abdulqawi, A. (2000), 'Technology Transfer in the Global Environmental Agreements: A New Twist to the North-South Debate', in Surendra J. Patel, Pedro Roffe and Abdulqawi A. Yusuf (eds), International Technology Transfer: The Origins and Aftermath of the United Nations Negotiations on Draft Code of Conduct, The Hague: Kluwer Law International, pp. 313–20.

4. Economic Globalization and Equity in East Asia

Chia Siow Yue

The 1990s witnessed a growing debate over the benefits and challenges of globalization, particularly whether poor countries and poor people benefited from globalization and economic growth. Two opposing views have emerged. One view, represented by the Dollar and Kraay (2001) study, is that growth is not anti-poor. The study found that globalization raises the incomes of the poor by about as much as it raises the incomes of the non-poor. The alternative view, espoused by Oxfam (2000) and others, is that current patterns of growth and globalization are worsening income disparities and thereby hindering poverty reduction.

East Asia is one of the most globalized regions in the world, with high levels of international trade and international investment. Globalization has generally been perceived as playing a critical role in the East Asian 'Economic Miracle', generating growth, employment and opportunities. However, with the onset of the East Asian financial crisis in 1997 and the subsequent economic downturn, analysts and policymakers have begun to question the high costs of globalization. This chapter focuses on the East Asian experience with globalization and more particularly the impacts on poverty and income inequality.

In the aftermath of the 1997–98 regional financial crisis, East Asia approached the twenty-first century in a mood of uncertainty. The optimism from decades of high and sustained economic growth and global integration through trade and investment gave way to questions about the fragile foundations of the economic miracle and the export-led model of development. The Asian crisis demonstrated that economic growth might not be sustainable and the social costs of global integration could be unacceptably high. The crisis threw millions of people in East Asia out of work or into poverty without adequate social safety nets. Thus, the crisis underscores that the developing and transitional economies of East Asia must discover how to balance the benefits of globalization against the risks and costs.

GLOBALIZATION BENEFITS REVISITED

East Asian countries are among the major beneficiaries of the global open-trading system. Access to the global store of knowledge, including medical science, has lengthened life expectancies and has led to better living standards. Access to global resources and markets enabled East Asian economies to achieve economic progress beyond that achievable with the limited domestic resources and markets of individual economies.

International Trade

Trade enables the East Asian economies to access the world's resources, technology and ideas; enables greater efficiency and productivity; and provides wider consumer choice. Trade affects not only the level of gross national product (GNP) but also its growth rate through exploiting comparative advantages, scale economies, competition and innovation, and imports of capital goods, intermediate inputs and technology help to improve productivity. Many East Asian economies in the early stages of development and industrialization have been able to utilize their abundant labor to break into global markets for manufactures and for services. Export-led growth forms the centerpiece of an industrial policy that created millions of factory workers who improved their lives by finding urban jobs and leaving crowded, rural, rice-growing areas. An open trading regime also pressures domestic producers to become more efficient and innovative to meet the challenge of import competition.

Foreign Direct Investment (FDI)

FDI enables host East Asian economies to access not only global capital, but also technology, managerial and marketing expertise and marketing networks. While foreign firms may compete with domestic enterprises, they also bring new industrial and technological capabilities, enabling the less-developed economies to catch up with the more advanced economies. FDI has helped the local economies and production units to integrate with the global and regional production networks, and it has also enabled East Asian nations to become major producers and suppliers of dynamic products, such as electronics.

Empirical evidence shows the positive impact of globalization on national economic growth and per capita income. However, the causality in the globalization-growth relationship is not absolute. A country's ability to reap benefits from globalization depends on various factors, including its stage of development, economic competitiveness and institutional flexibility. Countries best able to reap benefits from globalization tend to be not only those characterized by openness to the outside world, but also those able to balance economic growth with domestic policies and institutions to minimize any negative impacts on vulnerable groups and individuals.

GLOBALIZATION CONCERNS AND DISCONTENT

Concerns about globalization have heightened since the 1997–98 financial crisis brought the East Asian economic miracle to an end. The social costs of globalization have become visibly high, and studies on poverty and income inequality have shown that not all groups in society have benefited from globalization.

Volatility and Vulnerability

Globalization increases domestic exposure to disturbances in global markets for goods, services and finance. For example, East Asian economies have imported advanced industrial economies' business cycles through their exporting activities. Financial instability has generated the most concern in recent years. The region suffered terribly when the inward surge of short-term capital suddenly reversed, leaving behind collapsed currencies, weak banking systems and corporate bankruptcies.

Market Fundamentalism

Market fundamentalists argue that market inefficiencies are relatively small, while government inefficiencies are relatively large. Stiglitz (2002) argues that the discontent with globalization arises not just from the dominance of economics, but more particularly from the dominance of market fundamentalism as represented by the 'Washington Consensus'. Since the Asian crisis, East Asian policymakers, analysts and entrepreneurs have begun to question and criticize the Washington Consensus. Malaysia's Prime Minister Mahathir was a particularly high profile and vocal East Asian critic of the Washington Consensus.

Uneven Global Trading

Critics accuse the World Trade Organization (WTO) and multilateral trading system of maintaining an uneven playing field. While the rich countries push poor countries for more trade liberalization, they simultaneously impose barriers against agriculture and labor-intensive manufactures. Poor countries view the rich countries' push to incorporate labor, environmental and health regulations through the WTO as veiled efforts at protectionism. East Asian exports are often restricted by outside anti-dumping measures and health and environmental standards.

Access to Technology

Rich countries are the main sources of technology for the developing world, which raises issues over both access and pricing. Critics contend that the Uruguay Round strengthened the intellectual property rights regime in favor of rich country producers and ignored the dire needs of poor countries. Drug companies market essential drugs for AIDS, malaria and tuberculosis to poor country users at unaffordable prices. A second issue is uneven access to information technology. The new high-tech economy threatens the traditional competitive advantage of poor countries (cheap labor) and there are growing concerns that an emerging digital divide will reinforce the traditional income divide. More recently, however, developing economies such as India and the Philippines have become major beneficiaries of corporate outsourcing.

Rising Job Insecurity

In the rich countries, workers with the skills and mobility to exploit opportunities in global markets win, while low-skilled workers lose jobs and earnings due to labor-intensive imports from low-wage countries or because their employer shifts to overseas production or business outsourcing. But in East Asia, the unskilled and semi-skilled workers benefit from exports and FDI, through improved employment prospects and higher earnings. However, there is also growing job insecurity as export demand and employment face boom-and-bust cycles. Multinational corporations may relocate their factories to new centers of competitive advantage. Worse, the 1997–98 crisis led to massive unemployment and social disorders. Increasingly jobs and livelihoods seem at the mercy of global forces.

Social Disintegration

Globalization is perceived to undermine traditional values and cultural identities, due to the increasing intrusion of global, primarily Western, norms, practices and values. The Internet has accelerated this process. Domestic institutions, norms and practices have little time to adapt and respond to these rapid challenges

Eroding Sovereignty

Globalization poses a challenge to the role of government in East Asia. In an increasingly borderless world, government control has become ineffective or even counterproductive. With financial globalization, states have lost part of their sovereignty to capricious capital markets and speculators. New technology and fewer border controls have allowed trans-border crimes such as commercial fraud, drug and human trafficking, money laundering, environmental pollution and terrorism to proliferate. And while globalization raises the demand for the government to provide social safety nets, it reduces the ability to provide them, as governments cannot raise taxes lest business and skilled labor migrate to lower tax havens.

Negative Impact on Equity

Globalization has contributed to a growing divide between the haves and have-nots, as will be discussed in a later section.

EAST ASIA'S RECORD WITH GLOBALIZATION

East Asia represents one of the most globalized regions in the world, with high levels of participation in international trade and international investment. The East Asian 'Economic Miracle' from the 1960s to mid-1990s exemplifies the upside experience of globalization, while the East Asian Financial Crisis of 1997–98 exemplifies the downside. There is a voluminous literature on each phenomenon. Since the crisis, there has been increasing discussion about the benefits and costs of globalization and a search for a more sustainable, less volatile and more equitable development model.

Table 4.1 East Asia–GNP and GDP Growth Rates

Country/ Region	GDP growth rate 1965–96 %	GDP per capita growth rate 1965–96 %	GDP growth rate 1990– 2001 %	GDP growth rate 1997 %	GDP growth rate 1998 %	GDP growth rate 1999 %
China	8.5	6.7	10.0	8.8	7.8	7.1
Hong Kong	7.5	5.6	3.9	5.0	–5.3	3.0
South Korea	8.9	7.3	5.7	5.0	–6.7	10.9
Singapore	8.3	6.3	7.8	8.5	0.0	6.9
Indonesia	6.7	4.6	3.8	4.5	–3.2	0.9
Malaysia	6.8	4.1	6.5	7.3	–7.4	6.1
Philippines	3.5	0.9	3.3	5.2	–0.6	3.4
Thailand	7.3	5.0	3.8	–1.4	–10.8	4.4
Cambodia	na	na	4.8	3.7	1.5	6.9
Laos	na	na	6.4	6.9	4.0	7.3
Myanmar	na	na	na	5.7	5.8	10.9
Vietnam	na	na	7.6	8.2	4.4	4.7
East Asia and Pacific	7.4	5.5	7.5	na	na	na

Economic Miracle

Table 4.1 shows the growth performance of East Asian economies over the past four decades. Between 1965 and 1996, China, Hong Kong, South Korea and Singapore, as well as Indonesia, Malaysia and Thailand, enjoyed aggregate growth rates of at least 6.5 per cent per year. In the 1990s, while China continued its remarkably buoyant growth, the pace slowed in the other East Asian economies, particularly Hong Kong, Indonesia, the Philippines and Thailand.

Table 4.2 shows East Asia's extensive integration into the global economy through international trade and FDI. The trade/GDP ratios for 2001 were extremely high, with around 250 per cent for Hong Kong and Singapore, and over 100 per cent for Malaysia and Thailand. Even China's continental-sized economy registered a ratio of 44 per cent. The region's economies are also among the largest recipients of FDI among non-Organization for Economic Co-operation and Development (OECD) countries. FDI into China grew

Table 4.2 Trade and FDI Indicators of Economic Openness in East Asia

Country	Merchandise exports 2001 US$mill	Merchandise imports 2001 US$m	Total merchandise trade 2001 US$m	GDP 2001 US$m	Trade/ GDP ratio 2001 %	Manufactures % share of exports 2000	FDI Inflows Annual Average	
							1990–95 US$m	1996–2001 US$m
China	266,155	243,567	509,722	1,159,017	44.0	88	19,360	42,684
Hong Kong	190,676	202,252	392,928	162,642	241.6	95	4,859	24,327
South Korea	150,653	141,116	291,769	422,167	69.1	91	978	5,399
Singapore	121,731	115,961	237,692	92,252	257.7	na	5,782	8,594
Indonesia	56,716	31,170	87,886	145,306	60.5	57	2,135	−9
Malaysia	88,521	74,384	162,905	87,540	186.1	80	4,655	4,095
Philippines	33,589	31,373	64,962	71,438	90.9	92	1,028	1,355
Thailand	64,223	60,190	124,413	114,760	108.4	76		
Cambodia	1,531	1,476	3007	3,384	88.9	na	80	218
Laos	320	437	757	1,712	44.2	na	33	61
Myanmar	1,760	2,461	4,221	na	na	na	180	324
Vietnam	15,100	16,000	31,100	32,903	94.5	na	947	1,694

Sources: World Development Report (2003); World Investment Report (2002).

dramatically in the 1990s to reach an annual average of $43 billion during 1996–2001. Hong Kong and Singapore also absorbed large volumes of FDI.

Up to the mid-1960s, the economic advancement of East Asia (excluding Japan) was largely resource-based and countries of the region were integrated into the global economy as exporters of agricultural and mineral primary products and importers of manufactures and capital goods. Since then, export-oriented industrialization and FDI inflows have increased dramatically. In East Asia, industrialization occurred in three waves. It began with Hong Kong, Singapore, South Korea and Taiwan; Indonesia, Malaysia, the Philippines and Thailand soon followed, then lastly China and Vietnam. Import substitution was used to create infant industries, protect existing industries and nurture domestic entrepreneurship. But import substitution was limited by the size and growth of the domestic market and suffered from the lack of domestic competition. From the mid-1960s, South Korea, Taiwan and Singapore adopted export manufacturing in earnest, exporting labor-intensive products to markets in Europe, the United States and Japan. For Southeast Asia, this transition came in the mid-1980s, after the collapse of international oil and commodity prices which had provided the foreign exchange income to support the import-substitution drive. Southeast Asia also widely encouraged inflows of FDI, capitalizing on the emerging trend of FDI outflows from Japan and South Korea, Taiwan and Singapore.

China embarked on wide-ranging economic reforms from the late 1970s, including rapidly opening up to international trade and FDI. Exports surged from $10 billion in 1978 to $195 billion in 1999 and the export/GDP ratio rose from less than 7 per cent to about 20 per cent. At first, FDI inflows focused primarily on the special economic zones in the southeast coastal region. However, by the early 1990s, China had emerged as the largest recipient of FDI in East Asia and subsequently ranked second only to the United States as a recipient of FDI globally.

The economic success of East Asia has been well documented, highlighted by the 1993 publication of the World Bank's *The East Asian Miracle*. Export-led industrialization, and the accompanying FDI and technology inflows, largely explain the success. The growth rates in GDP and per capita GDP more than doubled that of other developing regions and the OECD. Its growing trade openness is seen in rising trade/GDP ratios as well as rising share of global trade. Factors which have been identified as crucial to East Asia's economic and industrial success include: macroeconomic stability (low inflation rates, positive real interest rates; fiscal balance); rapid accumulation of physical and human capital; and committed governments and competent bureaucracies. Furthermore, with industrialization, East Asia's export structures shifted away from primary products towards more dynamic manufactures. The success of industrialization, and of export manufacturing in particular, is evident in the rising share of manufactures in GDP and in exports. Table 4.2 shows the share of manufactures in merchandise exports reaching over 80 per cent for most countries. But as exports of electronics and other goods grew, several East Asian countries became vulnerable to the global electronics cycle and to the business cycles in the United States and EU.

Even before the onset of the crisis in 1997, the region's remarkable economic leap had generated debate about the pattern and determinants of East Asian development. One major controversy concerns the role of government, particularly industrial policy. Some studies argue that government intervention played a vital role in the industrial development of Korea, Taiwan, Singapore and Malaysia. Others believe that East Asian countries succeeded in spite of misguided and costly government policies.

A second major controversy is over the relative importance of factor accumulation and growth in total factor productivity (TFP). Growth accounting studies found that factor inputs matter, while increases in TFP represented a relatively small contribution to overall output growth (Young 1992; Krugman 1994). Kim and Lau (1995) estimated trans-log production functions for Hong Kong, Korea, Singapore and Taiwan and concluded that TFP accounted for only one-third of the growth of real GDP as compared to 80 per cent for the United States during 1948–90. These empirical results face problems of data deficiencies – national accounts provide data on investment, not capital stocks; workers have different demographic and economic characteristics; and the rate and direction of productivity growth differ from the elasticity of substitution between capital and labor. Some economists such as Hayami (1998) cautioned that the role of TFP could vary with the stage of development. For the advanced economies, the relative contribution of TFP growth to GDP growth is higher, while the relative contribution of factor accumulation is lower. As an economy moves closer to the technological frontier, the relative contribution of TFP growth rises. The East Asian region is a relatively late developer – in the initial growth period, factor accumulation mattered more and TFP growth mattered less.

Financial Crisis

The crisis began in Thailand in July 1997 and spread quickly to the rest of the region. South Korea, Indonesia, Malaysia, the Philippines and Thailand were hit hardest. The crisis led to sharp economic contractions in several countries, with the Indonesian economy plunging 13.2 per cent, followed by Thailand (–10.8 per cent), Malaysia (–7.4 per cent), South Korea (–5.3 per cent), Hong Kong (–5.3 per cent) and the Philippines (–0.6 per cent).

The crisis generated a voluminous literature on its causes, cures, implications and lessons. In brief, macroeconomic fundamentals had deteriorated, while massive short-term capital surges, overvalued exchange rates, and weak domestic financial systems rendered these economies vulnerable to financial panics. Poor policy prescriptions and inadequate state and corporate governance aggravated the crisis and delayed the recovery.

Macroeconomic Failures

International investor and creditor confidence eroded from the early 1990s as macroeconomic fundamentals deteriorated. Exports slowed, current account deficits rose, capital inflows became increasingly tied to short-term loans and portfolio investment rather than longer-term FDI, while real exchange rates, external debts and the number of non-performing loans rose. There were also individual factors at play – Korea, Singapore, Malaysia and Thailand were affected by the cyclical downturn in the global electronics industry, while Indonesia and the Philippines saw food production drop because of the El Niño drought. Throughout the region there were also asset bubbles in real estate and the stock market and serious excess capacity in several industries.

Short-term Capital Surges

Beginning in the early 1990s, East Asia experienced massive short-term capital inflows, in the form of commercial bank borrowings and portfolio investments, followed by sharp reversals which combined to trigger the infamous Asian financial crisis in 1997. The inward surge was a response to the economic boom, capital account liberalization and domestic financial market liberalization. As an example of the magnitude of these shocks, in the six quarters prior to July 1997, capital inflows into South Korea, Indonesia, the Philippines and Thailand totaled $86.8 billion; in the subsequent six quarters, there was a huge outflow of $77.9 billion (Woo 1999). These funds were largely unhedged against exchange rate risks, and exceeded the levels of official foreign reserves. The pegged exchange rate had provided an implicit government guarantee against an exchange rate risk and encouraged domestic borrowers to seek cheaper international funds. Short-term debt was used to finance longer-term investments, resulting in overlapping maturity dates.

Government efforts to defend the exchange rate proved costly and futile. The depletion of reserves and resulting currency devaluation triggered a financial panic among creditors and investors. The sharp capital outflow resulted in soaring interest rates and inflation, plunging stock market levels, declining real estate prices and sharp economic downturns. Eichengreen (1995) and others have shown that countries are more likely to be able to contain speculative pressure when they are not yet integrated into global financial markets. For example, China did not succumb to the crisis because Beijing retained its own capital controls. China's large foreign reserves also provided a sizeable war chest to defend its currency against speculators.

Flawed Domestic Finance

The crisis revealed serious flaws in the financial systems of many East Asian economies: inadequate regulations, lax accounting standards, unreliable financial data, poor corporate governance, and high exposure to real estates and stock markets. Banking systems could not absorb the capital inflows and direct them to efficient users. Non-performing loans escalated and insolvency became a serious problem.

Poor Policy Responses

The crisis was prolonged and aggravated by the inappropriate and inadequate responses on the part of both national governments and international financial institutions. Governments in the region were simply unprepared to handle the crisis, partly due to incompetence and corruption. In hindsight, governments should have been more careful in opening their capital accounts and financial markets. With massive, volatile short-term capital movements, maintaining the currency peg drained foreign reserves and contributed to financial panic.

While Malaysia undertook unilateral reforms and capital controls, South Korea, Indonesia, the Philippines and Thailand accepted IMF rescue packages. Critics questioned the IMF approach (Woo 1999; Stiglitz 2002). Initially, the IMF applied its standard prescription of fiscal and monetary restraint, making no distinction between East Asia's financial crisis, caused by external private-sector debt, and the more orthodox financial crises elsewhere, typically caused by profligate public sectors. IMF conditionalities also included many structural and institutional reforms which delayed the political willingness of governments to accept the rescue packages and led to public protests in Korea and Thailand and rioting in Indonesia. As the real economy deteriorated alarmingly, the IMF had to loosen its stringent monetary and fiscal targets.

GLOBALIZATION, POVERTY AND INEQUALITY

Table 4.3 shows poverty and income distribution in East Asia. Using national poverty lines, the poverty incidence (percentage of population below the

Table 4.3 Poverty and Income Distribution for East Asia

Country	National Poverty Lines % of population below poverty line					International Poverty Line					
	Survey year	Rural	Urban	National	Survey year	US$1 per day		US$2 per day		Survey year	Gini Index[b]
						% population	% poverty gap[a]	% population	% poverty gap[a]		
China	1998	4.6	<2	4.6	1999	18.8	4.4	52.6	20.9	1998	40.3
Hong Kong	na	na	na	na	na	na	na	na	na	1996	52.2
South Korea	na	na	na	na	1993	<2	<0.5	<2	<0.5	1993	31.6
Singapore	na	na	na	na	na	na	na	na	na	na	na
Indonesia	1999	na	na	27.1	1999	12.9	1.9	65.5	21.5	1999	31.7
Malaysia	1989	na	na	15.5	na	na	na	na	na	1997	49.2
Philippines	1997	50.7	21.5	36.8	na	na	na	na	na	1997	46.2
Thailand	1992	15.5	10.2	13.1	1998	<2	<0.5	28.2	7.1	1998	41.4
Cambodia	1997	40.1	21.1	36.1	na	na	na	na	na	1997	40.4
Laos	1993	53	24	46.1	1997	26.3	6.3	73.2	29.6	1997	37
Myanmar	na	na	na	na	na	na	na	na	na	na	na
Vietnam	1993	57.2	25.9	50.9	na	na	na	na	na	1998	36.1

Notes:
a. Poverty Gap is the mean shortfall below the poverty line, counting the non-poor as having zero shortfall, expressed as a per centage of the poverty line. This measure reflects the depth of poverty as well as its incidence.
b. Gini Index measures the extent to which the distribution of income deviates from a perfectly equal distribution.
Source: World Development Report (2003).

Table 4.4 Poverty Changes in East Asia, 1975–95

Country	No. of people in poverty (millions)				Headcount index (%)				Poverty gap (%)			
	1975	1985	1993	1995	1975	1985	1993	1995	1975	1985	1993	1995
Indonesia	87.2	52.8	31.8	21.9	64.3	32.2	17.0	11.4	23.7	8.5	2.6	1.7
Malaysia	2.1	1.7	<0.2	<0.2	17.4	10.8	<1.0	<1.0	5.4	2.5	<1.0	<1.0
Philippines	15.4	17.7	17.8	17.6	35.7	32.4	27.5	25.5	10.6	9.2	7.3	6.5
Thailand	3.4	5.1	<0.5	<0.5	8.1	10.0	<1.0	<1.0	1.2	1.5	<1.0	<1.0
Laos	na	2.2	2.2	2.0	na	61.1	46.7	41.4	na	18.0	11.5	9.5
Vietnam	na	44.3	37.4	31.3	na	74.0	52.7	42.2	na	28.0	17.0	11.9
China	568.9	398.3	351.8	269.3	59.5	37.9	29.7	22.2	na	10.9	9.3	7.0

Notes: Except for Laos, poverty numbers are based on the international poverty line of US$1 per person per day at 1985 prices.

Source: Barry Eichengreen (January 2002), *Capitalizing on Globalization*, Table 5.

poverty line) remains over 35 per cent for Cambodia, Laos, Myanmar, Vietnam and the Philippines. However, inter-country comparisons are problematic because different countries adopted different poverty lines. Using the common international poverty line of $1 per day, the poverty incidence ranges from a high of 26.3 per cent in Laos and 18.8 per cent in China to under 2 per cent in South Korea and Thailand. Poverty incidence is also sensitive to the choice of the poverty line. As the table shows, raising the international poverty line from $1 to $2 a day leads to a sharp jump in poverty incidence in China, Indonesia, Thailand and Laos.

Eichengreen (2002) shows that poverty in East Asia declined sharply between 1975 and 1995, whether measured by the absolute number of people below the international poverty line or the proportion of the population below the poverty line calculated by poverty incidence or headcount index (Table 4.4). The numbers below the poverty line in Indonesia, Malaysia, the Philippines and Thailand fell from 108.1 million in 1975 to 40.2 million in 1995, with Indonesia showing the largest absolute fall (because of its large population) and the Philippines showing a rise in absolute poverty; for China the numbers fell dramatically from 568.9 million to 269.3 million. Poverty incidence, as measured by the headcount index, was falling in all countries from 1975 to 1995. It dropped from 64.3 per cent to 11.4 per cent for Indonesia, 59.5 per cent to 22.2 per cent for China, 35.7 per cent to 25.5 per cent for the Philippines, and to under 1 per cent for Malaysia and Thailand. The crisis wiped out much of these gains.

Table 4.5 shows the trends in income inequality roughly from the 1970s to the mid-1990s. The Gini index shows varying patterns, with rising inequality in China, Hong Kong, the Philippines and Thailand, falling inequality in Malaysia and Singapore, and stable inequality trends in Indonesia and Vietnam.

It is difficult to isolate the effects of globalization on growth, inequality and poverty. The globalization outcome depends on a number of related factors, including a country's initial conditions and the economic and social policies that accompany the process of external liberalization. Deeper micro-empirical work on growth and distributional change is needed to better understand initial conditions and to identify the specific policies and programs that affect poverty and inequality.

An OECD study (Kohl and O'Rourke 2000) showed that globalization is not the major cause of income inequality and poverty, although it contributed to the poor performance of a number of developing economies. Globalization amplified the effects of pre-existing inequalities in the distribution of human capital and other assets and in access to infrastructure and other productive resources. In countries where inequalities were high, globalization tended to make inequality worse. The implications for development policy are two-fold.

Table 4.5 Inequality Indicators in East Asia

Country	Year	Share of income or consumption 1987–98 Poorest 20%	Richest 20%	Year	Gini coefficient First year	Last year
Indonesia	1996	8.0	44.9	1970–95	0.349	0.342
Malaysia	1995	4.5	53.8	1973–95	0.501	0.485
Philippines	1997	5.4	52.3	1985–94	0.410	0.429
Thailand	1998	6.4	48.4	1975–92	0.364	0.462
Vietnam	1998	8.0	44.5	1992–98	0.357	0.361
Cambodia	1997	6.9	47.6			
Laos	1992	7.6	40.3	1993		0.304
China	1998	5.9	46.6	1985–95	0.299	0.388
Hong Kong	1980	5.4	39.9	1971–91	0.409	0.450
Taiwan	na			1985–95	0.290	0.317
South Korea	1993	7.5	39.3	1970–88	0.333	0.336
Singapore	na			1973–89	0.410	0.390

Source: Mari Pangestu (2001), 'The social impact of globalization in Southeast Asia'.

First, for globalization to be pro-poor, it needs to be complemented by policies which create a more equal distribution and access to productive resources, particularly for vulnerable groups affected by the increased competition from globalization. Second, the speed and sequencing of external and domestic liberalization must take into consideration the institutional capacity to undertake economic transformation and manage risks.

Korea and Taiwan embarked on rural development and land reforms prior to industrialization, resulting in low-income inequalities which continued into much of the industrializing period. Indonesia, Malaysia, the Philippines and Thailand started off with higher income inequalities, having failed to embark on comprehensive land and rural reforms in the pre-industrial period, compounded by geographical concentrations of natural resources and ethnic concentrations of wealth. In Indonesia, Java is heavily overpopulated while the country's vast oil and other mineral resources are located in the outer islands. In Indonesia, Malaysia and Thailand, much wealth is concentrated in (as well as generated by) the ethnic Chinese minority. In the Philippines, much wealth is concentrated in the landed oligarchy. In Malaysia, ethnic inequalities have narrowed following government efforts at agricultural and rural development and redistribution in favor of the largely rural Malay *bumiputras*. Regionally, Thailand had the sharpest disparities, with growth and income concentrated in Bangkok and its central district, which accounted for only 15–20 per cent of Thailand's population but about 50 per cent of the country's GDP in the 1980s and increased to 55 per cent in 1987–91.

Pangestu (2001) notes that natural resources and a farm sector absorbing much of the population made for good initial conditions in Indonesia, Malaysia, the Philippines and Thailand. Revenue from commodities, especially oil in Indonesia and Malaysia and agricultural exports in Thailand earned foreign exchange to finance imports for industrialization. With growth, poverty fell. And with resource sectors located away from urban-industrial areas, the impact on regional and rural–urban inequalities softened. For example, during the Indonesian financial crisis and the massive depreciation of the Indonesian rupiah, sharp increases in commodity prices (in rupiah currency), and strong external demand boosted exports of several primary exports from the outer regions of Indonesia.

The Dollar and Kraay (2001) study looked at 18 Asian countries and found that economies which liberalized after 1980s had higher growth rates, no significant change in household income inequality and less poverty. Some groups lost in the short run and safety-net programs might ease the transition for them. Rodrik (1997) noted that opening trade and investment did not produce higher growth and that macroeconomic policies and investment are what mattered. Thus a combination of policies produces growth and the type of growth that leads to better social results.

THE CRISIS, POVERTY AND INEQUALITY

The Asian financial crisis worsened poverty incidence in East Asia, but its impact on inequality trends is more mixed. The effects on the poor were generally smaller than originally anticipated, with several possible explanations. First, the economic downturns turned out to be less protracted than originally feared. Second, some of the urban workers returned to their villages. Third, some agricultural and mineral exports garnered higher soft-currency prices because of the massive currency devaluation. Finally, the safety-net programs, however inadequate, helped cushion the social impact. Poor households also coped by dipping into savings and cutting back on non-essential purchases. Although the crisis affected broad segments of China's

Table 4.6 Measures of Inequality in East Asia

Country	Fall in poverty rates	Change in poverty due to growth	Change in poverty due to changes in inequality	Residual
Indonesia:				
1970–78	3.8	7.6	−2.7	−1.1
1978–84	26.7	18.5	3.4	4.8
1985–95	23.6	22.4	−3.1	4.3
Malaysia:				
1973–89	19.1	16.4	3.9	−1.2
Philippines:				
1985–88	5.0	5.2	−0.3	0.1
1988–91	−1.2	2.9	−4.1	0.0
1991–94	1.7	0.8	1.0	−0.1
Thailand:				
1975–86	−1.9	6.1	−11.0	3.0
1986–92	10.0	10.0	−1.5	1.5

Source: Mari Pangestu (2001),' The social impact of globalization in Southeast Asia'.

urban population, including the wealthy entrepreneurial class, the low-income groups, people without savings or safety nets, suffered the most.

Poverty

Evidence to support the proposition that globalization is generally poverty-reducing is presented in two stages. First, there is the positive relationship between globalization and economic growth. Countries that are more open to trade tend to enjoy higher rates of growth (Asian Development Bank 2001). Second, there is the relationship between economic growth and poverty reduction. Globalization raises job productivity in developing countries. And as poor countries break into global markets for manufactures and services, poor people can move from the vulnerability of grinding rural poverty to better jobs in urban areas. Also, globalization tends to increase the demand for unskilled and semi-skilled labor, which developing countries have in abundance. This relationship is exemplified by Hong Kong, South Korea, Singapore and the Southeast Asian economies, where the development of export-oriented industrialization resulted in rapid income growth and poverty reduction. Income grew at an average rate of over 6 per cent during 1987–98, while poverty incidence declined from 23 per cent to 9.6 per cent (World Bank 2000). Pangestu (2001) notes that Indonesia, Malaysia, the Philippines and Thailand had high poverty incidence and high inequality when they began industrialization in the early 1970s. During the following two decades, growth averaged at least 5 per cent, although growth was more uneven in the Philippines. Growth's effect on poverty was dramatic. The greatest decline in poverty rates came from economic growth, not improved distribution (Table 4.6).

In the two East Asian transitional economies, labor-intensive exports created employment opportunities for poor migrants from the rural sector (World Bank 2002). China's poverty reduction was massive, with the number of rural poor declining from 250 million in 1978 to just 34 million in 1999, while in Vietnam the level of absolute poverty halved in a decade. Therefore globalization, when accompanied by appropriate domestic policies, can promote poverty reduction. However, globalization also increases economic volatility and job insecurity.

Oxfam (2000) challenges the conclusion that economic growth is closely associated with poverty reduction and that globalization and openness bring the same benefits to the poor as to the non-poor. It criticizes the Dollar and Kraay study on two counts. First, globalization is anti-growth, since high inequality dampens pro-poor growth. However the evidence does not support this contention. Second globalization is anti-poor, because it ignores the critical role of income distribution on poverty reduction. The poor frequently lacked adequate access to productive resources and human capital, and improving income distribution would strengthen the linkage between growth and poverty reduction. On a more positive note, Oxfam found that East Asia is the only developing region that is on track to halve poverty by 2015 (Table 4.7). In East Asia, high growth rates have been accompanied by high poverty reduction, with each percentage point of growth producing four times as much impact on poverty reduction as in Latin America.

Warr (2002) provides an empirical study on the relationship between economic growth, poverty and inequality in Indonesia, Malaysia, the Philippines and Thailand. The limited availability of long-term time-series data proved a serious obstacle to the study of poverty incidence in the region. Warr pooled the time series for the four countries to obtain a total of 36 observations for a period stretching from the 1960s to 1999. Interpreting the results of pooled observations always poses a problem, however, because countries differ in their definitions of poverty lines and in their economic structures.

The Warr study found that the four cases have each achieved significant reductions in poverty incidence in recent decades (Table 4.8). Poverty

Table 4.7 Regional Poverty Indicators

Region	Number of poor (million)		Headcount index		Required rate of poverty reduction to meet 2015 target	Actual rate of poverty reduction 1990–1998
	1990	1998	1990	1998		
East Asia	452	278	27.6	15.3	2	2.40
South Asia	495	522	44.0	40.0	2	0.50
Sub-Sahara Africa	242	290	47.7	46.3	2	0.17
Latin America	74	78	16.8	15.6	2	0.15
All developing and transitional economies	1276	1190	29.0	24.0	2	0.62

Source: Oxfam (2000), 'Growth with equity is good for the poor', Table 1.

incidence is based on the headcount measure, and change in poverty incidence is divided into three parts – change in rural poverty incidence, weighted by the rural population share; change in urban poverty incidence, weighted by the urban population share; and rural–urban migration weighted by the rural–urban difference in poverty incidence. The achievement of poverty reduction was overwhelmingly attributable to the aggregate growth rate. In testing the impact of changes in the sectoral composition, the study found the impact limited, and the poverty reduction is strongly related to growth of agriculture and services, but *not* to the growth of industry (Table 4.9). This finding for Indonesia, Malaysia, the Philippines and Thailand contrasts with studies done on India (Ravallion and Datt 1996) and Taiwan (Warr and Wang 1999). The Indian study found strong negative effects of industrial growth, reflecting a pattern of industrialization focusing on import substitution in heavy industry. In contrast, the study on Taiwan found that growth of industry was strongly associated with poverty reduction, reflecting a pattern of industrialization focusing on labor-intensive exports and large absorption of semi-skilled and unskilled workers. The pattern of industrialization and its impact on poverty in Indonesia, Malaysia, the Philippines and Thailand lies somewhere between the experiences of India and Taiwan.

Some caution in interpreting poverty numbers and trends is necessary. Poverty incidence depends on how the poverty line is defined. In Indonesia, for example, raising the poverty line by 25 per cent more than doubled the poverty incidence from 11 per cent to 25 per cent. There are also significant urban–rural, regional, gender and ethnic differences in poverty incidence. The number of urban poor has grown due to rural–urban migration. Ethnic disparities in poverty incidence were the most politically sensitive in Malaysia, where most Malays were rural farmers, while the ethnic Chinese were employed mainly in urban business and industry (in part due to restrictions on land ownership). In 1970, the poverty incidence among Malays was a high 65 per cent, as contrasted with only 26 per cent among the Chinese. Unequal economic status led to racial riots in May 1969 and led the government to introduce the New Economic Policy to improve inter-ethnic income and wealth equity.

Inequality

There is no consensus on the impact of globalization on inter-country inequality. While some analysts argue that globalization has enabled the faster development of poor countries and a convergence of growth rates, others argue that globalization is impoverishing poor countries even more. The World Bank (2002) views globalization as mostly reducing inter-country inequality, noting that during the 1990s, the per capita growth rate for the rich countries was 2 per cent, but for the group of "new globalizing" developing countries, which encompasses some 3 billion people, the growth rate was 5 per cent per capita and the poverty incidence of those living on less than 1 a day declined by 120 million during 1993–98. East Asia's developing economies belong to this group of new globalizers. However, critics of globalization point to the widening GNP per capita between the world's rich countries and the world's poorest countries as evidence of globalization leading to rising inequality. The two conclusions on inter-country inequality are not inconsistent, since the faster growth rate of developing economies can still result in a wider absolute gap between advanced and developing economies. More significantly, there is also the large group of poor countries, encompassing about 2 billion people, which has not benefited from globalization, due to unfavorable physical geography or weak economic management, institutions and governance.

The World Bank (2002) believes that there is little basis for the widespread concern that globalization is leading to heightened inequalities within countries, pointing to evidence which shows that globalization has not *on average* affected within-country inequality. However, a statistical average masks wide variations in inequality, including inequalities based on rural–urban, region, ethnicity or gender.

The evidence on growth and inequality in East Asia is mixed. Some studies indicate general stability in inequality coefficients during the early years of globalization and industrialization, but, generally, inequality appeared to be rising in the 1990s. Oxfam (2000) argues that there is substantial evidence that current patterns of growth are reinforcing existing income inequalities across

Table 4.8 Aggregate Growth and Composition Effects on Poverty Reduction

Country	Actual	Estimated		
		Constant	Growth	Composition
			% change per year	
Indonesia:				
Aggregate	−1.11	2.01	−2.97	−0.14
Urban	−0.19	0.43	−0.55	−0.07
Rural	−0.42	2.71	−3.05	−0.07
Migration	−0.50	−1.13	0.63	0.004
Malaysia:				
Aggregate	−1.48	−0.25	−3.11	1.88
Urban	−0.70	−0.02	−0.66	−0.08
Rural	−0.50	−0.19	−2.12	1.82
Migration	−0.27	−0.03	−0.39	0.14
Philippines:				
Aggregate	−1.29	1.36	−2.46	−0.19
Urban	−0.55	−0.03	−0.42	−0.10
Rural	−0.58	2.02	−2.51	−0.10
Migration	−0.16	−0.63	0.47	0.00
Thailand:				
Aggregate	−1.97	2.43	−4.24	−0.17
Urban	−0.32	0.46	−0.70	−0.09
Rural	−1.68	2.62	−4.21	−0.08
Migration	0.03	−0.65	0.67	0.00

Table 4.8 continued

Country	Actual	Normalized (aggregate = 100)		
		Constant	Growth	Composition
Indonesia:				
Aggregate	100	−182	269	13
Urban	17	−39	49	7
Rural	38	−245	276	7
Migration	45	102	−57	0
Malaysia				
Aggregate	100	17	210	1
Urban	48	2	41	1
Rural	34	13	143	1
Migration	19	18	26	−0.03
Philippines:				
Aggregate	100	−105	30	15
Urban	43	2	10	8
Rural	45	−156	41	8
Migration	12	49	−20	−0.4
Thailand				
Aggregate	100	−124	215	8
Urban	16	−23	35	4
Rural	85	−133	214	4
Migration	−2	33	−38	0

Note: GDP growth data from national government statistical agencies.

Source: Peter Warr (2002), Poverty Incidence and Sectoral Growth: Evidence from Southeast Asia, Tables 4a–4d.

Table 4.9 Poverty Reduction and Sectoral Growth Decomposition

	Actual	Estimated				
		Constant	Agriculture	Industry	Services	Population
Indonesia:						
Aggregate	−1.11	2.01	−0.46	0.14	−2.65	−0.14
Urban	−0.19	0.43	−0.15	−0.13	−0.27	−0.07
Rural	−0.42	2.71	−0.62	0.02	−2.45	−0.07
Migration	−0.50	−1.13	0.31	0.26	0.06	0.00
Malaysia:						
Aggregate	−1.48	−0.25	−0.62	1.95	−2.56	−0.02
Urban	−0.70	−0.02	−0.17	−0.45	−0.06	−0.01
Rural	−0.50	−0.19	−0.59	2.34	−2.06	−0.01
Migration	−0.27	−0.26	0.20	0.00	−0.18	0.00
Philippines:						
Aggregate	−1.29	1.36	−0.39	0.09	−2.16	−0.19
Urban	−0.55	−0.03	−0.13	−0.08	−0.22	−0.10
Rural	−0.58	2.02	−0.53	0.01	−1.99	−0.10
Migration	−0.16	−0.63	0.26	0.16	0.05	0.005
Thailand:						
Aggregate	−1.97	2.43	−0.36	0.19	−4.06	−0.17
Urban	−0.32	0.46	−0.12	−0.17	−0.41	−0.09
Rural	−1.68	2.62	−0.49	0.02	−3.75	−0.08
Migration	0.03	−0.65	0.24	0.34	0.09	0.00

Table 4.9 continued

	Actual	Normalized (aggregate = 100)				
		Constant	Agriculture	Industry	Services	Population
Indonesia:						
Aggregate	100	−182	42	−13	240	13
Urban	17	−39	13	12	24	7
Rural	38	−245	56	1	221	7
Migration	45	102	−28	−23	−6	0
Malaysia:						
Aggregate	100	17	42	−132	173	1
Urban	48	2	12	30	4	1
Rural	34	13	40	−158	139	1
Migration	19	18	−13	0	12	−0.03
Philippines:						
Aggregate	100	−105	30	−7	167	15
Urban	43	2	10	6	17	8
Rural	45	−156	41	−1	154	8
Migration	12	49	−20	−12	−4	−0.4
Thailand:						
Aggregate	100	−124	18	−10	206	8
Urban	16	−23	6	9	21	4
Rural	85	−133	25	−1	190	4
Migration	−2	33	−12	−17	−5	0

Note: GDP growth data from national government statistical agencies.

Source: Peter Warr (2002), Poverty Incidence and Sectoral Growth: Evidence from Southeast Asia, Tables 4a–4d.

a broad spectrum of countries. For example, in China, there is the widening income gap between coastal and interior areas. In Vietnam, average income in the northern region increased by 31 per cent between 1993 and 1998, less than half of the level recorded in the southeast region. Poverty rates in the northern region are 59 per cent compared to 8 per cent in the southeast.

Ravallion (2000) uses data on poverty and inequality obtained from household surveys in which random samples of households are interviewed using a structured questionnaire, and he uses the Gini coefficient to measure inequality. He concludes that there is little or no correlation between growth in average household income per capita and the Gini coefficient. He had the same conclusion as that reached in the Dollar and Kraay study: there is little or no correlation between changes in inequality and policy reforms, including greater economic openness. Ravillion, however, cautions against drawing policy implications from the seeming lack of correlation between policy reforms and changes in overall inequality, and he suggested several possible explanations for the weak correlation. One possibility is measurement error. Another relates to the methodological problem – aggregate inequality and averages may change relatively little over time and fail to capture the losers and near losers, as panel data have found considerable churning under the surface. A third explanation is that starting conditions vary among countries. Obviously further research is necessary to cast better light on the growth-inequality nexus, including the role of initial conditions, the pattern of growth and the impact of policies.

Evidence on Indonesia, Malaysia and the Philippines points to varying inequality trends until the early 1990s. From the mid-1970s to mid-1980s, the Gini coefficient declined steadily for Indonesia and Malaysia, rose in Thailand, but remained stable in the Philippines. From the mid-1980s until the onset of the crisis in 1997, inequality rose in Indonesia and Malaysia, fluctuated in the Philippines and continued to rise in Thailand until 1992 when it started to decline (Pangestu 2001).

How has distribution affected poverty incidence? Pangestu found that the fall in poverty in Indonesia for much of the period was due mainly to growth rather than inequality changes. In Malaysia, policies that improved inequality, such as the New Economic Policy and rural development, helped reduce poverty. But growing inequality offset somewhat the growth-driven poverty reduction in Thailand. Aggregate inequality trends mask inequalities between rural and urban, between regions, between gender and between ethnic groups.

China

A study by Zhang, Shao and Su (2002) concludes that China has greatly benefited from its 1979 economic reforms and opening to the outside world. China's 44 per cent trade/GDP ratio is very high for such a large economy. And China's inward FDI growth has made it the largest FDI recipient in East Asia. During this period, China's GDP grew at 9.7 per cent annually. The impact of reform and openness on poverty reduction is widespread, with the number of poor people falling by 10 million each year. Official data show that in urban areas, the poorest quintile quadrupled their income during 1986–99, while in the rural areas the poverty incidence fell from 30.7 per cent in 1978 to less than 5 per cent currently. However, rural poverty and rising urban unemployment (with massive rural–urban migration) are increasingly becoming political and social problems.

While there has been widespread poverty reduction, the reforms also led to sharply rising inequality. In the pre-1979 period, China had a very egalitarian Marxist society with high poverty incidence. The Gini coefficient rose from 0.3 in 1978 to 0.45 in 2000. But Zhang cautions against any simplistic conclusion that openness creates inequality. In fact, rising inequality is a result of differing degrees of participation in globalization and the lack of mechanisms to redistribute benefits and costs between winners and losers.

China's pattern of inequality is dominated by regional and rural–urban disparities. Until the mid-1980s, China's regional growth rates were converging. Initial reforms in the late 1970s focused on the agricultural sector and strengthening property rights, freeing prices and creating internal markets. In the 1980s, the reform focus shifted to urban and industrial sectors, resulting in diverging growth rates and rising regional disparity. The eastern coastal region accounts for an overwhelming share of China's international trade and inflows of FDI. It is geographically advantaged, with easy access to cheap and efficient sea transportation, as well as investments from the ethnic Chinese of Hong Kong, Taiwan and Southeast Asia. The eastern coastal region also contained China's first special economic zones, created with special tax incentives and physical infrastructure to attract FDI. Since the initial ethnic Chinese investments, the coastal region has also increasingly attracted investments from Japan, Europe and the United States. Conversely, the interior regions of China are handicapped not only by physical geography but also by poor infrastructure and neglect. However, concern over the widening regional disparity, and its potential for political and social unrest, caused the central government to adopt the 'Go West' policy and to invest heavily in the interior region since the mid-1990s.

In 2000 China's urban–rural income ratio stood at 2.75 (Zhang, Shao and Su 2002). This gap can be traced back to the industrial strategy embraced during the early years of the People's Republic of China. To ensure low production costs for heavy industry, the government suppressed agricultural prices to subsidize the urban cost of living. The government also limited the urban–rural migration through a strict residence system to prevent rising urban unemployment. Thus, at the beginning of reforms in 1979, China's urban–rural income ratio was already a high 2.57. In the initial years of reform, focusing on the rural agricultural sector, the ratio dropped sharply, reaching a low of 1.82 in 1983. From the mid-1980s the reform focus shifted to urban industrial sectors and global integration. While industrial zones were given various fiscal incentives, the rural areas continued to be burdened by hefty taxes and mandated low grain prices. The Xinhua news agency cited an Agriculture Ministry source which reported that the average urban income in Shanghai could be as much as eight times that of some interior provinces. And in the first half of 2002, per capita income in cities was 3,942 yuan as compared to only 1,123 yuan in the rural areas. To ensure political and social stability and raise rural living standards, China's leaders have called for priority to be given to agricultural and rural problems.

The role that globalization played in urban–rural disparity is still debatable. In a study by Shang Jin Wei and Yi Wu (2001), cited by Zhang, the authors found that 'cities that experience a greater degree of openness in trade also tend to demonstrate a greater decline in urban–rural income inequality; thus globalization has helped to reduce, rather than increase, urban–rural income inequality'.

South Korea, Indonesia, Malaysia, the Philippines and Thailand

The financial crisis appeared to have little impact on overall inequality in South Korea, Indonesia and Thailand. But notwithstanding the aggregates, the crisis affected various groups in varying degrees. South Korea experienced the highest rise in urban poverty incidence, from 7.5 per cent in early 1997 to a peak of 22.9 per cent in 1998. The poverty rate reflected the sharp rise in unemployment, from 2 per cent to 6.8 per cent as well as substantial declines in real wages. In urban Korea, although the Gini coefficient on household consumption changed very little, the Gini coefficient on income rose from 0.271 to 0.301 during 1997–98, reflecting the poor's efforts to maintain consumption despite the loss of income.

Indonesia was hardest hit, with a combination of financial damage, drought and political crisis. Household poverty incidence rose from 11.3 per cent in 1996 to 16.7 per cent in 1998, with an additional 10–12 million people thrown into poverty. High inflation heavily affected real wages and incomes, which fell a whopping 34 per cent in the formal sector and 40 per cent in agriculture. Open unemployment recorded only a moderate rise from 4.9 per cent to 5.5 per cent, as retrenched workers moved to the informal sector or returned to their villages. The nominal Gini coefficient changed little, but due to the sharp increase in food prices, the urban poor and rural workers were affected more, while rural producers benefited from higher export earnings (Pangestu 2001). As in Korea, the poor protected basic consumption, so household consumption fell by only 3 per cent despite the economic contraction of 14 per cent in 1998. While Jakarta and cities in West Java were badly hit, some outer islands actually enjoyed a boom in farm exports. Adjusting the Gini coefficient to reflect deflated household incomes, the results indicate a slight drop in urban inequality (0.299 to 0.289) but an increase in rural inequality (0.265 to 0.289).

In Malaysia, a simulation study suggested a 36 per cent rise in poverty, with poverty incidence rising from 8.2 per cent in 1997 to 11.2 per cent in 1998. The increase in unemployment was relatively moderate, from 2.5 per cent to 3.2 per cent, as foreign workers (estimated at 20 per cent of the labor force) bore the brunt of retrenchments.

In the Philippines, more than 90 per cent of families reported being adversely affected by higher prices of food and other commodities, whereas 17 per cent reported job loss within the Philippines, and a further 5 per cent reported job loss as migrant workers in other East Asian economies. The unemployment rate rose to 13.3 per cent. Households dependent on overseas remittances were badly hit when host countries retrenched and repatriated their foreign workers.

In Thailand, the poverty headcount grew from 11.4 per cent in 1996 to almost 13 per cent in 1998, with an additional 1.1 million people sinking below the poverty line. Real wages fell by 20–25 per cent between 1998 and 1999. The largest rise in poverty was in the more urban south and central regions. Rural poverty incidence rose from 15 per cent in 1997 to 17.2 per cent in 1998. Cuts in government spending, combined with reduced household expenditures on health and education, were expected to have severe, long-term consequences. But the effects have been mixed, as health care spending and school enrolment did not decline as sharply as expected.

INADEQUATE SOCIAL SAFETY NETS

The financial crisis challenged an underlying assumption in most of East Asia, namely that economic growth obviates the need for formal social safety nets. Prior to 1997, government-provided safety nets were scarce, as countries relied on rapid economic growth, new jobs, families and villages to bridge any gap. The government limited its social services to education and health care.

These gaping holes in the social safety nets became highly visible during the financial crisis. Governments were unable to respond adequately because they had few distribution channels and little information, combined with declining fiscal revenues. Countries attempted to expand existing social safety nets and launched new programs to create jobs, protect social expenditures, cushion the impact of rising food and medical prices and discourage parents from withdrawing their children from school because of the hard times. Korea went the furthest, with its share of GDP for social protection rising from 0.6 per cent in 1997 to 1.26 per cent in 1998 and to almost 2 per cent in 1999.

Safety nets operate at three levels, and many East Asian countries adopted all three strategies.

Create New Jobs

All crisis countries used public works to generate employment. In South Korea, most of the jobless were unable to benefit from unemployment insurance, so the government introduced a new public works program in May 1998, which created over 400,000 jobs by January 1999. Indonesia created work that annually benefited more than 400,000 people.

Income Maintenance

Among South Korea, Indonesia, Malaysia, the Philippines and Thailand, only Seoul had a pre-existing unemployment insurance scheme, which it expanded to cover all firms with at least five employees, as well as temporary and day laborers; this raised the coverage from 5.7 million in January 1998 to 8.7 million by end of year. The government also shortened the contribution period required to activate eligibility and extended the duration of benefit payments. South Korea also implemented a wage-subsidy program, which paid one-third to two-thirds of a worker's wage if the firm could demonstrate a need for economic adjustment; in 1998 the program covered 800,000 workers and in 1999 the duration of subsidy increased from six to nine months. It is debatable as to whether wage subsidies save jobs. A survey of Korean enterprises found that only 22.3 per cent of jobs would have been lost without the subsidy. Severance pay, unemployment insurance, and wage subsidies largely benefit formal sector workers. Korea, Malaysia and Thailand also modified their severance schemes. Thailand extended the maximum amount of severance pay to 10 months and set up a fund to pay workers whose firms had gone bankrupt. Malaysia allowed workers who quit voluntarily to receive severance pay. In Korea, the government expanded the means-tested Livelihood Protection Program which provided cash and in-kind assistance to those unable to work.

Maintain Basic Spending

Countries tried to maintain health and educational spending, particularly after the IMF relaxed its fiscal restraint condition, with varying success. In Indonesia total public expenditure on health care fell 8 per cent in 1997–98 and 12 per cent in 1998–99, while public expenditure on education plummeted 41 per cent between 1996–97 and 1997–98, before rebounding somewhat in 1998–99. Basic foodstuffs were a serious concern in Indonesia and Philippines, where the impact of the El Niño drought was most severe. Indonesia offered cash, goods-in-kind and a targeted rice subsidy program to replace the general rice subsidy. Education scholarships and block transfers through the Indonesia Stay-in-School campaign helped families with tuition costs. Thailand expanded its low-income health insurance program. In Thailand the worst hit were younger, less-educated workers in rural areas and small firms; few of these workers received severance pay. Households and individuals ultimately fell back on informal means, such as extended family, informal credit networks, community projects and charity provided by Buddhist temples and Chinese clan groups.

How effectively did these governments respond to the social consequences of the crisis? Atinc (2003) found that governments implemented largely sensible policies to expand some safety-net programs and to protect expenditures in key sectors. But the governments were clearly hampered by a lack of preparedness, poor information, few existing programs to expand or upgrade and poor coordination.

Countries began to realize they could no longer take uninterrupted economic growth for granted and rely on growth and full employment to provide social safety nets. Nobel Laureate Amartya Sen (1999) cautioned that the days of unmitigated economic success, with all ups and no downs, are over for East Asia, and people need protection from sudden destitution. Urbanization and industrialization are eroding the traditional systems based on family and community at the same time globalization and intense competition make many jobs insecure. Safety nets work more effectively if they are already in place before a crisis outbreak.

Now the question is what type of safety nets to implement. Marshall and Butzbach (2003) caution East Asian countries against a total commitment to social insurance, given resource constraints and suggests beginning with health, education, housing and family services. There is no consensus on the utility and desirability of unemployment insurance, as East Asia has sizeable rural populations and large informal sectors that would be excluded. Thailand abandoned a permanent unemployment insurance scheme in favor of more poverty-targeted fiscal measures (Warr 2002).

For the poor without unemployment coverage, targeted transfers of cash, food, and in-kind services can reduce their financial vulnerability. Investment in education and health care are also forms of human capital development, and they can contribute to economic competitiveness. Public works programs have proven to be relatively efficient, but these work programs must be well designed to have a long-term impact. Microcredit programs have been successfully adopted in South Asia and could provide alternatives to the formal sector. Finally, as noted by Amartya Sen, social safety nets should not be equated solely with handouts. Human security means human development, with better education, health and job opportunities for everyone.

MORE EQUITABLE OUTCOMES

Many observers argue that the problem is not globalization itself but how it has been managed (Stiglitz 2002). Globalization can succeed if appropriate domestic policy measures are undertaken to enable all segments of society to take advantage of the benefits of globalization and to cushion the impact on groups that are adversely affected (Rodrik 1997). How should states maximize the benefits and minimize the risks of globalization? Opening to international trade and capital flows makes countries vulnerable to external shocks. Countries can minimize this volatility with accurate, timely information and sound macroeconomic and financial management, based on a sound financial system. Global market forces are also likely to widen income gaps between countries and within countries, unless mitigated by international and national actions and efforts.

Should East Asia abandon its dependence on international trade and investment? High external dependence has rendered East Asian economies highly vulnerable to the downsides of globalization, and there are limited mechanisms for winners to compensate losers. Countries need to pursue a strategy of *balanced growth* to achieve sustainable growth with less volatility and more equitable outcomes. Given the diversity of development levels and economic and social institutions among East Asian countries, any generalization runs the risk of ignoring particular national circumstances that could require specific responses. For example, small economies such as Singapore and Hong Kong have little choice but to ride globalization for scale and efficiency, while larger East Asian economies can opt for more balanced development between export- and domestic-led growth.

International Trade and Economic Growth

The East Asia economies that have been more outward-looking and involved in international trade have enjoyed higher growth rates than inward-looking economies. However, in the aftermath of the 1997–98 crisis, the wisdom of the export-led development model has been questioned, not because it failed to generate growth, but because it also generated socially unacceptable costs. There is growing recognition of the need to temper export-led growth with more attention to broader-based and domestic-led growth and the development of agro-industries and services. Product and market diversification, integrated regional markets and institutional linkages with other regional trading blocs can also reduce vulnerability. Many countries expect that the newly launched WTO Doha Development Round will lead to greater market access for developing economies, but most East Asian developing economies have opposed the inclusion of labor standards and environmental standards in a new WTO round.

Regional economic cooperation can help East Asia's individual economies cope with the challenges of globalization by providing market access and market security as well as improving economic competitiveness through exploiting scale economies and comparative advantage. Unlike continental economic blocs in North America and Europe, East Asia is a fragmented economic region. The Association of Southeast Asian Nations Free-Trade Area (ASEAN-AFTA), established in 1992, remains the only regional or sub-regional zone in East Asia to date. AFTA brings together 10 Southeast Asian countries with a population of 500 million. However, ASEAN's aggregate GDP size is only less than 10 per cent of either NAFTA or the EU. The sub-region is also heavily dependent on external sources for investment capital and technology. AFTA is expected to enhance the competitiveness of individual ASEAN member states as a production base and attractive investment location. To be an integrated market, ASEAN must accelerate its pace of trade liberalization under AFTA, implement the ASEAN Framework Agreement on Services to liberalize intra-regional trade in services and implement the ASEAN Investment Area to liberalize and facilitate FDI from within the region and beyond.

Economic regionalism in East Asia is rapidly expanding beyond ASEAN and AFTA and encompasses trade and investment cooperation, monetary and financial cooperation, and development cooperation. The driving forces are the intense global competition for markets, the new trading blocs in North America and Europe, the uncertainties surrounding WTO-led global trade liberalization and the need for regional self-help. The East Asian states are exploring a variety of economic relationships. These include ASEAN economic partnerships with China, Japan, the United States and India. The ASEAN+3 monetary and financial cooperation involving the ASEAN-10 plus Japan, China and South Korea could evolve into an East Asian free-trade zone. A China–Japan–South Korea partnership is also under consideration. At the bilateral level, Singapore and Thailand are entering into FTAs with a growing number of economies around the world. South Korea and Malaysia are rapidly following suit with bilateral negotiations. All these free-trade agreements are aimed at better and more secure market access. The regional initiatives also incorporate developmental elements pertaining to human resources, infrastructure and investment and trade preferences aimed specifically at raising the developmental levels of Cambodia, Laos, Myanmar and Vietnam and thereby narrow the economic gap between rich and poor East Asian economies.

Macroeconomic Stability and Capital Inflows

While economists generally agree on the benefits of international free trade, there is less agreement over the benefits of uncontrolled international capital flows. In principle, portfolio investment permitted by capital-account liberalization should relax financial constraints on growth, deepen domestic financial markets and make direct investment more attractive. Klein and Olivei (1999) found that portfolio capital flows stimulate financial deepening and, by inference, growth in relatively high-income countries, where policy and market distortions are lowest; but such flows have a perverse effect on financial development in low-income countries. The interaction of portfolio capital flows with pre-existing domestic market distortions in some East Asian economies has heightened volatility and risk.

The financial crisis highlighted the risks posed by rapid capital account and financial market liberalization without the accompanying regulatory regimes being in place. There is no consensus on how to limit financial volatility and safeguard against financial crises. For the countries that have not fully opened up their capital accounts and liberalized their financial markets, namely China, Cambodia, Laos, Myanmar and Vietnam, policymakers are adopting a more cautious approach. The crisis shows that countries must maintain sound macroeconomic management policy to avoid inflation and undermining investor confidence; strengthen banking and money-market institutions; strengthen prudential supervision and regulation of financial systems and capital accounts; improve governance of the public sector, financial institutions and corporations; pursue an appropriate exchange-rate regime; and develop stock and bond markets to lessen dependence on short-term commercial bank loans to finance corporate investments.

At the height of the crisis, Malaysia imposed capital controls on short-term outflows. The response appeared to stabilize the financial market. It also generated an active academic and policy debate on the role and efficacy of capital controls. Whatever the merits of capital controls, it will become increasingly difficult for individual states to enforce them with increasingly globalized and integrated financial markets facilitated by Internet transactions. Capital controls could also pose a serious deterrent to longer-term FDI flows.

Also at the height of the crisis, affected states sought reforms in the international financial architecture to reduce the systemic risks generated by globalized financial markets. There has been limited action at this level and more attention is now focused on regional schemes. At the ASEAN level, finance ministers have put in place a regional surveillance mechanism to provide timely economic and financial information that will serve as early warning signals of emerging problems. There is also a new system of bilateral swaps among ASEAN central banks to assist members facing liquidity problems. Financial cooperation in surveillance and swap arrangements has been extended beyond the immediate ASEAN region. An Asian Monetary Fund to complement the role of the IMF is also being discussed and an Asian Bond Market is being implemented.

While the role of portfolio capital and commercial bank borrowings remains doubtful, there is greater regional acceptance of the role of FDI. FDI is typically less volatile than short-term capital inflows. East Asia, particularly Southeast Asia, is heavily dependent on FDI inflows to develop manufacturing capabilities as well as finance natural-resource development. The after-effects of the financial crisis, particularly recession, uncertain recovery and political instability have discouraged the return of FDI in Southeast Asia to pre-crisis levels. To improve the investment climate, countries have embarked on unilateral investment liberalization for both greenfield investments and mergers and acquisitions and to improve the legal framework and governance. However, ASEAN still needs to accelerate the pace of liberalization towards a fully integrated regional market and hasten the implementation of the ASEAN Investment Area to liberalize investments from within Southeast Asia and from external sources. Even then, ASEAN has to contend with the stiff competition for FDI posed by China's booming economy.

GROWTH WITH EQUITY

The capitalist pattern of economic development, with emphasis on the market and private sector, promotes efficiency and innovation, but also contributes to volatility and inequity. The market remains indifferent to the ethical dimensions of poverty and inequality. Hence governments need to step in. Traditionally governments have used monetary, financial and fiscal policies to limit economic volatility and redistributive mechanisms such as taxation and subsidies to reduce inequalities. In the transition economies of China and Vietnam, governments have abandoned confiscation and redistribution in favor of market-oriented economies. Now income and wealth inequalities have widened rapidly and governments are resorting to the fiscal system to redistribute wealth.

Stiglitz (2002) advocates a balanced view of the role of government, one which recognizes both market failures and government failures but which sees market and government working in partnership. Governments can make a difference in growth, stability and equity, no matter the country's stage of political or economic development. Stiglitz believes the governments of East Asia have performed their roles reasonably well in providing education, infrastructure, advanced technology and even in regulating the financial sector.

Two major areas in which governments can promote more equitable growth are rural development and human resource development.

Rural Development

There has been too much of an urban and industrial bias in East Asia's development models. Southeast Asia and China still have large rural populations and any significant efforts at reducing poverty and inequality must encompass rural development. Pangestu (2001) noted that unlike Korea and Taiwan, Indonesia, Malaysia, the Philippines and Thailand did not experience an export-oriented industrialization strategy accompanied by the spread of industrialization, including rapid increases in non-agricultural employment in the rural areas. Rising inequality in the 1990s reflects the widening urban-rural gap. Warr (2002) demonstrated that the Southeast Asian pattern of industrialization had a less distributional impact than the Taiwanese model, which emphasized more export-oriented and labor-intensive industrialization. When the economic reforms in China shifted to the urban industrial sector in the 1980s, inequality rose rapidly. More recently, China's leaders are calling for faster rural reforms, stressing that without developed agriculture and a prosperous countryside, there can be no well-off society nationwide.

Key elements in rural advancement include developing rural infrastructure, urban-rural linkages, land rights and land-use rights that encourage farm improvements, and easier access to low-cost credit. Urban-rural migration has often been proposed as solving the problem of poverty and rural surplus labor.

However, this depends on the capacity of cities to provide employment and social amenities such as housing and sanitation. Otherwise, migration leads to rising urban unemployment and severe pressure on social services.

Human Resource Development

In Southeast Asia, the availability of a pool of unskilled labor able to respond to the employment opportunities created by labor-intensive export manufacturing proved a success. But these economies need to upgrade, and economic restructuring is hampered by shortages of skilled labor. Unlike Hong Kong, South Korea and Singapore, Indonesia, Malaysia, the Philippines and Thailand did not move as fast to educate workers, so while labor markets are relatively flexible, the result is still growing inequality due to the sharp rise in skill premiums. To build capacity among the poor, there has to be more equal access to quality, affordable education. Education promotes both growth and equity. Education enables the poor to find more productive employment and secure higher earnings.

CONCLUSION

East Asia faces twin challenges from globalization: how to remain economically competitive and how to mitigate the volatilities and social inequities of the market.

On globalization and competitiveness, some economies are more prepared for the challenge than others. Economies such as Hong Kong, Korea, Taiwan and Singapore have unilaterally embarked on economic restructuring and upgrading, as their economies lose comparative advantage in low-wage and labor-intensive activities. Dynamic comparative advantage requires developing human resources and technology to be competitive in knowledge-based activities. The less-developed economies of Indonesia, the Philippines, Cambodia, Laos, Myanmar and Vietnam still retain considerable advantage in resource-based and labor-intensive activities. For them, the issue is better natural resource management and providing a policy and institutional environment which enables them to develop their competitiveness in labor-intensive activities. Malaysia and Thailand are in-between economies, with considerable resource advantages yet rising labor costs that necessitate industrial upgrading. For all economies to meet the challenge of global competition, emphasis has to be on improving efficiency, cost competitiveness and innovation. In addition to national initiatives, East Asia's developing economies are also actively pursuing regional economic cooperation and integration to improve market access and exploit economies of scale and regional specialization along the value chain. The ASEAN countries, increasingly concerned about global competition and competition from China and India, have developed a workplan to improve the sub-region's economic competitiveness through accelerated economic integration.

Traditionally, East Asian economies have experienced the price and demand volatility associated with exporting primary products. Diversification into manufacturing has been one solution. However, the concentration on the electronics industry exposed many economies to the global electronics cycle and the ever-shortening product cycle. Also, the regional financial crisis of 1997–98 highlighted volatility emanating from short-term capital flows. Apart from national policy responses, countries in the region have also embarked on regional monetary and financial cooperation in an effort to maintain regional financial instability.

As demonstrated by the regional financial crisis, the vulnerability and volatility associated with globalization can impose severe shocks on the finances of individuals, households, businesses and governments. The low-income groups have been particularly vulnerable in the absence of social safety nets. Programs to provide social insurance for the poor in normal times have to take into consideration the financial capability of governments and corporate responsibility in a world of increasingly mobile capital. For crisis situations, it is crucial that institutional capacity exists to execute relief packages for the vulnerable poor.

While economic growth has led to significant reductions in poverty in East Asian economies, income inequality has been rising. The emphasis on export-led industrialization has widened the urban-rural gap and the gaps between regions within the country. Skills scarcity and the premium on entrepreneurship and innovation have also widened the divide between the unskilled and semi-skilled and the professional, managerial and entrepreneurial class. Each country will have to determine what is the politically and socially tolerable level of social inequity and adjust the economic growth rate and growth pattern accordingly. Political and social tolerance requires removing social inequities associated with corruption and market power. For many economies, the export-led industrial model will have to be tempered by more balanced growth, with greater emphasis on rural and agricultural development, development of small and medium enterprises, and more widespread human resource development.

REFERENCES

Asian Development Bank (2001), *Asian Development Outlook 2001: Special Chapter – Asia's Globalization Challenge*, New York: Oxford University Press.

Atinc, Tamar Manuelyan (2003), 'How the East Asian Crisis Changed the Social Situation,' in Katherine Marshall and Oliver Butzbach (eds), *New Social Policy Agendas for Europe and Asia: Challenges, Experience and Lessons*, Washington, DC: World Bank, pp. 55–80.

Dollar, David and Aart Kraay (2001), 'Growth is good for the poor', Washington, DC, World Bank Policy Research Department Working Paper No. 2587.

Eichengreen, Barry (2002), *Capitalizing on Globalization*, Manila: Asian Development Bank.

Hayami, Yujiro (1998), *Toward the Rural-based Development of Commerce and Industry: Selected Experiences from East Asia*, Washington, DC: World Bank.

Kim, John Il and Lawrence J. Lau (1995), 'The role of human capital in the economic growth of the East Asian industrialized countries', *Asia-Pacific Economic Review*, **1** (3), 3–22.

Klein, Michael and Giovanni Olivei (1999), 'Capital Account Liberalization, Financial Depth and Economic Growth', Boston, Federal Reserve Bank of Boston Working Paper No. 99-6.

Kohl, Richard and Kevin O'Rourke (December 2000), 'What's New About Globalization: Implications for Income Inequality in Developing Countries'. Paper presented at the Organization for Economic Co-operation and Development conference 'Globalization and Income Inequality in Developing Countries, Paris, 30 November–1 December 2000.

Krugman, Paul (1994), 'The myth of Asia's miracle', *Foreign Affairs*, **73** (6), 62–78.

Marshall, Katherine and Oliver Butzbach (eds) (2003), *New Social Policy Agendas for Europe and Asia: Challenges, Experience, and Lessons*, Washington, DC: World Bank.

Oxfam (June 2000), 'Growth with equity is good for the poor', www.oxfam.org.uk/what_we_do/issues/debt_aid/growth_equity.htm, June.

Pangestu, Mari (2001) 'The Social Impact of Globalization in Southeast Asia', Paris, OECD Development Centre Technical Paper No.187.

Ravallion, Martin (2000), 'Growth, Inequality and Poverty: Looking Beyond Averages', Washington, DC, World Bank Policy Research Working Paper No. 2527.

Ravallion, Martin and Gaurav Datt (1996), 'India's checkered history in the fight against poverty: are there lessons for Europe?' *Economic and Political Weekly*, **31** (35–37), 2479–86.

Rodrik, Dani (1997), *Has Globalization Gone too Far?* Washington, DC: Institute for International Economics.

Sen, Amartya (1999), *Beyond the Crisis: Development Strategies in Asia*, Singapore: Institute of Southeast Asian Studies.

Stiglitz, Joseph E. (2002), *Globalization and its Discontents*, New York: W.W. Norton.

Warr, Peter (2002), 'Poverty Incidence and Sectoral Growth: Evidence from Southeast Asia', Helsinki, United Nations University, World Institute for Development Economics Research (WIDER) Discussion Paper No. 2002/20.

Warr Peter and Wen-Thuen Wang (1999), 'Poverty, Inequality and Domestic Responses', in Gustav Ranis and Hu Sheng-cheng (eds), *The Political Economic of Development in Taiwan: Essays in Honour of John C.H. Fei*, London: Edward Elgar, pp. 133–65.

Woo Wing Thye (1999), 'Understanding the Asian Financial Crisis'. Paper presented at the ASEAN Roundtable organized by the Institute of Southeast Asian Studies, Singapore, November 1999.

World Bank (2000), 'Poverty in an Age of Globalization', World Bank Globalization Briefing Paper, October.

World Bank (2002), *Globalization, Growth and Poverty: Building an Inclusive World Economy*, New York: Oxford University Press.

Young, Alwyn (1992), 'A Tale of Two Cities: Factor Accumulation and Technical Change in Hong Kong and Singapore', *National Bureau of Economic Research Macroeconomic Annual 1992*, pp. 13–54.

Zhang Yunling, Shao Zhiqing and Su Zuegong (2002), *Impact of Globalization on Economic Disparity: Comparing Southeast Asia and China*, Beijing: Institute of Asia Pacific Studies, Chinese Academy of Social Sciences.

5. Globalization, Equity and Poverty: The South Asian Experience

Sisira Jayasuriya

In South Asia today official development strategies stress the need for opening domestic economies to the global economy through liberalization of trade and investment regimes, deregulation of domestic markets and privatization of state enterprises. They accept the pivotal role of the private sector in the growth process.[1] In this sense 'globalization' is seen as the path to economic development. This is an almost complete reversal of the policy stance of the 1970s, when import-substitution industrialization (ISI), incorporating protectionism in foreign trade and pervasive state intervention in the domestic economy, dominated the theory and practice of development. The economic, political and social implications of this shift in development strategy will have profound implications both regionally and globally. After all, South Asia, united by shared culture and history and divided by contested state boundaries, religion, language, ethnicity, caste, class and a myriad of other divisions, is home to more than one-fifth of the world's population and one-third of the world's poor (see Table 5.1).[2]

South Asian countries have followed broadly similar trajectories in their post-independence economic policies. They inherited relatively open 'liberal' economic regimes from British colonial rule, moved to progressively more stringent *dirigiste* policies and then shifted to the current strategy of 'opening up' and 'liberalization'. This policy shift was prompted by the ISI strategy's clear failure to deliver fast economic growth and development. Now, a decade or more since the change in development strategy, the question often asked is: Has globalization accelerated economic growth, reduced poverty and produced equitable development? This chapter assesses the empirical evidence and draws some preliminary conclusions, though the many differences among this group of countries necessarily precludes any simple generalizations.

137

Table 5.1 South Asia: Selected Socio-economic Indicators, 2000

	Bangla-desh	India	Nepal	Pakistan	Sri Lanka	World
Population (millions)	130	1,016	24	138	19	6,054
Per capita income ($)	380	460	220	470	870	5,150
Per capita income (PPP$)	1,650	2,390	1,360	1,960	3,470	7,350
Average GDP growth rate 1990–2000	4.8	6.0	4.8	4.1	5.3	2.6
Average per capita growth rate 1990–2000	3.2	4.2	2.4	1.6	4.0	1.2
% share of industry in GDP	25	27	20	23	27	31
Life expectancy						
1970	44	49	42	49	64	–
2000	61	63	58	63	73	66
Adult illiteracy	59	44	60	55	9	–
Gini coefficient	0.336	0.378	0.367	0.485	0.344	–
Population (%) below $1 day	29.1	44.2	37.7	31.0	6.6	–

Source: World Bank (2002b).

The chapter is organized as follows. First, a brief historical background traces how the first phase of globalization, from the late nineteenth century through World War I, and the economic and political changes leading to World War II and independence affected South Asia. This is followed by an analysis of the behavior of key economic variables during the post-independence period with particular emphasis on the liberalization period. The chapter concludes with a summary of the main lessons.

HISTORICAL BACKGROUND

Historically South Asia has been a major participant in international trade. Trade attracted the interest of the first 'modern' Western powers, starting with the Portuguese in the late fifteenth century. But until drawn into the global capitalist system as part of the British Empire, South Asia experienced only a marginal impact on its basic patterns of production and consumption. In the region's historical memory, the exposure of South Asia to nineteenth-century globalization is associated with painful experiences. Opening the national economies to the world economy was accompanied by the subjugation and exploitation of the native population. Nationalist interpretations of this experience view the impact of British rule as primarily destructive, replacing a prosperous pre-exiting social order, immiserating the country and benefiting only a privileged local elite. [3] These memories color South Asian attitudes to this day, even as the region grapples with the challenges of the new wave of globalization.

In reality the experience was more complex. Certainly British rule, particularly in the early years, was characterized by violent repression of challenges to colonial rule, taxes on an already impoverished peasantry, neglect of agricultural infrastructure (such as irrigation facilities) and the decline of traditional industries unable to compete with cheap imports from Britain. Most peasants, particularly those cultivating food grains, remained mired in chronic poverty and vulnerable to famines and near-famine conditions throughout British colonial rule. [4] However, once British rule had been consolidated and a centralized administrative system set in place, the British began to build physical infrastructure, including ports, road and rail networks and postal and telegraphic communications systems. Local economies were further helped by significant inflows of capital and skills and experienced economic growth and population increases.

From the second quarter of the nineteenth century to the start of World War I, growth rates in India and Sri Lanka matched that in Britain and raised average per capita income, despite significant population growth (Roy 2002;

de Silva 1981). Benefits from growth were certainly not uniformly distributed. Regions and groups that possessed the right kind of skills and resources to exploit the new commercial opportunities did better, while most peasants remained impoverished. Greater market integration led to a more productive allocation of resources. Further, by challenging (if not overthrowing) long-established caste and gender relations, capitalist penetration opened new horizons to millions who had for millennia lived at the bottom of the social and economic ladder. But war interrupted this process. No longer insulated from the world economy, South Asia experienced much economic distress during the interwar years and World War II. In India, the difficult struggle for independence, the catastrophic famine of 1943, partition and its bloody aftermath left bitter memories of the last years of British rule.

Nevertheless, at independence South Asia was far from an economic basket case. The region was well integrated into the global trading system, and per capita incomes were not far behind those in most Southeast and East Asian economies. But over the next two decades, a period of rapid and sustained growth of the global economy associated with even faster growth in international trade, South Asia turned its back on the world trading system, erecting barriers to international trade and investment. It increasingly turned to state controls and centralized planning, fueled by an ideological commitment to an import-substitution industrialization strategy. Despite some partial, half-hearted and short-lived attempts at liberalization, by the mid-1970s South Asia had some of the most inward-oriented economies in the world, outside the centrally planned economies, and had been reduced to a bit-player in the global trading system. Plagued by persistent external-sector imbalances and slow growth, the region slipped well behind the high-performing East Asian economies. These trends contributed to an attitudinal shift among the political elite that built up a powerful constituency for reforms.

Change began in the late 1970s with Sri Lanka embracing liberalization in 1977–78. The 1980s saw Bangladesh, Nepal and Pakistan all move towards more liberal policies. India, confronted with a major balance-of-payments crisis in 1991, finally joined the reform process in the early 1990s.[5] The desirability of this shift in policy was widely questioned at first, but the policy dialogue now tends to focus more on the pace and scope of reforms. The liberalization process in South Asia now appears irreversible.

LIBERALIZATION AND GROWTH

However, the liberalization process in South Asia remains limited and partial – though extensive and radical in comparison with the previous policy

Table 5.2 Status and Indicators of Liberalization in South Asia (mid–late 1990s)

	Bangladesh	India	Nepal	Pakistan	Sri Lanka
Exchange rate	Unitary	Unitary	Unitary	Unitary	Unitary
Exchange rate determination	Managed Float	Managed Float	Pegged	Managed Float	Managed Float
Payment restrictions Current					
Capital	No	No	No	No	No
	Yes	Yes	Yes	Yes	Yes
State monopolies in external trade	Yes	Yes	Yes	Yes	Yes
Import licenses	Yes	Yes	Yes	Yes	Yes
Simplification of tariffs	Yes	Yes	Yes	Yes	Yes
Average tariff – 1995 (unweighted) %	42	48	17	51	24
Maximum tariff rate – 1997	45	40	110^3	45	35
Extensive non-tariff barriers	No	Yes	No	No	No
Trade as % of GDP 1990 and 2000	20–33	17–31	33–54	39–35	67–91

Source: Samaratunga (1999); Weerakoon (1998); UNCTAD (2002); UNDP (2002).

Table 5.3 Significance of FDI in Domestic Economy

Country	FDI inflows as % of gross fixed capital formation		FDI stock as % of GDP	
	1990–95	2000	1990	2000
Bangladesh	0.1	2.7	0.5	2.1
India	0.9	2.3	0.5	4.1
Nepal	0.7	–	0.3	1.8
Pakistan	4.4	3.9	4.8	11.2
Sri Lanka	4.3	3.9	8.5	15.0
China	9.8	10.5	7.0	32.3
Malaysia	19.4	16.5	23.4	58.8
Thailand	4.4	10.4	9.6	20.0

Source: UNDP (2002b).

regimes. Generally it has been a rather protracted process, with episodes of radical reforms, though late starters (like India) have tended to move faster. By the mid-to-late 1990s, these countries still had a considerable distance to go to become fully open economies (Table 5.2). When economies have been insulated for long periods of time, domestic and international markets do not become integrated overnight even if all policy barriers are removed, and certainly not when liberalization is limited and partial. This is the case with both goods and factor markets. Despite significant progress with trade liberalization, the region still has many trade restrictions and controls on capital markets. Continuing restrictions on capital movements, perceived high risk and underdeveloped financial institutions have restricted portfolio capital flows.

There has been greater progress with foreign direct investment (FDI). With fewer restrictions and stimulated by the privatization of utilities and other state economic enterprises, FDI flows have grown in recent years. Bangladesh received almost no FDI during 1980–85 but received $280 million in 2000. During this period, Pakistan's FDI inflows grew from $75 million to $305 million, Sri Lanka's from $42 million to $178 million, while India's FDI surged from $62 million to $2.3 billion (UNCTAD, *World Investment Report*, various issues). But FDI flows are still rather small in terms of their significance relative to the size of the domestic economy and as a proportion of total investment (Table 5.3). They are also well below those in East and Southeast Asia. For example, even India's FDI flows, which increased to $3.4

billion in 2001, pale in comparison with China's at $47 billion for the same year. Thus while policy liberalization has reduced some of the barriers to globalization, South Asian economies have yet to be exposed to the broader currents of globalization like the East and Southeast Asian countries.

The debate about the link between growth and openness – with openness linked to exposure to globalization – has generated an immense literature and continues to attract scholarly and public interest. Given the many factors that can affect growth performance, this is not an issue that can be settled by looking at relatively short-term growth outcomes, though such comparisons may still be useful as suggestive indicators of longer-term trends. Because this region's experience with globalization is rather brief and limited in scope, conclusions based on its empirical experience about the links between globalization and equity/poverty outcomes (or any other causality) must be drawn with much caution and care. Further, the liberalization measures themselves have been part of broader economic policy packages implemented by governments responding to a variety of political pressures and driven by a range of motives. Some of the observed developments may be due to policies that have nothing to do with globalization.[6] All this means is that observed outcomes should not be directly or fully attributed to the liberalization measures or to the globalization process. Simple pre- and post-liberalization comparisons, in particular, may be quite misleading in identifying cause and effect or the likely impact of more extensive globalization. In this situation, predictions about the likely impact of globalization on South Asia must draw on theoretical analyses, empirical models (such as applied general equilibrium models) and the experience of other countries that have had greater exposure to globalization, particularly the East Asian countries.

Looking at both growth rates for incomes and broader measures of wellbeing, it is clear that there have been significant improvements in South Asia in recent decades. Real per capita incomes in the region have grown substantially since the late 1970s, though at different rates (Figure 5.1). Consequently inter-country income disparities have widened over time. Improvements have not been confined to incomes alone; as shown in Table 5.4, the Human Development Index (which incorporates health and education indicators as well as income) has recorded significant positive changes. But care must be exercised in attributing these improvements to globalization or even to policy liberalization as some analysts have done. Bhalla (2002), for example, has claimed that South Asia has grown faster due to globalization because per capita incomes increased at 3 per cent per year on average during 1980–2000. He labels the 1980–2000 period as the 'globalization' period, contrasting it with 0.55 per cent annual growth from 1960 to 1980 (Table 5.5).

Figure 5.1 South Asia: Real Per Capital Income (PPP basis)

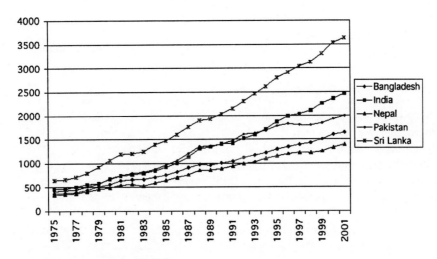

Source: World Development Indicators.

This is a misleading comparison. South Asia's average per capita growth rate, indeed any statistic for South Asia as a whole, is skewed by India, the dominant economy of the region. Some South Asian countries experienced policy liberalization during the 1980s, and the picture of generally superior post-1980 growth performance is largely true for most South Asian countries (see Figure 5.2).[7] But serious liberalization in India – the country that really matters for region-wide averages – started only after 1991.[8] As Srinivasan and Tendulkar (2003, 29–30) put it, 'The hallmark of the pre-1991 policy regime was that there were few economic activities except for those in agriculture and the unorganized sector that could be undertaken without government permission. The Indian economy was correctly regarded as one of the most regulated economies of the world'. Most analysts would concur that India's post-liberalization growth performance – now over a decade old – has been quite outstanding, placing it among the ten fastest growing economies in the world. But the average growth rate for the 1980–2000 period mixes the essentially pre-liberalization 1980s and the post-liberalization 1990s. The high average for these years reflects the fact India experienced a period of high growth prior to liberalization. In fact a simple comparison of growth rates between the 1980s and the 1990s shows only a marginal difference in performance. But the key point, as Ahluwalia (2002) notes, is that the 1980s

Figure 5.2 Real Per Capita GDP Growth Rates in South Asia (%)

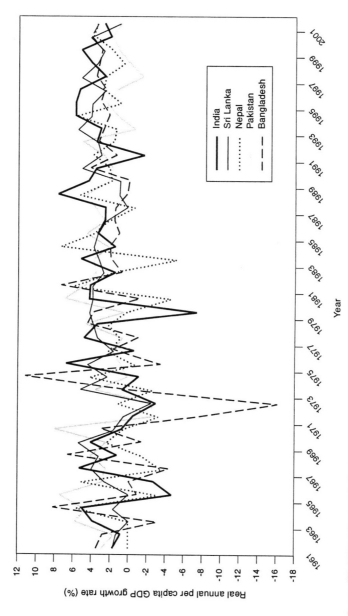

Source: World Development Indicators.

145

Table 5.4 Human Development Index in South Asia: 1975–2000

Country	1975	1980	1985	1990	1995	2000
Bangladesh	0.335	0.353	0.386	0.416	0.445	0.478
India	0.407	0.434	0.473	0.511	0.545	0.577
Nepal	0.289	0.328	0.370	0.416	0.453	0.490
Pakistan	0.345	0.372	0.404	0.442	0.473	0.499
Sri Lanka	0.616	0.650	0.676	0.697	0.719	0.741

Source: UNDP (2002).

Table 5.5 Growth Rates of Per Capita Income (PPP $1993) (annual averages): 1960–2000

Region	1960–1980	1980–2000
South Asia	0.55	3.00
East Asia	2.85	6.12
Latin America	3.13	0.08
World	2.50	2.65

Note: Figures for real per capita income based on national accounts match these closely.

Source: Bhalla (2002).

growth performance, fueled by a buildup of external debt that culminated in the 1991 balance-of-payments crisis, was simply unsustainable. Though the analytical problems of isolating the role of particular variables to go beyond mere growth-liberalization correlations are formidable, as the huge literature on this topic attests, liberalization must be judged on the extent to which it raises the sustainable level of longer-term growth. [9]

Most economies, despite some limited liberalization during the 1970s or 1980s, really were still 'more closed than open'; even when policy liberalization had progressed, actual globalization in terms of domestic and international market integration remained low. For example, Sri Lanka did implement major liberalization in 1977–78, but it was in the 1990s, following the so-called 'second wave' of reforms, that it even approached (but did not equal) the openness of Southeast Asian economies. Even at the end of the 1990s, India's import-weighted tariffs were still above 30 per cent – among the highest in the developing world (Ahluwalia 2002; Srinivasan and Tendulkar

2003). In any case, as shown by the experience of Pakistan in the late 1990s (which had also implemented significant though partial liberalization) and that of many other countries both in South Asia and elsewhere, liberalization by itself does not guarantee either continuing high growth or stability.

So what, if anything, can we conclude? The South Asian experience is still too short and too mixed to assert that globalization definitively accelerates growth. But, fortunately, the world is larger than South Asia, and there is a wider body of theory and experience to draw on that has applicability for countries of this region. In the past most analysts and policymakers blithely dismissed the experience of other countries as irrelevant to the 'special circumstances' of South Asia. This is no longer the case. Nowadays, most South Asian analysts familiar with the complex economic and political history of the region will not accept that the region would have performed better in the 1990s (or will do better in the future) with less openness to the world. When the South Asian liberalization experience is considered in conjunction with the longer record of China and East Asia (notwithstanding the 1997 Asian economic crisis and aftermath), it is difficult to argue convincingly that rapid, sustainable growth can be achieved by insulating a national economy from the contemporary global economy. As Bhagwati and Srinivasan (2002, 182) point out, 'No country that has been close to autarkic has managed to sustain a high growth performance over a sustained period'. Furthermore, China and India, the two largest developing countries that have opened their economies to the world (albeit gradually and partially) have achieved unprecedented rates of growth over more than twenty years and ten years, respectively. The issue that really confronts the region is how to open and exploit the growth opportunities while ensuring that other social objectives – in particular poverty alleviation, equity and maintaining national cohesion and stability – are not undermined. Understandably, reports about China's alarmingly rapid increase in post-liberalization inequality and rising social tensions ring alarm bells in the politically volatile South Asia, which contains the world's largest concentration of poor people.

GROWTH AND POVERTY

How successful has post-liberalization growth been in reducing poverty in South Asia? It is difficult to identify trends in poverty and equity and establish causal links between them and policy changes when many aspects of the broader environment are changing. As is well known, poverty measurements raise complex conceptual and methodological problems. The simplest measures of poverty are based on incomes. But even if poverty is defined narrowly as a person's inability to obtain certain minimum levels of consumption of goods and services, often income is not a reliable predictor of a person's true capacity to obtain a specific bundle of goods and services. Economists usually prefer consumption (expenditure) to income as a more reliable indicator of poverty, because economic agents tend to smooth consumption over time in line with their overall net wealth position. Therefore consumption tends to be more stable than income and a better indicator of household wealth. But few South Asian countries have data sets that go sufficiently far back in time for meaningful comparisons.[10] More generally, inter-temporal comparisons are often difficult because of changes in survey design, implementation and data collection methods. This is a major problem in every South Asian country, including India, which has the best data series in the region.

But even when the required income or consumption data are there, they provide at best only a partial picture of poverty and equity. An understanding of poverty – following Sen (1983, 2000) – as deprivation of a person's basic capabilities, implies that low income, while clearly a major cause of poverty, is not its only important determinant. Because low incomes are often correlated (though imperfectly) with poverty, income or consumption is often taken as a reasonable indicator of poverty, though it is recognized that other factors associated with poverty (i.e. access to literacy and education, health services, absence of various forms of discrimination, even political freedoms) must also be taken into account when assessing the level or intensity of poverty and its changes over time. Unfortunately, the many attributes of poverty or welfare cannot be satisfactorily aggregated into a single quantifiable indicator. Hence attempts to look at poverty trends over time with a broader definition of poverty confront even greater data and measurement problems.

Table 5.6 summarizes some of the key measures relating to income or consumption poverty for the post-reform periods in South Asia. It cannot be too strongly emphasized that data presented in this table suffer from major issues of comparability and reliability. They should be treated as suggestive of trends only. Nevertheless, though individual country experiences have been diverse, the data do point to some important common trends during the 1980s and 1990s.

Headcount poverty, typically considerably higher in rural areas compared to urban areas, fell significantly during the 1990s in India. However, the picture is mixed for the rest of South Asia.[11] There has been considerable concern that poverty was not falling in India after liberalization despite growth: the 1993–94 estimates of poverty (35 per cent) were not much different from those of the mid-1980s. But official estimates based on 1999–2000 data suggested a steep drop in poverty – even a halving – which gave rise to an intense debate as data from the most recent survey were not strictly comparable with the

Table 5.6 Poverty and Inequality Indicators: South Asia

Country	Poverty (headcount)			Gini (consumption)		
	Rural	Urban	National	Rural	Urban	National
Bangladesh[a]						
1983–84	53.8	40.9	52.3	0.246	0.298	–
1991–92	52.9	44.9	58.8	0.243	0.307	0.259
2000	43.6	26.4	39.8	0.271	0.368	0.306
India[b]						
1983	61.1	35.7	43.0	0.301	0.334	0.320
1993–94	36.7	30.5	35.0	0.277	0.339	0.315
1999–00	26.8	24.1	21.4			(0.378)
Nepal[c]						
1984–85	43.1	19.2	41.4	0.29	0.32	0.302
1995–96	46.6	17.8	44.6	0.31	0.43	0.347
Pakistan						
1984–85	49.3	38.2	49.3	0.263	0.314	0.284
1990–91	36.9	28.0	34.0	0.267	0.316	0.287
1998–99	35.9	24.2	32.6	0.251	0.353	0.296

Sri Lanka[d]	Rural	Estates	Urban	National	Rural	Estates	Urban	National
1980–81	25.9	25.0	16.9		0.38	0.27	0.44	0.43
1985–86	35.6	20.5	18.4	30.9	0.43	0.31	0.48	0.46
1990–91	22.0	12.4	15.0	19.9	0.42	0.25	0.62	0.47
1995–96	27.0	24.9	14.7	25.2	0.48	0.44	0.46	0.43

Notes:

a. Bangladesh figures based on Annex Tables 3 and 4 in Bangladesh Ministry of Finance (2002), except for the Gini figures for 1991–92 and 2000, which are from Table 2.

b. Poverty data for 1983 and 1990–91 and the National Gini coefficients are from the World Bank (http://www.worldban.org/research/povmonitor/countrydetails/India.htm), poverty figures for 1999–00 (official) from Deaton and Dreze (2002) and rural and urban Gini coefficients are from Jha (2000). The Gini given for 2000 is the figure for 1997.

c. Rural and urban Gini coefficients for Nepal in 1984–85 are those for Rural East Terai and Urban Kathmandu, respectively; both Gini coefficients and poverty incidence figures draw on Tables 2 and 3 in the background paper on 'Poverty Over Time' in Prennushi (1999).

Table 5.6 (continued)

d. In Sri Lanka, the Ginis are for income; consumption Gini for 1995–96 was 0.33. 1995–96 was affected by drought that probably resulted in a higher than normal level of 'current year income' poverty; data from a survey that was conducted by the Central Bank in the following year estimated national poverty to be almost the same as that in 1990–91, though the surveys are not strictly comparable.

Source: Deaton and Dreze (2002); Bangladesh Ministry of Finance (2002); Sri Lanka Ministry of Policy Development and Implementation (2000); Jha (2000); Prennushi (1999); World Bank (2002a).

earlier surveys due to changes in survey design. Datt and Ravallion (2002) and particularly Deaton and Dreze (2002) have examined the potential biases involved. Estimates adjusted to overcome some of the data problems support the view that income poverty fell significantly in the 1990s, though not as much as official estimates indicated.

Other countries show mixed results. Bangladesh follows a rather similar pattern to India, with income poverty falling from 58.8 per cent in 1990–91 to 39.8 per cent in 2000. It has also been quite successful in terms of improving broader human development indicators. Significant declines in fertility, infant and child mortality and child malnutrition, as well as improved literacy and primary education, have been major achievements. In Sri Lanka, reliable poverty estimates are not available prior to the 1980s, but poverty seems to have fallen from the mid-1980s to 1990–91 and then increased in the mid-1990s (from 19.9 per cent in 1990–91 to 25.4 per cent in 1995–96). This finding is contentious: other data suggest that poverty may not have changed much during the 1990s.[12] In any case, no significant fall in poverty can be observed during the 1990s. In Pakistan, there was at best only a minor decline in poverty rates during the 1990s, with headcount ratios almost unchanged around the 32–34 per cent range; indeed, poverty may have actually increased in the latter half of the 1990s when the economy slowed down sharply. In Nepal, too, poverty appears to have worsened in the early 1990s (from 41.4 per cent in 1984–85 to 44.6 per cent in 1995–96), and may well have increased further in the latter half of the decade.

There are two issues of importance when looking at the poverty–growth link. One is whether growth reduces poverty, and the other is the extent to which it does so. When the trends in poverty reduction are linked to per capita growth rates, there is evidence of a negative growth–poverty link, though of course the growth rate is not the only determinant of poverty reduction. The rigorous analysis of the link between growth and poverty reduction for India reported by Datt and Ravallion (2002) is particularly revealing. Pre-1990s' growth was poverty-reducing in India (Ravallion and Datt 1996) with no evidence that it tended to increase income inequality (Bruno, Ravallion and Squire 1998). Similarly, growth continued to have a poverty-reducing impact in the 1990s, suggesting that liberalization has certainly not reversed the nature of the growth–poverty link.

But on the second issue, there are serious grounds for concern about the pace of poverty reduction. India's growth in particular seems to be relatively less effective in reducing poverty than has been the case in other parts of Asia (but states which invested in improving literacy and agricultural growth, such as Kerala and West Bengal, performed quite well). Warr (2000) has examined the degree to which overall growth in India (prior to the early 1990s) was poverty-reducing, compared with growth in a group of East and Southeast Asian economies. The estimated growth elasticities of aggregate poverty (which measure the proportional change in absolute poverty incidence in response to GDP growth) suggest that though growth does reduce poverty in India, its impact is much weaker than in the more open economies of Indonesia, Malaysia, Thailand and Taiwan; only the Philippines had a comparable (low) elasticity.[13] While the results are subject to several qualifications, it is difficult to avoid being struck by the remarkably close association between the degree of openness of the country and the growth elasticity of poverty: the poor benefit more from growth generated by open economies. Warr links this association to the fact that the more open economies implemented development strategies that emphasized labor-intensive patterns of industrialization, whereas India (as well as the Philippines) followed industrial strategies that protected capital-intensive manufacturing industries, thereby effectively discriminating against labor-intensive industries as well as agriculture. The resulting impact was anti-labor – the single most important resource owned by the poor.

Evidence at a sectoral level supports this view. More open trade regimes, in combination with more pro-FDI policies, attracted foreign investors and fueled rapid growth in the export-oriented, labor-intensive garment manufacturing sector in both Bangladesh and Sri Lanka. As a result of the large expansion of these industries, manufacturing exports and rural female employment grew rapidly and helped maintain employment and wage levels at a time of considerable economic difficulties. This experience highlights the complementary role of investment liberalization for exploiting the potential gains from trade liberalization: it was the combination of trade and investment liberalization that proved critical, as either of these alone would not have produced a similar outcome.[14] Taking into account the Chinese experience, it may be argued that a slower pace of trade liberalization and more restrictive policies towards FDI may have prevented India from achieving a faster rate of unskilled employment increasing in manufacturing industries, thereby slowing down poverty reduction.

Another aspect of globalization that likely has had a large impact on employment, and thereby on poverty, is the emergence of an international market for relatively unskilled labor, initially in the Middle East and more recently in East Asia.[15] Policy liberalization in the source countries eased the barriers on international travel and payments. Of course, the push for overseas employment might have been weaker if South Asian countries had achieved faster growth in labor-intensive industries. The extensive participation of females in the migrant labor market, from societies with gender-related discrimination, has also had a large pro-equity social impact.

In summary, the evidence from South Asia favors the view that growth associated with liberalization has been poverty-reducing. But its effectiveness seems to be considerably weaker in countries whose policies do not favor growth in labor-intensive industries. Deeper and more extensive reforms – in terms of faster trade liberalization coupled with investment liberalization – may produce growth with a greater pro-poor bias. The impact of growth on the poor is at the heart of the debate about the distributional implications of globalization. The overall Asian experience indicates that more, rather than less, openness may be pro-poor. The next section examines the growth–equity links that emerge from the South Asian experience.

GROWTH AND EQUITY

Table 5.6 presents figures for the Gini coefficients of consumption distributions, divided between urban and rural sectors.[16] There is no indication, either from these Ginis or from other sources, that a sharp deterioration in household consumption inequality has occurred anywhere in South Asia after liberalization, but there are indications that inequality is widening at several different levels.

In India, as well as in other parts of South Asia, increasing inequality in urban areas is quite visible. This has moderated the decline in the urban poverty rate in response to growth. Deaton and Dreze (2002) point out that this effect is particularly pronounced in some Indian states, such as Kerala and Madhya Pradesh. Overall in India, if there had been no change in inequality, the headcount ratio in 1999–2000 would have been 1.3 per cent lower. In Bangladesh, if inequality had not worsened, poverty would have fallen 17 per cent, nearly twice the rate it actually did.[17] The combination of rising inequality in urban areas and faster growth in incomes – a common phenomenon throughout the region – is widening both the urban–rural income gap and overall inequality.

Regional (inter-provincial and inter-state) or spatial inequality is also widening throughout South Asia. This trend often aggravates pre-existing differences, paralleling trends seen in China (see, for example, Hu and Fujita 2001) that are causing much concern.[18] The importance of ethnic, religious, caste and other divisions in South Asia implies that trends in inequality across these dimensions are also of concern. Though the evidence is not conclusive that increased inequality is a direct and immediate cause precipitating conflict, poverty-related factors are often an underlying determinant (Peiris 2000). Sometimes these divisions have a distinctly spatial dimension. Thus widening regional disparities are cause for concern. Such disparities are linked to differences in human skill attainments and endowments; education in particular is a major determinant of who benefits from post-liberalization growth. With respect to caste, there can be little doubt that economic changes that have undermined traditional society in India have increased the political power of traditionally depressed castes. But the immediate impact of liberalization on caste-related inequality also depends on access to human capital and marketable skills.

Deaton and Dreze's broad conclusion on the basis of state-wide data from India is more generally applicable to other parts of South Asia. 'Except for the absence of rising intra-rural inequality within states,' they write, 'we find strong indications of a pervasive increase in economic inequality in the 1990s. This is a new development in the Indian economy: until 1993–94, the all-India Gini coefficients of per capita consumer consumption expenditure inequality in rural and urban areas were fairly stable. Further, it is worth noting that the rate of increase in economic inequality is far from negligible' (2002, 3740). The fact that the benefits of growth appear to accrue mostly to those states with low poverty incidence again mirrors broader trends. Datt and Ravallion (2002) attribute the lower rate of overall reduction in poverty that is observed in the 1990s to the sectoral and geographical pattern of growth favoring states with better initial conditions; states with low levels of initial rural development and human capital development were not well suited to reduce poverty in response to economic growth. The importance of human capital as a factor in widening inequality in the post-liberalization conditions is seen in other parts of South Asia as well. For example the 'estates' sector in Sri Lanka, which has poor human capital, appears to have experienced both widening inequality and rising poverty in the 1990s.[19]

An important aspect of equity, particularly relevant to South Asia, is the impact of liberalization on gender equity. The evidence on this issue is sketchy, but improvements in literacy, life expectancy and overall mobility observed through most parts of South Asia suggest improvement, at least across some dimensions. Where demand for female labor has increased substantially (as in Bangladesh and Sri Lanka, with the expansion of the garments industry and access to overseas employment), gender equality tends to improve across many dimensions. However, women may now have to carry a double burden; that is, be a breadwinner at the same time as they also do the bulk of household work and caregiving. Deaton and Dreze (2002) point to another issue of concern in India: with access to prenatal sex-determination technology and sex-selective abortions, female–male ratios among children appear to have declined. They argue that this is not merely a technological phenomenon: the impact of liberalization and globalization on social inequalities depend on access to human capital and market opportunities and are mediated through prevailing attitudes and preferences. Though the latter can change through exposure to global currents of thought and value systems, some entrenched attitudes such as male preference in children is unlikely to change very quickly.

LIBERALIZATION AND DISTRIBUTIONAL OUTCOMES

Recent changes in poverty and inequality in south Asia have several common features. Growth associated with liberalization has tended to reduce consumption poverty and improve broader dimensions of human development. However, though income inequality has not yet increased in any dramatic way, there are signs that inequality is increasing across several other dimensions (spatial, urban–rural etc.). But it is not always clear how much these increases in inequality should be attributed to liberalization, how the long-term effects of growth may differ from the more immediate consequences of stabilization and adjustment policies and what would be the relevant counterfactual scenario.

Despite the large and growing literature on the distributional outcomes of liberalization, there are both theoretical and empirical problems in ascertaining the relative contributions of various exogenous factors.[20] At the simplest level, drawing upon the Stolper–Samuelson theorem, a shift to patterns of economic growth based on comparative advantage, which in the case of South Asia lies in low-skilled, labor-intensive activities, is likely to improve distributional outcomes by increasing relative labor demand. But this is only one aspect of a complex reality. Both present and past policies also matter. It is undeniable that India's dramatic successes in the software and information technology sectors, which produces a very skewed distributional impact, is related to its education policies that created a large pool of highly skilled labor while also allowing huge numbers of poor to remain completely illiterate. Other outcomes, such as regional and spatial disparities in growth, may not only reflect past urban bias in government policies but also, and perhaps even more so, the dynamics of agglomeration forces that are given a freer rein in more liberalized economies. But there is no persuasive evidence from South Asia that globalization has been bad for the poor in general. Indeed, more extensive globalization may have had an overall positive effect on labor employment and incomes and thereby on the poor.

But the evidence of increasing inequality is definitely a cause for concern. Can South Asia manage the opportunities and risks of globalization without aggravating inequality and jeopardizing social and political stability? Liberalization reforms are unavoidably accompanied by profound distributional changes. Even when reforms led to faster growth and higher average incomes, these gains from reforms are not distributed equally. At least in the short term, there are likely to be significant losers. In addition, the policy and institutional changes associated with liberalization can increase not only actual inequality but also perceived inequality, with perceptions magnifying changes in expected gains and losses.[21]

Such reforms have profound effects on the underlying determinants of asset returns (through the revaluation of skills and other human capital, social capital embodied in ethnic and religious networks, as well as physical capital) so the net wealth positions of households and individuals are redefined. These actual or potential distributional changes – even if they are of relatively short duration – can be a potent source of social and political conflict. Such conflicts often develop along existing social fault lines – class, ethnic, religious and regional – particularly if liberalization does not quickly expand the total economic pie. However, the social impact of policy reforms is not confined to the effects on wealth and on inequalities. Liberalization does not abolish rent seeking; the very process of liberalization creates new opportunities for rent-extraction through access to political power and regulatory institutions. The scale of potential gains also can expand. The extent to which such rents may be appropriated by groups or individuals depends on the specificities of the political and social environment. Again the experience of South Asia appears to increasingly parallel the developments in the former planned economies, such as China: rampant corruption aggravates social dissatisfaction generated by rising inequality.

These distributional issues cannot be lightly dismissed on the grounds that greater labor mobility and lower absolute poverty will make these changes acceptable.[22] The short- to medium-term distributional considerations do matter for policy: measures that may improve overall growth and thereby reduce poverty in the long run cannot be effectively implemented and sustained unless the accompanying distributional consequences are managed politically. Policies that may be beneficial in the longer term, such as agricultural trade liberalization, may nevertheless generate politically unsustainable impacts in the short run. In many parts of Asia, food trade liberalization may increase poverty among vulnerable segments of the population, unless there are ways to absorb more labor into non-agricultural sectors. This emphasizes the need to link food trade liberalization in net-food importing developing countries to greater market access for labor-intensive products in developed country markets; in other words, globally coordinated action. The observed changes in poverty and distribution in South Asia also highlight the need for, and the beneficial impact of, well-directed public action to improve access to human capital and physical infrastructure. These are the key determinants of post-liberalization success. Here, the region can gain from the experience – both positive and negative – of Sri Lanka.

Sri Lanka is often presented as an exemplar of a failed strategy that placed social welfare expenditures ahead of productive investment. During the 1950s, Sri Lanka channeled funds into social programs to provide primary health care and nutrition, universal access to education and enhanced human development, producing an educated workforce, political stability and human development indictors far above those seen in countries with comparable (or even considerably higher) per capita incomes. The resulting socio-political stability permitted Sri Lanka to spend typically less than 0.5 per cent of GDP on defense, a level among the lowest in the world. Social expenditures substituted for defense expenditures.

Slow growth eventually made the burden of social expenditures unbearable and finally led to their demise. It is commonly asserted that slow growth occurred because potential investment funds were diverted to 'welfare' expenditures. In Joan Robinson's (1958) widely cited words, Sri Lanka 'tasted the fruit before planting the tree' by investing too much on social expenditures. But this is a misinterpretation of the true causes of Sri Lanka's slow growth. Certainly better targeting of expenditures, such as those on staple food subsidies, could have made a slightly larger surplus available for investment. But focusing on this inefficiency masks the main reason for Sri Lanka's poor growth. The primary culprit for sluggish growth was not social expenditures but the shift towards an inward-oriented development strategy in the late 1950s which held back growth by turning the country away from the dynamism and opportunities of world markets and discouraged both domestic and foreign investment. The well-educated and healthy workforce and social and political stability were assets which could have become the basis for exploiting the huge opportunities which arose in the global trading system starting in the 1950s. But instead the country turned inward and closed up, embracing the dead-end strategy of import-substitution industrialization. This turn away from the global economy ultimately led Sri Lanka to being left behind the dynamic

East Asians in both economic growth and human development. With slow growth, it was unable to maintain its investments in human capital and poverty alleviation or to undertake necessary infrastructure investments.

Unfortunately, social expenditures, particularly food subsidies, became the main target of liberalization proponents. [23] From the very beginning liberalization was accompanied by – and identified with – attacks on social expenditures, particularly food subsidies, with equity issues treated disdainfully. The result was predictable: deep-rooted social and political tensions exploded into violent conflict and dragged the country into ethnic and political strife, ending the peace and tranquility that had been the hallmark of Sri Lanka. Military expenditures now replaced social expenditures, increasing from the less than 0.5 per cent of gross domestic product (GDP) figure that prevailed till the early 1970s to more than 6 per cent of GDP by the mid-1990s.

A quarter-century after initiating liberalization, Sri Lanka remains unable to secure the most basic precondition for economic development: an end to political instability and civil conflict.[24] The real lesson of Sri Lanka's experience – both before and after liberalization – is that growth can be maintained only through integration with the world economy, but such growth will be politically unsustainable unless policies are implemented to ensure that the fruits of growth are equitably shared.

CONCLUSION

By the 1990s all the states of South Asia had liberalized economic policies to open their states to globalization. Their experience with globalization, therefore, remains limited both in scope and time. Though much has been achieved, domestic goods and factor markets are still significantly insulated from global markets.

The results of liberalization have been mixed. India, the largest economy of the region, has demonstrated unprecedented growth momentum. Taken in conjunction with the Chinese experience, this suggests strongly that more open policies can produce faster and more sustainable growth. Further, growth under liberalization has led to poverty reduction. Though the precise extent to which poverty has fallen in India during the 1990s remains contentious, there is clear evidence that absolute poverty has fallen significantly. This poverty growth link is reinforced when policies tend to promote labor-intensive industries in which the region in general has a comparative advantage. However, the equity outcomes are a matter for concern. Though overall income inequality across households has not deteriorated significantly, the evidence suggests increasing inequality across other dimensions (i.e. regional, urban–rural etc.).

The benefits of growth under more liberal policies accrue largely to those who have the human and physical assets that enable them to exploit more efficiently the new expanded opportunities.

As South Asia embraces globalization, at a time when the global economy itself faces challenges to its stability and continuing growth, it must address the underlying causes of rising inequality that are amenable to state intervention. Public action to provide less privileged households, communities and regions with broader access to resources such as education, transport and telecommunications will determine whether gains from liberalization will be distributed equitably. Otherwise, given the social, ethnic and religious fault lines that run through the region, growth and rising prosperity will not be politically sustainable, the opportunity for growth and prosperity will be in jeopardy and the current embrace of globalization may trigger a rise in populist xenophobia and a new phase of political and social instability.

NOTES

1. In this chapter the term 'South Asia' is used to refer mainly to Bangladesh, India, Nepal, Pakistan and Sri Lanka, though the region also includes Bhutan and Maldives. The term 'globalization' is interpreted here to mean the process of integrating domestic and international markets in goods, services and factors (particularly capital) facilitated by policies that remove barriers to their mobility both within and across national boundaries.

2. Based on an international poverty line of $1 per day (Datt and Ravallion 2002).

3. Some Indians attributed the destruction of that idyllic society to the twin effects of Mogul invasions and British rule.

4. In Sri Lanka, 'After a century of rule, the British colonial administration had not succeeded in improving the living standards of the rural population in most parts of the country. Peace and stability they certainly had brought, but they had alleviated little of the hardships of the Sinhalese peasants' (de Silva 1981, 314) Cases of peasants losing land due to colonialism in India appear to have been highly exaggerated (Roy 2002).

5. For discussions of the policy changes in individual countries, see, for example, Ahluwalia (2002), Joshi and Little (1994), Kreuger (2002) and Srinivasan (2000) for India; Poudyal (1988) and Sharma (1999) for Nepal; Hasan (1998) for Pakistan; Athukorala and Jayasuriya (1994, 2000) and Dunham and Kelegama (1997) for Sri Lanka.

6. In the early 1980s several enthusiastic proponents of liberalization attributed rapid growth in post-1977 Sri Lanka to liberalization when the primary factor causing the surge in growth in the immediate post-liberalization period was a huge public sector investment boom that not only proved unsustainable but also undermined the potential longer-term positive impacts of trade liberalization (Dunham and Jayasuriya 2000).

7. Pakistan's performance was quite poor during the late 1990s.

8. There had been some limited deregulation of industry with relaxation of licensing in India.

9. Guha-Khasnobis and Bari (2000) find that total factor productivity growth – an important source of long-term sustainable growth – has increased in South Asia during recent years, which has also experienced liberalization.

10. However, in developing countries, both income and expenditure measures can be subject to considerable margins of error depending on factors such as specific circumstances that influence reporting accuracy, cultural attitudes and so forth. Arguably, expenditure-based measures may be worse than income measures when analyzing distributional changes in countries implementing liberalization programs. Typically they undertake financial reforms as a core component of the reform program. But a better performing financial market provides greater saving opportunities for (richer) net savers and greater borrowing opportunities for (poorer) net borrowers. Hence post-reform expenditure inequality will fall even if there is no change in the wealth distribution, thus biasing the results towards underestimating any post-reform increase in inequality.

11 Note that absolute numbers of poor may continue to increase even when the poverty *rate* is falling.

12. Note that data from the late 1980s is limited in coverage as they effectively exclude the eastern and northern regions of the country, which were the scene of military conflicts and a massive humanitarian disaster. There is also evidence that the increase in poverty in 1995–96 may reflect transient (i.e. severe drought) conditions that may have overestimated the general level of poverty as large numbers of people have incomes just around the poverty line and hence the headcount index is very sensitive to even relatively small changes in incomes; similarly the 1990 figure probably overestimated the fall in poverty in the late 1980s. Data from a survey in 1997 carried out by the Central Bank of Sri Lanka, though not strictly comparable, suggests little change in overall poverty, though urban poverty appears to have declined somewhat.

13. The estimated elasticities are: India: –0.9; Indonesia: –0.1.4; Malaysia: –2.1; Philippines: –0.7; Thailand: –2.0; and Taiwan: –3.8.; Warr's figure for India is broadly comparable with other estimates.

14. Athukorala and Jayasuriya (2000) discuss this link in greater detail.

15. Migrant worker remittances are a major income source of in Bangladesh, Pakistan and Sri Lanka and some states in India,

16. For Sri Lanka, three sectors (rural, urban and estates) are distinguished because the 'estates' (primarily tea and rubber plantations) have a large population of workers of relatively recent (from late nineteenth century) 'Indian' origins who have been restricted in terms of both spatial and sectoral mobility because of problems with the legal status of their citizenship, language barriers and lower human capital due to poor access to education facilities.

17. Temple (2002).

18. See the sources cited in Table 5.6.

19. This needs further confirmation because of data comparability problems between surveys and

differences in poverty lines.

20. No attempt is made here to provide an exhaustive list of relevant references. Vito Tanzi and Ke-young Chu (1998) provides a survey of some of this literature. Bhagwati (1998) is a particularly useful survey of the trade theoretic models that inform the discussion of the distributional outcomes of liberalization.

21. On this see also Bardhan (1997) and Dunham and Jayasuriya (2000).

22. As argued by, for example, Sachs, Rajpai and Ramiah (2001).

23. The endresult of years of slow growth must not be confused with the causes of slow growth. As Bruton (1992, 368) pointed out, 'If Sri Lanka had done nothing different except abolish food subsidies, the consequence would have been that a large share of the population would have been hungry, not that the economy would have grown faster.'

24. The central place given to food subsidies as the prime culprit for Sri Lanka's slow growth itself has a political economy explanation. For a discussion of this issue, see Dunham and Jayasuriya (2000).

REFERENCES

Ahluwalia, Montek S. (2002),'Economic reform in India since 1991: has gradualism worked?', *Journal of Economic Perspectives*, **16** (3), 67–88.

Athukorala, Prema-chandra and Sisira Jayasuriya (1994), *Macroeconomic Policies, Crises and Long-Run Growth: Sri Lanka 1966–86*, Washington, DC: World Bank.

Athukorala, Prema-chandra and Sisira Jayasuriya (2000), 'Trade policy and industrial growth in Sri Lanka', *World Economy*, **23** (3), 387–404.

Bangladesh Ministry of Finance, Division of Economic Relations (2002), *Bangladesh: A National Strategy for Economic Growth and Poverty Reduction*.

Bardhan P. (1997), 'Method in the madness? A political-economy analysis of the ethnic conflicts in less developed countries', *World Development*, **25** (9), 1381–98.

Bhagwati, Jagdish (1998), 'External Sector and Income Distribution', in Vito Tanzi and Ke-young Chu (eds), *Income Distribution and High Quality Growth*, Cambridge, MA: MIT Press, pp. 251–90.

Bardhan P. (1997), 'Method in the madness? A political-economy analysis of the ethnic conflicts in less developed countries', *World Development*, **25** (9), 1381–98.

Bhagwati, Jagdish and T.N. Srinivasan (2002), 'Trade and poverty in the poor countries', *American Economic Review*, **92** (2), 180–83.

Bhalla, Surjit (2002), *Imagine There's No Country: Poverty, Inequality and Growth in the Era of Globalization*, Washington, DC: Institute of International Economics.

Bruno, Michael, Martin Ravallion and Lyn Squire (1998), 'Equity and Growth in Developing Countries: Old and New Perspectives on the Policy Issues', in Vito

Tanzi and Ke–young Chu (eds), *Income Distribution and High Quality Growth*, Cambridge, MA: MIT Press, pp. 117–46.

Bruton, Henry J. (1992), *Sri Lanka and Malaysia: The Political Economy of Poverty, Equity and Growth*, Oxford, UK: Oxford University Press.

Datt, Gaurav and Martin Ravallion (2002), 'Is India's economic growth leaving the poor behind?', *Journal of Economic Perspectives*, **16** (3), 89–108.

De Silva, K.M. (1981), *A History of Sri Lanka*, Berkeley, CA: University of California Press.

Deaton, Angus and Jean Dreze (2002), 'Poverty and inequality in India: a re-examination', *Economic and Political Weekly* (7 September), 3729–48.

Dunham, David and Sisira Jayasuriya (2000), 'Equity, growth and insurrection: liberalization and the welfare debate in contemporary Sri Lanka', Oxford Development Studies, **28** (1), 99–110.

Dunham, David and Saman Kelegama (1997), 'Does leadership matter in the economic reform process? Liberalization and governance in Sri Lanka, 1989–93', World Development, **25** (2), 179–90.

Guha-Khasnobis, Basudeb and Faisal Bari (2000), 'Sources of growth in South Asian countries', www.saneinetwork.org/pdf/grp/Basudeb.pdf, November.

Hasan, Parvez (1998), *Pakistan's Economy at the Crossroads: Past Policies and Present Imperatives*, Karachi: Oxford University Press.

Hu, Dapeng and Masahisa Fujita (2001), 'Regional disparity in China 1965–1994: the effects of globalization and economic liberalization', Annals of Regional Science, **35** (1), 3–37.

Jha, Raghbendra (2000), 'Reducing Poverty and Inequality in India: Has Liberalization Helped?' Helsinki, United Nations University, World Institute for Development Economics Research (WIDER) Working Paper No. 204.

Joshi, Vijay and Ian Little (1994), *India: Macroeconomics and Political Economy 1964–1991*, Washington, DC: World Bank.

Krueger, Anne O. (2002), ‚Supporting Globalization.' Remarks at the 2002 Eisenhower National Security Conference on "National Security for the 21st Century: Anticipating Challenges, Seizing Opportunities, Building Capabilities", Washington, DC, 26 September, www.imf.org/external/np/speeches/2002/092602a.htm.

Peiris, G.H. (2000), 'Poverty, development and inter-group conflict in South Asia: covariances and causal connections', *Ethnic Studies Report*, **18** (1), 1–45.

Poudyal, S.R. (1988), *Foreign Trade, Aid and Development in Nepal*, New Delhi: Commonwealth Publishers.

Prennushi, Giovanna (1999), 'Nepal: Poverty at the Turn of the Twenty First Century: Main Report and Background Studies', Washington, DC, World Bank, South Asia Region Internal Discussion Paper No. IDP 174.

Ravallion, Martin and Gaurav Datt (1996), 'How important to India's poor is the sectoral composition of economic growth?' *World Bank Economic Review*, **8** (1), 1–25.

Robinson, Joan (1958), 'Economic Possibilities of Ceylon', in Prema-chandra Athukorala (ed), *The Economic Development of South Asia,* volume 1, Aldershot, UK and Brooksfields, US: Edward Elgar, pp. 76–82.

Roy, Tirthankar (2002), 'Economic history and modern India: redefining the link?' *Journal of Economic Perspectives*, **16** (3), 109–30.

Sachs, Jeffrey, Nirupam Bajpai and Ananthi Ramiah (2002), ,Understanding Regional Economic Growth in India', Cambridge, MA, Harvard University, Center for International Development, Working Paper No. 88.

Samaratunga, R.H.S. (1999), 'Essays in Trade Policy and Economic Integration with Special Reference to South Asia', Ph.D. dissertation, La Trobe University, Melbourne.

Sen, Amartya (1983),'Poor, relatively speaking', *Oxford Economic Papers*, **35** (2), 153–69.

Sen, Amartya (2000), *Development as Freedom*, New York: Oxford University Press.

Sharma, Kishor (1999), *Trade Liberalization and Manufacturing Performance in Developing Countries: New Evidence from Nepal*, Commack, NY: Nova Science Publishers, Inc.

Sri Lanka, Ministry of Policy Development and Implementation (2000), Department of External Resources (2000), *Sri Lanka: A Framework for Poverty Reduction.*

Srinivasan, T.N and Suresh D. Tendulkar (2003), *Reintegrating India with the World Economy*, Washington, DC, Institute for International Economics.

Tanzi, Vito and Ke-young Chu (eds) (1998), *Income Distribution and High-Quality Growth*, Cambridge, MA: MIT Press.

Temple, Frederic T. (2002), 'Growth and Poverty Reduction in Bangladesh', Lecture delivered at National Defence College, Dhaka, 27 May.

UNCTAD (2002), *World Investment Report 2002*, New York, United Nations Conference on Trade and Development.

UNDP (2002b), *Human Development Report 2002*, New York, United Nations Development Program.

Warr, Peter (2000), 'Poverty reduction and economic growth: the Asian experience', *Asian Development Review*, **18** (2), 131–47.

Weerakoon, Dushni (1998) 'SAPTA/SAFTA: Implications for Sri Lanka', *Upanathi: Journal of the Sri Lanka Association of Economists*, **9** (1–2).

World Bank (2002a), *Pakistan Poverty Assessment – Poverty in Pakistan: Vulnerabilities, Social Gaps, and Rural Dynamics*, World Bank, Washington, DC: World Bank Report No. 24296–PAK.

World Bank (2002b), *World Development Report 2002*, Washington, DC.

6. Institutions and the Commonwealth of Independent States

Ksenia Yudaeva

Disentangling the effect of globalization on the economies of the twelve Commonwealth of the Independent States (CIS) member states is a challenging task. The globalization era in these countries coincided with the process of transition from planned to market economies. Hence, most of the literature about the region concentrates on the process of transition, not globalization. At the same time, opening the economy and deepening integration into the world economy were part of the reform strategy of all transition countries. As a result, the CIS states were not left out of the globalization process.

The Soviet Union was a closed economy with a state monopoly on international trade, a non-convertible currency and state control over foreign direct investment (FDI). The countries which emerged after the USSR disintegrated have much weaker regulations regarding foreign trade, foreign exchange and foreign capital flows. The breakup of the USSR brought about an increase in trade, capital flows and individual travel from CIS to non-CIS countries, although trade among the CIS countries somewhat decreased. This chapter investigates the link between growth, inequality and poverty in the CIS countries and changes in trade policy and globalization. Data from the CIS countries suggests that how globalization affects growth, inequality and poverty depends crucially on the quality of state institutions. Hence, while other studies have tried to show whether globalization or institutions are more important for growth (Dollar and Kraay 2003; Rodrik, Subramanian and Trebbi 2002), this study points to the key interaction between these two factors.

What effect does globalization have on countries with weak institutions? The experience of the CIS countries, such as Russia, shows that they can suffer from 'passive globalization'. Due to the weakness and corruption of customs authorities in such countries, import levels can be higher, and tariff collection lower, than the current tariff regime allows. This may result in a substantial increase in trade flows, a part of which finance capital flight. However, in contrast to active globalizers, such countries fail to reorient their exports from extractive to manufacturing or high-tech industries.[1] Weak institutions are also a barrier to FDI inflows, even in the most profitable natural resources extractive sectors. Russia shows that income inequality in such countries may assume enormous proportions because of the increased gap between incomes in exporting and import-competing industries, which is not compensated by inter-sectoral labor mobility or a well-functioning social security system. As shown by Kolenikov and Shorrocks (2002), such an increase in inequality can lead to a rise in poverty rates. Only countries with strong governments, which can control integration and guarantee the rights of foreign investors, can benefit from globalization in terms of output growth without aggravating income inequality.

The chapter begins with a detailed analysis of trade policies, output and inequality in the CIS countries and argues that trade policy by itself was only a minor factor in the output and inequality changes which occurred in the CIS countries in the 1990s. Next it uses the case of Russia to show what effect globalization may have on output, inequality and poverty under conditions of weak institutions. The chapter then refers to cross-regional Russian data to demonstrate that globalization may be beneficial for CIS countries if institutional performance improves. The conclusion provides suggestions for further research.

CROSS-COUNTRY EVIDENCE

In their study of the economic effects of globalization, Dollar and Kraay (2001) show that in the last 20 years developing countries which liberalized their trade policy and increased their volume of trade with other countries have been more successful economically than the countries which continued protectionist policies. Countries which opened their economies have experienced an increase in growth rates and a decrease in poverty rates in comparison with the preceding periods. Since the list of these countries includes such large states as China and India, globalization has resulted in a massive decrease in the world poverty in the last 20 years. Dollar and Kraay (2001) refer to countries which opened their economies as 'globalizers'.[2]

When judged by policy measures taken during the 1990s, most of the CIS countries can also be viewed as globalizers. By 2002 only one country, Turkmenistan, had kept pervasive state control over international trade and massive restrictions on the convertibility of foreign exchange. Two others,

Table 6.1 EBRD Trade and Foreign-Exchange-System Index (2002)

Armenia	4	Moldova	4+
Azerbaijan	4–	Russia	3
Belarus	2+	Tajikistan	3+
Georgia	4+	Turkmenistan	1
Kazakhstan	3+	Ukraine	3
Kyrgyzstan	4	Uzbekistan	2–

Where:

1 = Widespread import and/or export controls or very limited access to foreign exchange

2 = Some liberalization of import and/or export controls; almost full current account; convertibility in principle but with a foreign-exchange regime that is not fully transpareent (possible multiple foreign-exchange rates).

3 = Removal of almost all quantitative and administrative import and export restrictions; almost full current-account convertibility.

4 = Removal of all quantitative and administrative import and export restrictions (apart from agriculture) and all significant export tariffs; insignificant direct involvement in export and imports by ministries and state-owned trading companies; no major non-uniformity of customs duties for non-agricultural goods and services; full current account convertibility.

4+ = Standards and performance norms of advanced industrial economies: removal of most tariff barriers; membership in WTO.

Source: European Bank for Reconstruction and Development (2002).

Uzbekistan and Belarus, also have extensive government intervention in international trade activities and non-transparent foreign-exchange regimes. But the nine other CIS countries have convertible currency and almost no government control over trade flows. Kyrgyzstan, Georgia and Moldova have already become members of the World Trade Organization (WTO) and have very low levels of tariff protection. Among the remaining countries, several regard WTO accession as their political priority and have begun to lower their tariff barriers. According to the European Bank for Reconstruction and Development (EBRD), at least five have trade and foreign-exchange levels near those of advanced industrial economics. (See Table 6.1.)

As the CIS countries liberalized their foreign-trade policies, they also increased trade flows with non-CIS countries, while trade with other CIS countries declined (Djankov and Freund 2001). Unfortunately, some of the

Table 6.2 Trade-to-GDP Ratio and Tariff Rates in CIS Countries

Country	1985	1990	1995	1999
Russia[a]	15.1[b]	53.3	37.4	36.8
Armenia		81.3	86.1	70.7
Azerbaijan			85.8	84.5
Belarus		90.4	104.8	126.5
Georgia			67.9	73.0
Kazakhstan			71.1	85.3
Kyrgyzstan		78.8	71.8	99.2
Moldova			130.3	114.8
Tajikistan				131.8
Turkmenistan			71.1	103.5
Ukraine		56.4	97.2	104.4
Uzbekistan		76.6	74.6	37.9

Notes:

a. trade with non-CIS countries only;

b. USSR.

Source: Narodnoe Khozyaystvo SSSR v 1989 Godu.

decline was not voluntary: countries which do not have a common border with Russia, such as Armenia or Kyrgyzstan, had to decrease their trade with Russia because their neighbors raised significant barriers for goods transiting their territory. Some of the decline in trade was also compensated for by worker migration into other countries of the former Soviet Union. Such guestworkers usually send substantial transfers to their families left in the home countries. These transfers certainly help to improve poverty situation in recipient countries.

The degree of increase in non-CIS trade was often comparable to that seen in globalizer countries (see Table 6.2). At the same time, it was not necessarily correlated with changes in trade policy. According to World Bank data, in countries with the most liberal trade policies (scoring 4 and 4+ on the EBRD index) the average trade in goods and services to gross domestic product (GDP) ratio in 1999 was equal to 88 per cent, which is slightly lower than the average trade-to-GDP ratio in countries with the least liberal (EBRD index between 1 and 2+) trade policies (89 per cent).[3]

As mentioned above, in addition to current-account liberalization in the 1990s, the CIS countries also undertook impressive capital-account

Table 6.3 FDI as a Percentage of GDP in CIS Countries, 1994–99

Country	% of GDP
Armenia	4.0
Azerbaijan	16.2
Belarus	0.8
Georgia**	3.5
Kazakhstan	5.8
Kyrgyzstan	3.3
Moldova	2.7
Russian Federation	0.3
Tajikistan**	1.1
Turkmenistan	3.6
Ukraine	1.0
Uzbekistan	0.5

Notes:
**average for 1996–99
Source: EBRD (2002).

liberalization. The first steps to liberalize FDI inflow were taken during the last years of the USSR, with most of the CIS countries liberalizing the FDI regime even further. Some legal obstacles to FDI inflows still exist in most CIS countries, but these obstacles are usually no higher than in countries which have been very successful in attracting FDI recently, such as China. Nonetheless, in terms of attracting FDI, the achievements of the CIS countries were quite modest by transition economy standards (Table 6.3). In 2000 and 2001 net average FDI inflows to these countries were 3.2 per cent and 3.1 per cent of GDP, respectively.[4] This is substantially lower than 5.5 per cent and 4.9 per cent observed in countries of Eastern and Central Europe and the Baltics. What is even more worrisome, however, is that most FDI has gone to oil- and gas-rich Kazakhstan, Turkmenistan and Azerbaijan, while FDI inflows to countries with few natural resources have been quite insignificant. Portfolio investments in the CIS countries were quite modest. The only country to attract significant amounts of portfolio investment is Russia (Garibaldi et al. 2002). Because of capital flight, Russia had net capital outflow throughout the 1990s, and in 2000–2002 even official Russian statistics indicated that outward FDI had exceeded its FDI inflows.

The growth performance of CIS countries throughout the 1990s seemed to depend very little on trade policy. Figure 6.1 shows the growth pattern of CIS

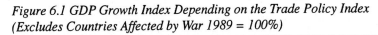

*Figure 6.1 GDP Growth Index Depending on the Trade Policy Index
(Excludes Countries Affected by War 1989 = 100%)*

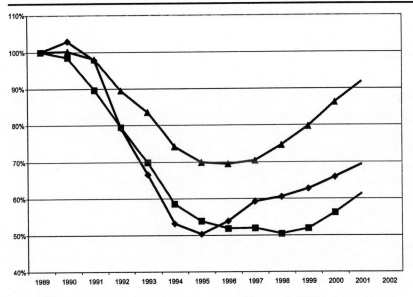

Source: European Bank for Reconstruction and Development (2001, 2002).

countries, not affected by war, in the 1990s depending on the EBRD index of external liberalization (see Table 6.1). The EBRD index refers to trade policy in the early 2000s. I use the index to group countries over the whole period of transition, because the rankings of countries according to external liberalization were more or less stable throughout the transition period. Figure 6.1 shows that countries which pursued the least liberal policies experienced a more drastic output decline and recovered faster than very liberal and modestly liberal countries. However, trade regime is not liberal in those countries, that undertook little reforms, and have rather autocratic governments. There are strong reasons to believe that output statistics in such countries overestimate economic growth, so the real difference between output patterns of various countries is probably smaller than the graph shows.

In transition states, the strength of institutions, particularly government, correlates more with growth performance than with levels of international trade (Sonin 1999; Popov 2000; Berglöf and Bolton 2002; Yudaeva et al. 2002). Government collapse in some CIS countries caused massive and protracted output declines. Weak governments cannot create an environment conductive to economic growth. The CIS countries which managed to keep stronger governments experienced a less dramatic output decline than countries unable to consolidate their governments. The nature of governing institutions seems to matter less than their overall ability to provide a growth-promoting environment. The high growth rates of Eastern and Central European countries can be explained by their success in building well-functioning market-economy institutions in the early years of transition. China has managed to establish a positive climate for growth and investment, while keeping some institutions of the planned economy intact. In fact, comparing the Chinese and Russian track records shows that institutional experimentation can be more beneficial for growth than rote copying of Western institutions (Mukand and Rodrik 2002).

Has globalization played any role in shaping transition-economy institutions? The answer appears to be yes, but only in the case of Eastern and Central Europe. Roland and Verdier (1999) argue that the desire of Eastern and Central European countries to become members of the European Union (EU) works as an expectation–coordination mechanism in building new institutions in these countries. Since all economic agents in these countries turn to EU institutions as a model, it is easier to make institutions function. By contrast, in the former Soviet republics, with the exception of Estonia, Latvia and Lithuania, there has been a lack of consensus on what kind of institutions are necessary. This has weakened the governments and has had a negative effect on growth. Moreover, almost none of the CIS countries have ever had independent governments in their history. Thus they had to build many institutions, such as customs, from scratch. This has delayed growth in some CIS countries.

In the Soviet Union the level of recorded inequality was quite low, comparable to that in most developed countries (Milanovic 1998; Atkinson and Micklewright 1992). At the beginning of transition, the level of inequality rose in all transition economies but in different proportions. In the Eastern and Central European countries the increase in inequality was smaller than in the CIS countries. As Figure 6.2 shows for Russia, most of the inequality increase occurred at the beginning of transition.

While all data on the CIS countries are of poor quality, data on poverty and inequality are particularly deficient and difficult to compare across countries. Measures of poverty and inequality are computed based on household surveys. Sampling of household surveys was poorly designed in the Soviet Union: it was biased towards the working population, among other faults (Klugman 1997). Some countries have improved the sampling of their household surveys since then, but in other states it has deteriorated even further. It appears also that in some countries no household surveys have been conducted in recent years, either by their own statistical agencies or by other organizations, such as the World Bank. Two other problems with household surveys in the CIS countries are a high non-response rate and an underreporting of incomes. In

Figure 6.2 Gini Coefficient in Russia

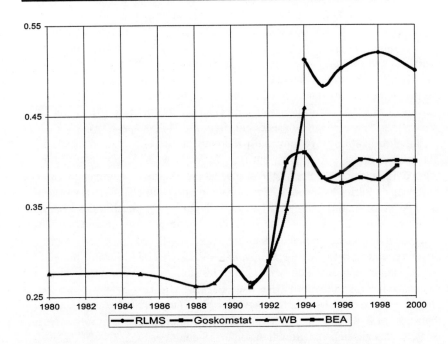

Source: Author's calculations, using data from the Russian Longitudinal Monitoring Survey (RLMS), Goskomstat, World Bank (WB) and Bureau of Economic Analysis (BEA).

the Russian Longitudinal Monitoring Survey (RLMS), for example, household expenditures exceed income by about 30 per cent. Therefore, inequality and poverty indexes computed using measures of expenditure are considered more reliable than the ones calculated using the income measure. Unfortunately, I could not find expenditure-based indexes of inequality for all CIS countries. This makes cross-country comparison of inequality indexes even less reliable.

Table 6.4 reports Gini coefficients for 1989, 1997 and 2001 in the CIS countries for which the data were available. Where possible, the numbers refer to per household member inequality of expenditure, but such information was not available for all countries. Where inequality of expenditure measure is unavailable, I use inequality of income. The table shows that inequality increased in all CIS countries but to a different extent. Of course, some of the cross-country variance in the measures of poverty and inequality can be

Table 6.4 Gini Coefficients in CIS countries

Country	1992	1994	1996	1997	1998	1999
Armenia	0.280		0.457			
Azerbaijan	0.317					0.311
Belarus	0.242				0.283	
Georgia	0.313			0.576		
Kazakhstan	0.291		0.354			
Kyrgyzstan	0.312					0.405
Moldova	0.264			0.466		
Russian Federation	0.264				0.487	
Tajikistan	0.318					
Turkmenistan	0.316				0.408	
Ukraine	0.248			0.313		
Uzbekistan	0.306	0.33				

Source: United Nations Development Programme.

explained by differences in calculation methodologies, but they still reflect the overall picture fairly accurately.

While in 1989 the values of the Gini coefficient were quite similar in all countries, by 1997 the level of inequality had widened significantly. The highest level of inequality was seen in war-torn Armenia, Georgia and Moldova, while the lowest level was registered in slow-reforming Belarus. Average levels of inequality over groups of countries with various levels of external liberalization are as follows: the most liberal countries show the highest (44.2 per cent) and the least liberal the lowest (34.0 per cent) levels of inequality. In all countries, the 1997 level is higher than that in 1989.[5] Unfortunately, data for years after 1997 are available only for a handful of countries. Available data suggest that the difference between groups of countries with various external liberalization strategies declined between 1997 and 2001, but the lack of data does not allow a strong conclusion to be drawn in this respect.[6]

Cross-country comparison of poverty levels is even more difficult than inequality comparisons. A comparable poverty line should be used for such analysis, but such data seems to be unavailable for the CIS countries. Table 6.5 reports headcount ratios and reveals an intuitive picture: countries affected by war have the highest poverty rates, but there seems to be no relationship between poverty rates and trade policy. Most of the poverty rate increase occurred in the early years of transition. The main cause of the poverty

Table 6.5 Poverty Rate in CIS Countries

	Year	Population in Poverty (%)	Year	Living on $1/day (%)
Armenia	1998	54.7		
Azerbaijan	1995	44.7	1995	<2
Belarus	1999	46.7		
Kazakhstan	2000	31.8	1996	1.5
Kyrgyzstan	1999	55.3		
Moldova	1999	53.4		
Russia	2000	28.9		
Tajikistan	1999	83		
Turkmenistan	1994	48	1998	12.1
Ukraine	1996	30		
Uzbekistan	1996	22	1993	3.3

Source: World Bank, www.economic-trends.org, Goskomstat.

increase was output decline, but the increase in inequality also had a significant impact on poverty. In fact, in Russia these two factors had impacts of a similar magnitude (Kolenikov and Shorrocks 2002). Poverty in the CIS states is also quite persistent: using the RLMS dataset, Luttmer (2002) shows that after accounting for transitory shocks, about 80 per cent of the poor in Russia remain in poverty for at least one year. As in the case of inequality, there seem to be no relationship between poverty rates and trade policy.

To summarize, the data on growth rates, inequality and poverty show either no or a negative relationship between external liberalization and indicators of welfare for the CIS countries in the 1990s. This result seems to contrast dramatically with the results reported by Dollar and Kraay (2001) for developing countries. The difference lies in the institutional performance of the CIS countries and developing globalizer countries. Most of the globalizer countries studied by Dollar and Kraay had fairly strong government institutions which, in addition to pursuing trade liberalization policies, managed to create a good investment climate. But in most of the CIS countries governments were weak, and, therefore, their trade policies did not affect growth. In fact, there are at least three countries on the Dollar and Kraay list which appear to be countries with weak governments, and their output, inequality and poverty indexes show dynamics very similar to that of the CIS countries. These countries are Rwanda, Nicaragua and Haiti. While these countries have registered a substantial international trade increase in the last 20 years, they

Table 6.6 Legislated and Collected Tariff Rates in Russia (%)

CEFIR calculations	1996	1997	1998	1999	2000
Weighted average legislated tariff rates (all countries)	14	14	12	8	
Collected tariff rates (collected tariffs/import)	4	7	7	5	
IMEI calculations	**1996**	**1997**	**1998**	**1999**	**2000**
Weighted average legislated tariff rates (non-CIS countries)	15	14	15	12	13
Collected tariff rates (collected tariffs/import)	9	12	8	9	9

have also experienced a GDP decline and an increase in poverty rates. Trade flows in most of the CIS countries have increased not because of a government policy aimed at opening up the economy, but because of the inability of the governments to close inter-state borders effectively. This phenomenon is 'passive globalization'.

PASSIVE GLOBALIZATION

In countries with weak and corrupt governments, an officially stated trade policy is not important by itself, because corruption can alter the effective rate of protectionism substantially. As an example, Table 5.6 reports official tariff rates and the ratio of collected tariffs to imports for Russia. Even if the official tariff rates are not very high in Russia, the ratio of collected tariffs to imports is even lower. But even this ratio may understate the degree of evasion: there is anecdotal evidence that goods which are subject to high tariffs are often declared as different commodity items subject to lower tariff rates.

Since trade barriers in countries with weak governments are not enforced, such countries can suffer from 'passive globalization'. In other words, these countries can achieve high trade flows, higher than mandated by their official trade policy, but experience no positive effects on growth, which globalization produces in developing countries with strong government institutions. The question is why passive globalization does not have such a positive effect on growth as active globalization. To answer this question, I look at the

Figure 6.3 Export Structure of USSR (1980, 1985) and Russia (1994–2000)
(%of total non-CIS exports)

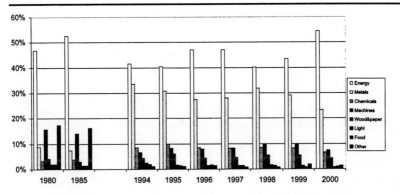

Source: Goskomstat.

trade structure first. Dollar and Kraay report that successful globalizers have changed their trade and production structure from natural resources and agriculture to manufactured goods. The CIS countries have not yet shown such a trend. Figure 6.3 compares the export structure of the Soviet Union and the largest CIS state – Russia.[7] During the 1980s, the Soviet Union's exports were already biased towards energy. Russia has retained this emphasis on natural resources' exports. The only difference between the Russian and Soviet export structures is that Russia exports much greater amounts of metals than the USSR did. Similar stories can be told about other CIS countries: in resource-rich countries, such as Kazakhstan, non-petroleum industrial sectors have almost disappeared since the beginning of transition (Kaluzhnova et al. 2002). Resource-poor countries, such as Armenia, have experienced a substantial increase in the share of agriculture in GDP at the expense of industry (Manasyan and Jrbashyan 2002; Iradian 2003). Comparative advantage and Dutch disease effects can only partially explain this dynamic. Berkowitz, Moenius and Pistor (2002) have demonstrated that weak institutions in the exporting country create obstacles to exports and, therefore, to the production of complex (diversified manufacturing) goods. Some of the CIS countries, for example Russia, began the transition rich with human capital. But instead of realizing and utilizing this comparative advantage, these countries lost a large part of their skilled labor force, who opted to emigrate. Hence, the collapse of governments in the CIS countries intensified their de-industrialization and concentration on the extraction of natural resources.

Another important difference between successful globalizers and transition countries is that, in most countries of the first group, inequality decreased after trade liberalization or increased only mildly, while in all CIS countries inequality increased, often quite dramatically. China is an important example of a successful globalizer, which has also experienced an increase in inequality over the last 20 years. Could passive globalization have played a role in such an increase in inequality? Traditional trade theory, such as the Heckchsher–Ohlin model, suggests that trade liberalization may lead to an increase in incomes related to factors used intensively in exporting sectors, and a decrease in incomes connected to inputs used intensively in importing sectors. Russian household survey data seem to suggest that this prediction holds for Russia, and it likely holds in other CIS countries as well.

RLMS, a household survey very popular among researchers, has begun to provide information on sectors of the economy where respondents are employed.[8] Detailed data on industries are available only for the rounds of the survey conducted in 1994–96. For the 1998 and 2000 rounds, I used the industry where the respondent was employed in 1996. This procedure may result in a wrong industry assignment in 2000, because of job change.[9] Therefore, the figures below should be interpreted as presenting information on wage and income development of people initially employed in relevant industries rather than as containing information on current wages and incomes of people employed in these industries.

All industrial types of activities reported by RLMS were assigned to one of eight groups of industries: machine-building, light, chemical, food, metallurgy, wood and paper, construction materials and repairs. Then I assigned all industries to one of the following groups: exporting (metallurgy, wood and paper), import-substituting (machine-building, light, food), nontradables (construction materials and renovation), and industries with large trade volumes in both directions (chemical).[10] To make the assignments I used information on the export-to-output ratio, import-to-output ratio, and intra-industry trade index of each industry. These ratios were constructed using data on industrial output obtained from the Russian state statistical agency, Goskomstat, and State Customs Committee data on export and import of goods.

Since wage data in RLMS are considered to be unreliable, I compare per capita expenditures of households across sectors where the head of the household is employed (Figure 6.4).[11] To construct the graph, I deflated expenditures by the regional poverty line. Incomes of households, where the primary income earner is employed in the exporting sector, are consistently higher than in households where income earners are employed in all other industries, with the exception of nontradables in 1998. The difference between exporting and importing sectors increases over time. As mentioned above, for

1998 and 2000 I assign to individuals the industry in which they were employed in 1996. Hence, my graphs trace income differentials not so much across industries, as across people initially employed in relevant industries. This comment is particularly important for the 2000 round, because many people reported changing jobs prior to this round. Since incomes of households where the primary income earner is employed in exporting and import-substituting sectors in 1996 diverge in 2000, Figure 6.4 provide weak evidence that globalization might add to an increase in income inequality. In terms of the effect on poverty, average per capita incomes are above the poverty line (and even above 1.5 times the poverty line) in all industries and all periods, but the risk of falling into poverty is higher for those working in import-substituting industries. Figure 6.5 shows that the poverty rate among those working (or those who previously worked) in import-substituting industries is close to 45 per cent during the 1996–2000 period, while among those who worked in export-oriented industries the poverty rate declined below 30 per cent in 1998–2000. The lowest poverty rate (20 per cent) in 2000 was documented among those employed in industries with a high index of intra-industry trade in 1996.

While RLMS data register some differences in poverty and inequality rates across sectors, they also register almost no differences across sectors in the probabilities of occupation change unemployment. Hence, the data seem to suggest that such a huge increase in inequality, as was observed in Russia, can be at least partially attributed to poor labor mobility and high correlation with family incomes. This problem may be especially relevant in Russia, because other CIS countries have much smaller territories and a smaller degree of regional economic specialization. However, I believe that, in one form or another, this problem exists in other CIS countries as well.

Low geographical mobility of labor in Russia can be only partially explained by large distances between cities and low population density, particularly in the eastern part of the country. Andrienko and Guriev (2001) show that a substantial part of the Russian labor force may be willing to move but lack financial resources to do so. Many Russian firms avoid paying their workers in cash in order not to provide potential relocation funds for workers (Friebel and Guriev 2000). Such labor hording, combined with wage arrears, was particularly common in Russia before the 1998 economic crisis. The Russian production system, with many industrial enterprises located in single-industry towns, made it easier for firms to resort to such practices (Earle and Sabirianova 2002). Employment in a single-industry town decreases the probability of changing a job or occupation (Sabirianova 2000).

Low labor mobility suggests that in Russia there were at least two sorts of governmental failures that contributed to globalization's negative effect on

Figure 6.4 Per Capita Household Expenditure, by Industry Employing Primary Income Earner (in poverty lines)

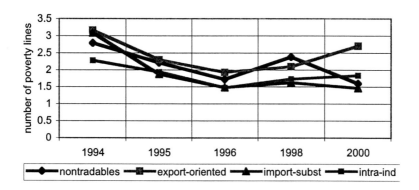

Source: Author's calculations using RLMS.

Figure 6.5 Poverty Rates by Industry Employing Primary Income Earner

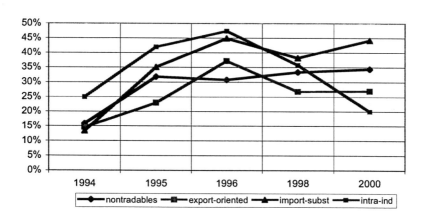

Source: Author's calculations using RLMS.

inequality. First, Russia lacks a social-security system, which would facilitate geographical and professional mobility of labor. In the 1990s Russian unemployment benefits were often very low, and in many regions they were not paid, so workers did not bother to register as unemployed. The lack of unemployment insurance added to the rise in inequality in the country. The government also failed to guarantee that firms met their obligations to workers: timely payment of wages in cash. Partly the wage-arrears equilibrium was maintained by the government itself: unable to create a properly functioning social-security system, it preferred labor hording, combined with wage arrears, to a more actively functioning labor market with higher labor mobility.

ACTIVE GLOBALIZATION AND RUSSIAN REGIONS

The above description of the effects of globalization on the CIS countries does not provide a clear answer to the question of whether it was government failure which prevented the CIS countries from reaping the benefits of globalization or whether these countries cannot gain from globalization under any circumstance. To address this issue, I use data from Russian regions. These data are more homogeneous than the cross-country data and show a wide variation in policies and outcomes.

In the 1990s regional authorities in Russia received substantial independence from the center. This was a result of President Boris Yeltsin's attempt to secure greater support from regional leaders to counter his lack of support in parliament. In exchange for political support, Yeltsin allowed regions to take 'as much sovereignty as they could swallow' (Zhuravskaya 2000; Berglöf et al. 2002). As a result, regional economic policies in Russia show substantial variation, often greater than allowed by federal legislation.

Regional variations are particularly significant for foreign (and inter-regional) trade and foreign investment policies. In 1993–94 some regions pursued a highly protectionist trade policy and even imposed trade barriers against the export and import of some goods. Policies regarding foreign investors also varied significantly. Despite the popular rhetoric that Russia would like to attract foreign investment, some firm owners and many regional governors are afraid of foreign investors and follow a number of informal policies to make their regions unattractive to foreigners.[12] Other regions, such as Novgorod Oblast, are known for creating a good investment climate. Such a wide variation in regional policies allows the Dollar and Kraay exercise to be repeated on Russian regions to see what effects policies aimed at integration into the world economy had on growth and income distribution at the regional level.

While there is considerable anecdotal evidence of regional trade barriers, no comprehensive data on such barriers exist, rendering classification of regions on the basis of differences in trade policies impossible. The situation with FDI is similar, because many procedures hostile to FDI are not formalized in regional legislations. Using trade data as a basis for country classification is also problematic. The import of goods from foreign countries is frequently channeled through particular regions thought to allow faster customs clearance and lower tariff and bribe payments. Hence, imports are usually not reported in the regions of their final destination. Inter-regional flows of goods are not reported at all.[13] Therefore I decided to use the FDI/gross regional product (GRP) ratio to classify regions as globalizers or non-globalizers. Of course, geographical factors, such as natural-resource endowment, can also play an important role in explaining regional distribution of FDI. However, Manaenkov (2000) and other authors have shown that regional policies are just as important in explaining FDI patters as geography.

To classify regions as globalizers or non-globalizers, they were ranked according to total FDI they received in 1995–99 and FDI per capita over the same period. Then, the 28 regions which appear in the upper part of the list and the 28 regions from the bottom part of the list were classified as globalizers and non-globalizers, respectively.[14] Both groups of regions are quite heterogeneous. The list of globalizers includes both natural resource-rich regions, such as Tyumen and Sakhalin, and regions known to be fast reformers, such as Samara, Sverdlovsk and Novgorod. The list of non-globalizers also includes two types of regions. In addition to underdeveloped Caucasian and Siberian ethnically identified republics, regions known as slow reformers, such as Ulyanovsk, appear on this list. Data on FDI, FDI per capita, international trade/GDP ratios in 2000, average GRP growth rates in 1997–99, and growth rates in 1999 for both globalizers and non-globalizers are reported in Table 5.7. It turns out that regions attracting more FDI also trade more with other countries.

The regional data confirm the hypothesis of Dollar and Kraay that globalizers grow faster than non-globalizers. In 1999, the average growth rate of globalizers was 5.5 per cent, while for non-globalizers it was 4.4 per cent. Because of the 1998 economic crisis, the average growth rate in 1997–99 was negative in both types of regions, although globalizers showed only a marginally negative growth of −0.1 per cent, while non-globalizers suffered a rather significant decline of −1.8 per cent. These results can be criticized for reversed causality: those regions which grow or are expected to grow at the fastest rate attract more FDI. It is difficult to find an indicator for fast-growing regions which is not correlated with FDI. To partially overcome this problem, I calculated average growth rates for the group of globalizers, excluding fast-growing Moscow and resource-rich Tyumen and Sakhalin. For the list of

Table 6.7 FDI, Trade Volume and GRP Growth Rates in Globalizer and Non-globalizer Regions

Region	Cumul. FDI 1995–99	Cumul. FDI per capita 1995–99	Trade/ GRP 2000	Av. growth rate 1997–99	GRP growth 1999
Globalizers					
Moscow city	9,807,567	1,147.6	0.75	3.7	6.9
Moscow oblast	2,046,579	318.0	0.61	3.7	5.2
Krasnodar krai	1,846,136	369.3	0.29	1.8	16.6
Sakhalin oblast	1,682,294	2,846.5	0.39	4.7	19.1
St. Petersburg	1,160,353	250.7	0.70	−0.2	6.2
Leningrad oblast	732,281	441.4	1.21	1.5	13.7
Novosibirsk obl.	569,896	208.7	0.27	−2.0	4.7
Tyumen oblast	514,291	158.0	0.76	0.1	1.9
Samara oblast	496,643	151.5	0.75	0.1	2.5
Sverdlovsk oblast	382,738	83.7	0.57	−3.1	1.8
Volgograd oblast	298,970	112.5	0.43	−2.6	1.2
Primorskii krai	260,183	120.7	0.40	0.0	6.5
Kaluga oblast	256,978	240.4	0.23	−3.3	1.5
Chelyabinsk obl.	245,633	67.3	0.51	−1.6	8.3
Magadan oblast	212,186	906.8	0.10	−8.3	−3.0
Khabarovsk krai	188,860	126.2	0.59	2.5	9.2
N. Novgorod obl.	186,976	51.5	0.32	0.4	3.4
Oryol oblast	179,862	201.9	0.23	3.4	1.2
Tatarstan republic	175,287	46.4	0.47	0.1	7.6
Orenburg oblast	147,274	66.6	0.66	0.3	9.0
Komi republic	131,138	116.5	0.49	−2.0	−3.7
Vladimir oblast	129,424	81.4	0.20	0.9	7.1
Stavropol krai	125,456	47.3	0.18	−1.8	4.1
Tula oblast	120,705	70.3	0.51	−3.4	−0.3
Novgorod oblast	103,353	143.5	0.45	3.1	6.5
Average	880,042	335.0	0.48	−0.1	5.5

Table 6.7 continued

Region	Cumul. FDI 1995–99	Cumul. FDI per capita 1995–99	Trade/ GRP 2000	Av. growth rate 1997–99	GRP growth 1999
Non-globalizers					
Tambov oblast	14,605	11.6	0.08	3.2	9.1
Bryansk oblast	13,468	9.5	0.23	−2.8	−4.1
Kamchatka oblast	12,600	32.8	0.23	−5.8	−7.0
Tver oblast	11,888	7.5	0.20	−0.5	4.9
Kemerovo oblast	10,351	3.5	0.61	−1.2	8.3
Amur oblast	10,344	10.4	0.08	−5.2	3.9
Kirov oblast	10,055	6.4	0.31	−1.5	4.7
Ivanovo oblast	9,871	8.2	0.41	−4.1	5.0
Dagestan republic	9,021	4.2	0.21	−1.8	1.8
Kostroma oblast	9,018	11.7	0.14	0.6	5.5
Smolensk oblast	8,393	7.5	0.49	5.6	25.5
Chuvash republic	8,109	6.0	0.13	−4.5	0.7
Penza oblast	7,368	4.9	0.09	0.6	12.1
Kabar–Balkar rep.	3,794	4.8	0.04	2.4	9.0
Buryat republic	3,786	3.7	0.18	1.4	8.0
Kara–Cherk rep.	3,469	8.0	0.05	−1.7	−2.8
Ulyanovsk oblast	3,180	2.2	0.19	0.0	6.0
Adygeya republic	2,616	5.9	0.05	−2.4	5.4
Mari–El republic	2,176	2.9	0.11	−0.8	0.2
Tuva republic	2,155	7.0	0.43	0.6	6.6
Kalmyk republic	1,641	5.2	0.77	−3.9	−6.0
Khakasia republic	1,563	2.7	0.92	−3.1	−0.8
Chita oblast	1,447	1.2	0.15	−3.7	9.8
Kurgan oblast	1,101	1.0	0.36	−0.2	3.0
Evrei autn. oblast	979	5.0	0.12	−7.3	5.1
Altai republic	117	0.6	0.85	−3.2	4.5
N. Ossetiya rep.	0	0.0	0.32	2.9	12.0
Chukotka aut. okr	0	0.0	0.02	−13.2	−7.6
Average	5,826	6.2	0.28	−1.8	4.4

Source: Goskomstat.

Table 6.8 Poverty and Inequality Changes in Globalizer and Non-globalizer Regions

Region	Poverty rate 1995	Poverty rate 1999	Gini coeff. 1995	Gini coeff. 2000	5 to 1 income quintile ratio 1995	5 to 1 income quintile ratio 2000
Globalizers						
Moscow city	19.1	23.3	0.52	0.56	19.7	27.8
Moscow oblast	31.2	27.6	0.26	0.30	4.0	5.3
Krasnodar krai	32.4	35.3	0.35	0.36	7.3	7.6
Sakhalin oblast	24.6	36.5	0.22	0.29	3.3	5.0
St. Petersburg city	20.0	33.2	0.35	0.32	7.3	5.9
Leningrad oblast	29.1	51.5	0.25	0.26	4.0	4.1
Novosibirsk obl.	39.8	61.1	0.29	0.31	5.0	5.6
Tyumen oblast	19.2	17.8	0.41	0.42	10.5	11.5
Samara oblast	21.2	23.4	0.30	0.39	5.2	9.2
Sverdlovsk oblast	29.5	35.6	0.30	0.31	5.3	5.6
Volgograd oblast	33.2	58.1	0.26	0.28	4.3	4.7
Primorskii krai	31.8	39.8	0.26	0.29	4.2	5.1
Kaluga oblast	26.6	47.0	0.35	0.29	7.3	4.9
Chelyabinsk obl	27.9	32.0	0.31	0.32	5.6	5.8
Magadan oblast	24.6	46.3	0.35	0.27	7.1	4.4
Khabarovsk krai	29.4	28.2	0.28	0.31	4.6	5.6
N. Novgorod obl.	22.0	38.0	0.29	0.31	5.0	5.7
Oryol oblast	22.7	35.9	0.35	0.33	7.3	6.2
Tatarstan republic	22.1	24.1	0.32	0.35	5.8	6.9
Orenburg oblast	49.3	35.6	0.27	0.28	4.3	4.6
Komi republic	19.2	22.1	0.30	0.36	5.1	7.5
Vladimir oblast	27.9	40.8	0.24	0.27	3.6	4.5
Stavropol krai	39.6	45.2	0.35	0.31	6.9	5.7
Tula oblast	16.2	31.2	0.29	0.26	4.8	4.3
Novgorod oblast	22.8	24.0	0.28	0.32	4.7	5.8
Average	27.3	35.7	0.31	0.32	6.1	6.8

Table 6.8 continued

Region	Poverty rate 1995	Poverty rate 1999	Gini coef. 1995	Gini coeff. 2000	5 to 1 income quintile ratio 1995	5 to 1 income quintile ratio 2000
Non-globalizers						
Tambov oblast	22.0	27.9	0.30	0.33	5.1	6.2
Bryansk oblast	22.7	45.0	0.27	0.29	4.4	5.1
Kamchatka obl.	22.7	33.6	0.35	0.31	7.1	5.7
Tver oblast	28.6	67.4	0.27	0.28	4.4	4.8
Kemerovo obl.	16.1	27.9	0.35	0.33	7.3	6.3
Amur oblast	37.9	44.9	0.40	0.30	9.6	5.3
Kirov oblast	32.0	56.6	0.24	0.27	3.7	4.3
Ivanovo oblast	33.7	64.9	0.26	0.29	4.0	4.9
Dagestan rep.	71.2	63.2	–	0.34	–	6.8
Kostroma oblast	30.5	38.1	0.35	0.30	7.3	5.3
Smolensk oblast	19.8	27.2	0.29	0.31	4.8	5.4
Chuvash rep.	27.3	68.2	0.24	0.28	3.6	4.8
Penza oblast	30.2	68.7	0.26	0.29	4.3	4.8
Kabar-Balk rep.	42.5	46.6	0.28	0.31	4.7	5.6
Buryat republic	55.2	50.5	0.39	0.37	9.1	8.2
Kara-Cherk rep.	45.7	64.6	0.28	0.33	4.7	6.3
Ulyanovsk obl.	16.3	31.4	0.28	0.33	4.8	6.2
Adygeya rep.	46.4	54.8	0.32	0.32	6.1	5.8
Mari-El republic	43.2	69	0.24	0.34	3.7	6.5
Khakasia rep.	25.3	45	0.27	0.28	4.4	4.7
Chita oblast	66.5	88.8	0.41	0.33	10.6	6.2
Kurgan oblast	50.4	56.5	0.27	0.35	4.4	7.1
Evrei autn. obl.	–	55.7	–	0.28	–	4.6
Altai republic	26.2	61	0.33	0.28	6.5	4.7
N. Ossetiya rep.	42.8	31.2	0.28	0.32	4.7	5.8
Chukotka aut.ok	–	70.9	–	0.31	–	5.7
Average	38.0	54.2	0.30	0.31	5.7	5.7

Source: Goskomstat.

non-globalizers, all Caucasian republics were excluded, as their scores may be affected by the region's various wars. As a result, the 1999 growth rate decreased to 5 per cent for globalizers, while for non-globalizers it increased to 4.5 per cent. The average growth rates in 1997–99 actually declined in both sets of regions to –0.5 per cent for globalizers and –2.1 per cent for non-globalizers. Still, even after these changes, globalizers look more successful in terms of growth rates than non-globalizers.

In terms of changes in poverty, globalizers and non-globalizers differ even more. Table 5.8 shows poverty headcount ratios in 1995 and 1999. Poverty increased between these two years in both sets of regions. However, in the case of globalizers the increase was 2.6 per cent smaller than the average Russian decrease, while the increase in poverty shown by non-globalizers was 4.3 per cent higher than the Russian average. Dropping resource-rich regions from the list of globalizers produces almost no changes in the poverty results, while excluding the Caucasus regions from the list increases poverty even further, because Northern Ossetia was very successful in terms of poverty reduction in 1995–99.

Table 6.8 also reports regional Gini coefficients in 1995 and 2000. These coefficients were computed from the information on income quintiles available for these two years.[15] There is almost no difference between the two groups of regions when absolute numbers are considered. Judging by the average difference from Russia's mean change between the two periods, non-globalizers appear to become more equal with time than globalizers. A comparison of the 1995 and 2000 ratios of the top and bottom income quintiles suggests that globalizers are more unequal than non-globalizers, and the gap increases with time. However, this result seems to be almost fully driven by Moscow, which is extremely unequal compared to all other regions, with inequality having increased dramatically from 1995 to 2000.

To summarize, there is weak evidence that more globalized regions in Russia grow faster than other regions. In terms of poverty changes, the results are even more convincing: While poverty increased in all regions, globalizers had a smaller increase than the Russian average, while non-globalizers had a greater increase. The results on inequality are mixed and depend critically on inclusion or exclusion of specific regions. Overall, inequality seems to be similar in both sets of regions, showing little change from 1995 to 2000.[16] The only region which differs substantially from all others is Moscow, with inequality increasing dramatically over time. Of course, globalization cannot fully explain Moscow's inequality, but it might have enhanced other factors making Moscow so unequal. For example, representatives of such well-paid professions as investment bankers or auditors are mainly located in Moscow, and the emergence of such professions in Russia was related to opening a

Russian capital account. Warner (2002) shows that the wages of managers working at multinational firms in poor countries are much less correlated with the level of GDP per capita than wages of unskilled workers. He hypothesizes that this difference exists because managers have access to the global labor market, while the market for less-skilled occupations is local. Clearly, there are many more occupations in Moscow for which the labor market is global, which may add to an increase in inequality of incomes in Moscow.

The results in this section are in line with the cross-country findings of Dollar and Kraay, who demonstrate that in globalizer countries growth rates have increased and poverty rates have decreased in the last 20 years, while non-globalizers have experienced a decline in growth rates.[17] The effect of globalization on income distribution is uncertain, with some countries becoming more equal and others less so. As the previous section suggests, low geographical and/or professional mobility can at least partially explain the increase in inequality in globalizer countries.

CONCLUSION

This chapter shows that institutional quality is an important factor affecting the results of globalization in transition countries. Countries with strong government institutions, that is the East and Central European countries and China, have benefited from globalization. The CIS countries, which mostly had weak governments when transition began, have globalized passively. While the share of foreign trade in GDP has increased in such countries, weak institutions prevent the development of advanced industries, leading to an over-reliance on the natural-resource extraction sectors. Globalization may also increase inequality: it increases the gap between incomes in importing and exporting sectors, or between skilled labor which can compete on the global market and unskilled labor, which can only compete on the local labor market. In many cases, however, the economic effects of globalization are intensified due to weak institutions. For example, it is true that globalization increases income inequality between import-substituting and exporting sectors. However, poor contract enforcement has prevented the production of complex goods from becoming an exporting sector in all CIS countries. Additionally, poor labor mobility, largely caused by poorly functioning labor markets and social-security systems, prevents labor reallocation between exporting and import-substituting sectors.

In countries with weak institutions, opening capital markets mainly provides more opportunities for capital flight, and in some cases may also attract unstable foreign portfolio investment. Of the CIS states, only Russia has been able to attract a large inflow of portfolio investment. At the same time, countries with weak institutions which do not protect property rights fail to attract FDI, one of the major sources of globalization's positive effects seen in successful countries.

While there is a large literature on the causes of output decline and growth in transition economies, the issues of income inequality and poverty have been studied insufficiently, and there have been almost no studies of the effects of globalization, trade and capital account liberalization on poverty and inequality. The greatest problem is the lack of data, particularly data comparable across countries and over time. One of the most interesting issues to study in this respect is the interaction between institutional factors and globalization. In the era of globalization, labor-market institutions and the social-security system perform two roles: they promote labor mobility across sectors and occupations and decrease income insecurity. In developed countries, there is a popular belief that globalization destroys social-security systems. The experience of transition countries, however, shows that countries where the social-security system functions better, that is Eastern and Central Europe, have managed to restructure faster and to reap more benefits from globalization. So a comparative study of the effects of labor-market policies on adjustments caused by globalization would help policymakers to better understand the effects of globalization and to reform labor-market institutions.

A more general issue of interaction between institutions and effects of trade policies also remains insufficiently studied. Recently, several studies have shown how weak institutions affect importers and exporters (Anderson and Marcouiller 2002; Berkowitz et al. 2002). It would be interesting to find out what particular features of institutions in the CIS countries prevent them from developing their economies and increasing their integration into the world economy and what the effects are on their poverty and inequality levels.

One more issue which needs to be studied is the effect of capital-account liberalization on income inequality. The effect of this policy is unclear. While opening a capital account may disproportionally increase the possibilities for the rich to diversify their income; it is also easier for wealthy individuals to overcome capital-control limits. Comparing the experience of Uzbekistan, which has multiple exchange rates and capital controls, with the situation in neighboring countries could provide useful insights in this respect.[18]

Globalization is not bad for the welfare of countries with weak institutions. In fact, it can partially compensate the population of such countries for government problems: capital flight is a way to escape some welfare-decreasing taxes, and low tariffs are a way to minimize corruption of customs officials. However, the experience of the CIS countries suggests that strong institutions, and particularly a strong government commitment to securing a good investment climate, are needed for globalization to positively affect transition and developing economies.

NOTES

1. One can argue that some or all CIS countries have comparative advantages in natural-resource-extraction sectors, and, therefore, they cannot diversify their exports towards other sectors. This is only partially true. First, a country's comparative advantage may change over time. For example, India in the last 20 years has gained comparative advantage in computer programming. Second, some CIS countries began the transition with comparative advantage in skilled labor. But because of weak institutions and poor management, they were unable to capitalize on this comparative advantage, and a substantial proportion of their skilled labor preferred to emigrate.

2. Birdsall and Hamoudi (2002) show that most of non-globalizers in the Dollar and Kraay classification are commodity-dependent countries, which experienced negative terms-of-trade shocks during the period under consideration. The reason for the poor performance by non-globalizers was this terms-of-trade shock, not poor trade policy.

3. Trade-to-GDP ratios change from year to year depending on the exchange rate, but no trade-policy-related pattern is observed in any of the years, or as an average for all years, for which data are available.

4. The gross FDI inflows to GDP ratio is somewhat higher: in 2000–2001 Russia made some FDI abroad.

5. According to some measures reported by United Nations Development Programme, Belarus may be an exception with its 1997 level of inequality being lower than the 1989 one.

6. Since 1997, the largest decreases in inequality have happened in war-torn countries.

7. In the case of Russia only the non-CIS export structure is considered.

8. The Russia Longitudinal Monitoring Survey (RLMS) covers about 4,000 households. It has been conducted since 1991, although pre-1994 data are considered to be of poor quality and do not form a panel with post-1994 data. Data are available for 1994–96, 1998 and 2000. The survey is conducted by the University of North Carolina at Chapel Hill together with the Institute of Sociology of the Russian Academy of Science.

9. In fact almost 80 per cent of all individuals who participated in the 2000 round reported that they had changed their jobs since the previous rounds of the interviews. This number looks too high, though, so there seem to have been a problem with this question in the survey.

10. These industries are subsequently referred to as to intra-industry trade industries.

11. Comparing wages as reported in RLMS provides strong evidence of an increase in the gap between exporting and import-substituting sectors during the 1990s.

12. The famous story of the Philips factory in Voronezh provides a good example of such policies. In the mid-1990s, Philips bought a TV production factory in Voronezh. Regional authorities did not allow Philips to adopt a restructuring plan and imposed multiple regulations on the

factory's operations. As a result, Philips terminated its operations in Voronezh, and sold the factory for $1.

13. There are statistics on inter-regional flows of some imported goods, but no summary statistics are available.

14. This section uses official Goskomstat regional data. Information was available on 80 regions, but I excluded Ingushetia, which has suffered greatly from the war in neighboring Chechnya.

15. For other years Goskomstat did not publish any information on regional inequality.

16. Data on Russia as a whole show substantial changes in inequality during this period, although due to lack of data it cannot be traced on the regional level.

17. Of course, a reverse causality explanation – that faster-growing economies can integrate into the world economy more successfully and attract more FDI – cannot be excluded. However, even in this case, good institutions are necessary preconditions for both growth and FDI.

18. In this chapter I do not discuss the role of the increased mobility of global capital on inequality and poverty in CIS countries. Since the inflow of foreign portfolio investment to these countries has been small so far, these effects are not large. It is well known, for example, that the 1998 financial crises led only to a short-lived recession in Russia and other CIS countries, followed by four years of high growth.

REFERENCES

Anderson, James E. and Douglas Marcouiller (2002), 'Insecurity and the pattern of trade: an empirical investigation', *Review of Economics and Statistics*, **84** (2), 342–52.

Andrienko, Yuri and Sergei Guriev (2001), 'Determinants of Inter-regional Mobility in Russia', Moscow, Center for Economic and Financial Research (CEFIR) Working Paper.

Atkinson, Anthony Barnes and John Micklewright (1992), *Economic Transformation in Eastern Europe and the Distribution of Income*, Cambridge, UK: Cambridge University Press.

Berglöf, Erik and Patrick Bolton (2002), 'The great divide and beyond: financial architecture in transition', *Journal of Economic Perspectives*, **16** (1), 77–100.

Berglöf, Erik, Andrei Kunov, Julia Shvets and Ksenia Yudaeva (2002), *The New Political Economy of Russia,* Cambridge, MA: MIT Press.

Berkowitz, Daniel, Johannes Moenius and Katharina Pistor (2002), 'Trade, law and product complexity', Department of Economics, University of Pittsburgh.

Birdsall Nancy and Amar Hamoudi (2002), 'Commodity Dependence, Trade, and Growth: When "Openness" is not Enough', Washington, DC, Center for Global Development Working Paper No. 7.

Djankov, Simeon and Caroline Freund (2001), 'Trade flows in the former Soviet Union, 1978 to 1996', *Journal of Comparative Economics*, **30** (1), 76–90.

Dollar, David and Aart Kraay (2001), 'Trade, Growth and Poverty', Washington, DC, World Bank, Working Paper No. 2615.

Dollar, David and Aart Kraay (2003), 'Institutions, Trade and Growth: Revisiting the Evidence', Washington, DC, World Bank, Working Paper No. 3004.

Earle, John S. and Klara Sabirianova (2002), 'Equilibrium Wage Arrears: A Theoretical and Empirical Analysis of Institutional Lock-In', Bonn, Institute for the Study of Labor, IZA Discussion Paper No. 196.

European Bank for Reconstruction and Development (2001), *Transition Report 2001: Energy in Transition*, London: EBRD.

European Bank for Reconstruction and Development (2002), *Transition Report 2002: Agriculture and Rural Transition*, London: EBRD.

Friebel, Guido and Sergei Guriev (2000), 'Why Russian Workers Do Not Move: Attachment of Workers through In-kind Payments', Washington, DC, Center for Economic Policy Research, Discussion Paper No. 2368.

Garibaldi, Pietro, Nada Mora, Ratna Sahay and Jeromin Zettelmeyer (2002), 'What Moves Capital to Transition Economies', International Monetary Fund, Working Paper No. WP/02/64.

Iradian, Garbis M. (2003), 'Armenia: The Road to Sustained Growth—Cross-country Evidence,' Washington, DC, International Monetary Fund, Working Paper No. 03/103.

Kaluzhnova, Yelena, James Pemberton and Bulat Mukhamediyev (2002), 'Economic Growth in Kazakhstan', Moscow, Economics Education and Research Consortium.

Klugman, Jeni (ed) (1997), *Poverty in Russia: Public Policy and Private Responses*, Washington, DC: World Bank.

Kolenikov, Stanislav and Anthony Shorrocks (2002), 'Regional Dimensions of Poverty in Russia', Department of Statistics, University of North Carolina at Chapel Hill.

Luttmer, Erzo F.P. (2002), 'Measuring Poverty Dynamics and Inequality in Transition Economies: Disentangling Real Events from Noisy Data', Washington, DC, World Bank, Working Paper No. 2549.

Manaenkov D. (2000), 'What Determines the Region of Location of an FDI Project? An Empirical Assesment', Moscow, New Economic School, Paper No. BSP/2000/036.

Manasyan, Hegine and Tigran Jrbashyan (2002), 'Explaining Growth in Armenia: Pivotal Role of Human Capital', Moscow, Economics Education and Research Consortium.

Milanovic, Branko (1998), 'Explaining the Increase in Inequality During the Transition', Washington, DC, World Bank, Working Paper No. 1935.

Mukand, Sharun and Dani Rodrik (2002), 'In Search of the Holy Grail: Policy Convergence, Experimentation, and Economic Performance', Washington, DC, Center for Economic and Policy Research, Discussion Paper No. 3525.

Popov, Vladimir (2000), 'Shock therapy versus gradualism: explaining the magnitude of the transformational recession', *Comparative Economic Studies*, **42** (1), 1–59.

Rodrik, Dani, Arvind Subramanian and Francesco Trebbi (2002),'Institutions Rule: The Primacy of Institutions over Geography and Integration in Economic Development', Washington, DC, Center for Economic and Policy Research, Discussion Paper No. 3643.

Roland, Gérard and Thierry Verdier (1999), 'Transition and the output fall', *Economics of Transition*, **7** (1), 1–28.

Sabirianova, Klara (2000), 'The Great Human Capital Reallocation: A Study of Occupational Mobility in Transitional Russia', Brown University, William Davidson Institute, Working Paper No. 309.

Sonin Konstantin (1999), 'Inequality, Property Rights, and Economic Growth in Transition Economies: Theory and Russian Evidence', Washington, DC, Center for Economic and Policy Research, Discussion Paper No. 2300.

Warner, Andrew (2002), 'International Wage Determination and Globalization'. Paper presented at the National Bureau of Economic Research–Harvard University conference 'Labor in the Global Economy', Cambridge, MA, May 2001.

Yudaeva, Ksenia, Maria Gorban, Vladimir Popov and Natalia Volchkova (2002), 'Up and Down the Stairs: Paradoxes of Russian Growth', Moscow, Center for Economic and Financial Research.

Zhuravskaya, Ekaterina (2000), 'Incentives to provide local public goods: fiscal federalism, Russian style', *Journal of Public Economics*, **76** (3), 337–68.

7. Transition, Globalization and Equity: Eastern and Central Europe

Grzegorz W. Kolodko

Equity issues in policymaking are difficult to resolve because they are linked to economic matters as well as social constraints and political conflicts. This problem is compounded by globalization – the historical process of first liberalizing the domestic economy and then integrating capital, goods and eventually labor into one world market. While globalization helps long-term economic growth to accelerate and creates opportunities for many countries and regions to catch up with more advanced economies, at the same time it causes inequality to increase, both between the countries and within them (Tanzi, Chu and Gupta 1999). On average, the global standard of living is growing, but so is the distance between the rich and the poor (World Bank 2002). Equity should always be a concern for policymakers, but it is particularly important in the early years of post-socialist change.

This chapter begins with a discussion of 'emerging markets', especially the position of post-socialist emerging markets in the global economy. Next, the characteristics of income distribution under central planning and the changes taking place during the transition to a market system are examined. Income patterns will shift and asset redistribution may in fact increase inequality, which will raise different policy options. Based on the experience of Eastern and Central Europe, inequality inevitably rises during transition, but policymakers can link income redistribution with growth in such a way that it improves its pace and durability.

THE POST-SOCIALIST EMERGING MARKETS

The concept of 'emerging markets' is fuzzy. It gets a different reading in the countries where it was coined, that is highly developed market economies (Mobius 1996; Garten 1998; Gilpin 2001), than in the countries to which it is now applied, including the post-socialist countries in transition (Kolodko 2002). It is easier to say with certainty what is *not* an emerging market than what it *is*. Emerging markets do not include, by definition, highly developed market economies which have long-evolved, mature institutional systems, or countries which have yet to set out on the path of market development. The former group comprises all the 'old' members of the Organization for Economic Co-operation and Development (except Turkey), and several countries which have attained a high development level in recent decades by acceding wholeheartedly to the world economy and liberalizing their economic regulations.

At the opposite end of the development spectrum are countries with one of four types of economies. The first group consists of the few remaining orthodox socialist (or communist) states, like North Korea and Cuba. The second group is made up of countries which, either by self-imposed isolation or by externally imposed sanctions, are largely isolated from the world economy. The third group consists of failed states, unable to take part in global economic exchange. Finally, the fourth group, which is the main source of candidates for emerging market status – comprises countries which have been hard at work with structural reforms, opening markets and liberalization and should soon be able to take advantage of global capital flows and international free trade. This group also contains several post-socialist countries which belatedly embarked on transformation, such as Turkmenistan or Uzbekistan.

Methodologically, it is also possible to treat as emerging markets all economic systems which cannot be considered fully mature, such as China, Libya and Mexico. But the purpose of this chapter is not to argue whether Singapore and Slovenia still count as emerging markets, as global investors would have it,[1] or whether Pakistan and Kazakhstan have already attained this status, although not as fast as some global corporations and the governments of the most highly developed economies would wish. This chapter narrows its focus to the post-socialist emerging markets. Does the fact that a country counts as an emerging market have a bearing on its socio-economic development and its chances for accelerated and equitable growth? These are questions that both the post-socialist markets and the advanced economies need answered.

In general (institutionally), developed and (materially) rich countries view 'emerging markets' instrumentally. Developed countries consider emerging markets as yet another segment of the expanding field of economic activity.By 'emerging', a new region of the world creates new opportunities to invest profitably, sell products and acquire resources such as cheap labor or highly qualified personnel. Hence, an additional demand 'emerges' – and becomes globalized – which now can be satisfied, as the political, cultural, economic and financial barriers used to block access to these regions are torn down.

Such an approach emphasizes not so much a commitment to the socio-economic development (including concern about 'equitable growth') of an emerging market, as the opportunity to increase one's own capacity to expand and to multiply the wealth of the already-rich countries. Sometimes outsiders seize opportunities that damage the emerging post-socialist economies; sometimes they provide benefits. The results depend on several factors, including geopolitics, but especially on the emerging country's own strategy for development and genuine political concern about equity issues and fair income distribution. However, the post-socialist markets are simultaneously joining the global economy and redistributing wealth at home. The growing inequality within the post-socialist economies is a consequence of both.

The emerging markets themselves have a totally different perspective. What matters from their point of view is not the additional outlet created in their territory for an influx of capital and goods from more advanced countries, but the rapid maturation of their domestic economic systems, and eventually becoming full-fledged market economies. In this interpretation, the principal goal is not to create new *sales markets* for outsiders, but to build a new *market system* which benefits the local market and progressively opens to an expanding range of outside contacts.

Such a system should ensure a higher level of efficiency and faster output growth, improving living standards and reducing concerns about equity issues. The object of the game is to produce market *economies* and civic *societies*, rather than just *markets*. This distinction is significant, for it emphasizes the main objective: rapid and equitable growth, generated by an inclusive, open, globally involved market economy with strong institutions (Kolodko 2002; World Bank 2002; North 2002).

THE LONG SHADOW OF CENTRAL PLANNING

Income distribution under a central planning system was more equal than earnings during the transition period as well as compared with the market economies at that same point in time. However, there was some income variation within the socialist economies, as indicated by examining these countries' Gini coefficients (reflecting here distribution of net disposable income). In the late 1980s, the Gini coefficient varied from a low of 0.20 (for

Table 7.1 Income Inequality Indexes in Eastern and Western Europe, 1986–87

Country	Gross Earning		Net Disposable Income	
	Gini Coefficient	Decile Ratio	Gini Coefficient	Decile Ratio
Czechoslovakia	0.197	2.5	0.199	2.4
Hungary	0.221	2.6	0.209	2.6
Poland	0.242	2.8	0.253	3.0
USSR	0.276	3.3	0.256	3.3
Great Britain	0.267	3.2	0.297	3.9
United States			0.317	
West Germany*			0.252	
Australia			0.287	

Notes:
*1981.

Source: Atkinson and Micklewright (1992); Milanovic (1998).

Slovakia), to 0.28 (for Uzbekistan), with an average between 0.23 and 0.24. Compared with the advanced market economies, the countries of Eastern Europe – excluding Yugoslavia – had Gini coefficients of about 0.06 points less than Western European countries (see Table 7.1).

Using the classification scheme proposed for the OECD (Atkinson, Rainwater and Smeeding 1995), none of the former centrally planned economies would exhibit high income inequality (Gini coefficient of 0.33–0.35), or even average income inequality (0.29–0.31). All of these economies would be either low income inequality (0.24–0.26) or very low income inequality (0.20–0.22). Therefore, before the transition commenced, the dominant pattern of income distribution should be considered as relatively equal, but definitely not egalitarian. If measured by the Gini coefficients in terms of distribution of disposable income, the situation was similar in Finland, Sweden, West Germany, the Netherlands and Norway.

Let us examine income distribution and inequality in the centrally planned economies compared to that of the market economies at that time. Income distribution in the Soviet bloc was rather sheltered from fluctuations in other parts of the world economy, especially due to the closeness of these economies and the inconvertibility of their currencies. Of course, the centrally planned system – significantly modified in Hungary and Poland and very little in most of the other socialist countries – played a major role here, too. This comparison will help to explain the qualitative changes that occurred later, during the first 15 years of the transition to a market economy. More significantly, however, there were two types of systemic differences between centrally planned and free-market economies, and they had different policy implications during the transition. These differences lie in primary nominal income distribution and the income redistribution mechanism.

Primary Income Distribution

In socialist economies, the dominant role of the state and collective ownership of the means of production minimized the role of capital gains, profits, rents and dividends. These forms of individual income did play a marginal role, but only in countries with a relatively significant private sector (Hungary, Poland and Yugoslavia) did it influence household income distribution.[2] However, the interest earned was not significant due to weak banking sectors and the lack of other financial intermediaries. Thus most households accumulated disposable income from wages and pensions.

Income Redistribution

Wage systems and policies were highly centralized, and only a few countries (again, Hungary, Poland and Yugoslavia) had market-oriented reforms that allowed for relatively greater wage diversification. In Poland in the 1970s, the Party determined that the highest-to-lowest-wage ratio should not exceed 6:1; although for about 90 per cent of the labor force, the actual wages ratio was closer to 3:1. Social and political pressures for a semi-egalitarian redistribution of income were very strong. These pressures, together with the socialist egalitarian ideology, were the driving force behind Poland registering more equal income distribution than elsewhere in the Soviet bloc (yet much less egalitarian than during the early years of socialism, the 1950s and 1960s), and heavily influenced labor allocation and productivity.

The state pension system was directly linked to the wage system. Therefore, the ratios of pensions for the retired and social benefits for the disabled were similar to the levels for salaries. Of course pensions were, on average, lower than wages, but their proportions were the consequence of a more or less egalitarian wage policy.

The socialist system also included other mechanisms to redistribute primary nominal income. The state provided an extensive range of subsidies on basic goods and services. In Poland in 1980 – the year the Solidarity movement emerged[3] – the subsidies accounted for as much as 10 per cent of the national income. However, their distribution, although mainly to the poor, did significantly increase the fairness of real income allocation or in-kind consumption. Subsidies were granted for goods and services with low income elasticity, mainly apartment rent and mass transportation. These subsidies targeted the lower-income groups (Cornia 1996), but also helped middle-income households, For example, larger apartments and more travel meant greater subsidies. Hence policies meant to reduce inequity in reality often caused it to increase still further.

Taxation did not play an important role in socialist economies. Direct taxes were of marginal significance in income dispersion – they accounted for no more than 2 per cent of gross salaries. For most of the population, gross remuneration was the same as net compensation, a situation that would create significant consequences and policy implications for the transition to a new system.

All of these economies suffered regular shortages. Although they differed among countries in goods, intensity and timing, shortages influenced the final distribution of real disposable income in a significant way (Kornai 1980; Kolodko 1986; Nuti 1989). The 'shortageflation' phenomenon – that is, vast shortages accompanied by open price inflation (Kolodko and McMahon 1987) – had a major effect on actual consumption. Income was often insufficient to acquire needed goods and services, so nominal demand could not be satisfied. Queuing, rationing schemes, parallel markets, forced substitution, involuntary savings and corruption overwhelmed the distribution system. Backdoor access to scarce goods and services sometimes was more important than nominal income. Hence, it is impossible to evaluate the income distribution based only on the data about monetary income dispersion.

This legacy affected the expectations and changes in income-distribution patterns in the post-socialist countries. Although 15 years have elapsed since the transition began, the shadow of socialist income-distribution patterns and policies still cloud popular attitudes and government policies.

EXPECTATIONS VERSUS REALITY

There is no doubt that one of the main reasons that socialism collapsed in Eastern and Central Europe was the common belief that the income-distribution system was unfair and unequal, contrary to political claims and the system's ideological foundations. It is difficult to say whether the people were more concerned about the absolute or relative level of their income, but perceptions of inequity certainly played a significant role in sparking the collapse of the old system. The desire for fair and equal income distribution was very strong and social dissatisfaction and political tensions were rising due to the growing disparity in real income (Kolodko 1989). Even in 2004, some people still did not want to move from relatively egalitarian socialism to widely non-egalitarian capitalism. There is still considerable naïveté that a market regime will bring higher and more equitably distributed income. In reality, however, markets increase income gaps.

At the beginning of the transition, there was a widespread conviction that this process would quickly bring both higher income and more equitable distribution of the fruits of a better-performing economy. As naïve as this attitude is, it is still present, even among some professionals and leading politicians familiar with economic and social realities. Optimism increased still further when eight of the transition countries, that is Czech Republic, Estonia, Hungary, Latvia, Lithuania, Poland, Slovakia and Slovenia concluded their accession negotiations with the European Union (EU) in December of 2002 and joined in May 2004. This development led some East Europeans to believe that the development gap between the transition countries and those in the 15 'older' member states would be closed within 10 years or so. Unfortunately, it will take much longer, if it ever happens at all (Kolodko 2002). The development gap is simply too large to close in a time span of just one generation.[4] The fact that Southern European members of the EU – Greece, Spain and Portugal – are still stuggling to catch up with the income of the richer countries is instructive here. Though EU members for two decades already, they still lag behind with their output levels and consequently the standards of living of their populations. Therefore, closing the existing development gap could be accomplished only if the rate of growth in Eastern and Central Europe were much faster than in Western and Southern Europe. Unfortunately, so far the opposite has happened. The severe collapse in output during the first years of the transition actually widened the gap between these two parts of the continent quite significantly (Figure 7.1).

Political leaders and trade union activists assumed that liberalizing prices and eliminating shortages would lead to more equal income distribution. Leaders in some countries, such as the Czech Republic and Russia, thought that privatization through free asset distribution would improve income distribution. Vast circles of professionals and politicians believed that reforming the transfer system – especially for pensions – would decrease income inequality. It did not. Short-term results did contribute to more equal income distribution. For example, price liberalization improved access to goods that earlier had been in short supply. But soon thereafter, other transition events, such as the severe contraction of real salaries and the rapid rise in unemployment, increased the number of poor, while sometimes also increasing the number of rich, due to rent-seeking and asset-grabbing.

Figure 7.1 GDP as a Percentage of PPP for 2002

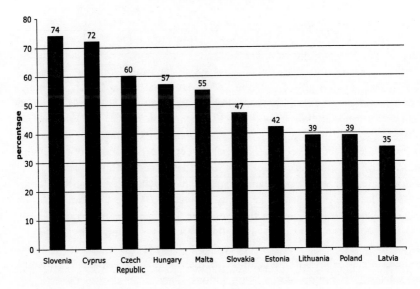

Source: EBRD (2003).

Over 12 years into the post-socialist transition, the poorest part of the society now receives a smaller portion of the national income than it did during the final stage of socialism. If participation in the national income is measured by the share of the poorest quintile (that is the poorest 20 per cent of the population) in total national income, then it fluctuates between less than 5 per cent in Russia and about 10 per cent in the Czech Republic and Hungary (Table 7.2).

The income distribution policies implemented since the 1990s have been, in a sense, a walk from one point-of-no-return to the next. Hence, societies have been forced to swallow any unexpected consequences, and they hardly welcome the results of such developments. The clearest example of this has been seen in Russia, where the gap between expectations and achievements has grown since the transition began. In Poland, initial expectations surpassed reality, because the accompanying costs proved too high. Thereafter, policy design was more realistic (Poznanski 1996; Kolodko 1996; Kolodko and

Table 7.2 Share of the Poorest Quintile in National Income, 1997–2001 (in %)

Country	%
Russian Federation	4.9
Georgia	6.0
Turkmenistan	6.1
Armenia	6.7
Bulgaria	6.7
Estonia	7.0
Moldova	7.1
Azerbaijan	7.4
Latvia	7.6
Poland	7.8
Lithuania	7.9
Tajikistan	8.0
Kazakhstan	8.2
Romania	8.2
Croatia	8.3
Belarus	8.4
Macedonia	8.4
Slovakia	8.8
Ukraine	8.8
Kyrgyzstan	9.1
Slovenia	9.1
Uzbekistan	9.2
Hungary	10.0
Czech Republic	10.3

Source: World Bank (2003).

Nuti 1997). However, because of unfair budgetary redistribution, inequality may increase still further after 2004, due to the corporate tax cut which has necessitated lower social spending.

So far, the greatest disappointment has been privatization. The higher the expectation for an egalitarian mass privatization, the greater the disappointment. Popular belief that post-socialism would evolve into a 'people's capitalism' – due to the free distribution of state assets – led only to frustration. Although many people did receive free shares, they got rid of them quickly. As privatization contiues, more and more shares are accumulating in fewer and fewer hands. The new owners are oriented more toward entrepreneurship and capital accumulation than consumption. There is nothing wrong with this type of redistribution as long as the people are not misled by their leaders, the emerging market rules are transparent, public interest is taken into account and redistribution patterns contribute to sound development (Shorrocks and van der Hoeven 2004). Unfortunately, this has not been the case in most of the transition countries.

REGIONAL VARIATIONS

In the centrally planned economies, income levels and living standards differed significantly by region. The largest differences were seen in the Soviet Union and Yugoslavia. The dissolution of those federations eased the regional tensions that had existed between the richest (i.e. Estonia and Slovenia) and the poorest (Tajikistan and Macedonia) republics. Other countries experienced contradictory expectations, which have had significant policy implications. People living in the more backward regions expected a quick improvement in their standard of living. Those living in the richer regions assumed they would be forced to transfer part of their income to the poorer regions, and they have been quite reluctant to do so.

Hence, people expected the transition to lessen regional differences and tensions. It has not. In certain areas they have even increased. For example, in Poland – if the country is divided into 44 regions according to the 'NUTS III' methodology taking into account the average regional income – the income per person in the richest region is equal to about 270 per cent of the country's average, while in the poorest region it is a meager 57 per cent. Therefore, the ratio between metropolitan Warsaw, with income per capita in 2004 hovering at about 120 per cent of the EU average, and the poorest region of the country, Chelm-Zamosc, a rural district in eastern Poland, with income per capita at about 25 per cent of the EU average, is roughly 5:1.

Such disparities are likely to grow still further because foreign direct investment and other funds are drawn to regions with the best physical infrastructure and high-quality human capital, not to the regions lagging behind. Paradoxically, the EU's regional development policy may actually increase the existing differences. However, if that does happen, it will take place at a higher absolute level, due to economic integration and convergence. Therefore, both the average standard of living and inequality will be higher.

Although income distribution varies among countries, all transition economies share some common features. Most importantly, income inequality is rising in all these countries. The fluctuations in people's income – first it fell, then it grew – have led to greater income inequality than most residents have seen in their lifetime. The greatest changes occurred during the early stages of transition, when real income contracted significantly, but the pace varied by income group. Hence, in a very short period, the income proportions have changed significantly. From this perspective, the transition economies can be divided into three groups (Milanovic 1998).

In the first group, consisting of Hungary, Slovakia and Slovenia (with a combined population of 18 million), income distribution, measured by quintile relations, has not changed. No quintile group gained or lost more than 1 percentage point, so the income shift did not occur between those groups but within them. The changes were rather minor. In Hungary, the Gini coefficient went up by 0.02 points (from 0.21 to 0.23), in Slovenia, by 0.03 points (from 0.22 to 0.25). In Slovakia, even more equal distribution was observed in 1993–95 than in 1987–88, since the Gini coefficient fell from 0.20 to 0.19 (see Table 7.3).

In the second group, which includes Belarus, the Czech Republic, Latvia, Poland and Romania (with a combined population of 84 million), moderate regressive transfers were noticed. Maximum losses were within the range of 1 to 2 percentage points and occurred only toward the three lower quintiles. At the same time, the gains of the top quintile varied from about 6 points (for the Czech Republic and Latvia) to below 2 points (for Poland). Thus, only the highest quintile benefited, and only in terms of income share. Due to the severe contraction, the absolute level of real income declined in all quintiles although the higher the quintile, the lower the decrease. In this second group of countries, the Gini coefficient rose by only 0.02 points in Poland (from 0.26 to 0.28), but by a significant 0.08 points in the Czech Republic (from 0.19 to 0.27).

In the third group, which consists of Bulgaria, Estonia, Lithuania, Moldova, Russia and Ukraine (with a combined population of more than 220 million), the changes were much greater. Income decline of the bottom quintile was 0.04 to 0.05 points, and the second and third quintiles lost similar margins of their earlier share. In Russia, Ukraine and Lithuania, the fifth quintile gained as much as 0.20, 0.14, and 0.11, respectively. The greatest shift occurred in Russia, where the bottom quintile share of income was halved – from 0.10 to 0.05 – while the top quintile jumped from the relative high of 0.34 to as much as 0.54. The Gini coefficient increased by 0.11 in Bulgaria, and doubled in Russia and Ukraine, jumping from 0.24 and 0.23 to 0.48 and 0.47, respectively.

After five or six years of transition, income distribution in the first and second groups of countries was, on average, still more equal than in the developed market economies. In the third group, especially in the former Soviet Union, income distribution continued to be less equal than in the old 24 OECD member countries. Lately, the process has taken another route.

Table 7.3 Changes in Income Inequality During Transition, 1987–2001 Gini Coefficient (income per capita)

Country	1987–88	1989	1993–95	1998	1999	2000	2001
Kyrgyzstan	0.26		0.55[b]			0.47	
Russia	0.24		0.48[b]			0.46	
Ukraine	0.23		0.47[a]			0.46	
Lithuania	0.23		0.37	0.36			
Moldova	0.24		0.36			0.39	
Turkmenistan	0.26		0.36		0.27		
Estonia	0.23		0.35[b]		0.40		
Bulgaria		0.23	0.34				.32
Kazakhstan	0.26		0.33			0.31	
Uzbekistan		0.28	0.33			0.27	
Latvia	0.23		0.31	0.32			
Romania		0.23	0.29[a]			0.30	
Poland	0.26		0.28[c]		0.31		
Belarus	0.23		0.28[b]			0.34	
Czech Rep.	0.19		0.27[a]			0.27	
Slovenia	0.22		0.25	0.28			
Hungary	0.21		0.23	0.24			
Slovakia	0.20		0.19	0.26			

Notes:

For most countries, the income concept for 1993–95 is disposable income. In 1987–88, it is gross income, since, at that time, personal income taxes were small, as was the difference between net and gross income. For the data for periods 1987–89 and 1993–95 income includes consumption in-kind, except for Hungary and Lithuania in 1993–95.

a. Monthly.

b. Quarterly.

c. Semiannual.

Source: UNDP (1996); Milanovic (1998); UNDP (2002); World Bank (2003).

Although income inequality has continued to grow in most of these economies, albeit at a much slower pace than before, a few have stabilized. More recently, this inequality has hovered around the dispersion structure that resulted from the changes that followed the earlier shocks. Only in Russia, some other post-Soviet republics and Slovenia it has still been growing in a meaningful way. Of course, the income of some households and professional groups still fluctuates, but the changes are not as remarkable as they were in the first half of the 1990s.

However, it must be stressed that income distribution in the post-socialist emerging markets is still in flux and continues to change much more – and rather toward still larger inequality – than it changes in other emerging markets, for example in Asia or Latin America. The greater shifts are due to the vast and ongoing structural and institutional changes that are still taking place in these countries (Kolodko 2003). Taking into consideration the significant lags for relevant data, the gap between the true situation in the post-socialist economies and the one sketched here on the basis of available data is probably greater than may be the case for other emerging markets. This discrepancy exists because in the latter cases there is not such a dramatic change in the income and assets distribution (and redistribution) pattern as the one occurring in post-socialist countries. In other words, the actual income inequality in 2004–2005 in the transition economies is definitely higher than what can be read from the dated statistical data, which is emerging much slower than these markets do.

TRANSFORMING SHADOW ECONOMIES

This is not the only reason these observations must be interpreted with proper caution. Although the transition economies are going through a vast, intensive process of liberalization, they still lack the sophisticated market mechanisms typical in advanced market economies. Instead, their common feature is an extensive shadow economy consisting of unregistered economic activities that produce considerable – but untracked – income. The shadow economy, estimated to contribute from 15 per cent to 30 per cent of GDP in these countries, affects inequality in a remarkable way.[5]

Because there are many types of unregistered activities, the real challenge is to find the most appropriate way to institutionalize the shadow economy; that is, to incorporate it into official markets rather than eliminate a fairly well-functioning arrangement. While some activities should be prohibited others should be made official. The parallel economy encompasses organized crime, which must be resolutely fought, but primarily it is composed of numerous small-scale businesses in many sectors that produce goods and provide services, jobs and income but – for the time being – no fiscal revenue.

This type of emerging entrepreneurship, which creates vital income for many households, should be tolerated and gradually assimilated into the official economy. The state should establish a friendly business climate by cutting red tape and diminishing the fiscal burden imposed on the firms, if state expenditures are adjusted correspondingly. Yet before this task is accomplished, considerable income will be made in the shadow economy and, simultaneously, a significant part of the total income will be redistributed through the parallel sector. These uncontrolled corrections in the dispersion pattern obviously complicate policies based on official income distribution data alone.

At the low end of the spectrum, many households engaged in the shadow economy – particularly in the trade, housing construction, maintenance, and some traditional service sectors – have higher income than is recorded formally in the household budget surveys. Although most – if not all – of the unemployed are officially counted in the bottom quintile, some should instead be counted in at least the second quintile, if not higher. Given the substance of the shadow economy and the methodological problems of accurately measuring unemployment, it is obvious that an important fraction of this group makes money outside the registered economy. Therefore, their true earnings are higher than the official statistics – or even the more comprehensive household budget surveys – show.

At the highest end of the spectrum, the official picture may be biased even more than for the poor, because many activities of the new entrepreneurial class are not recorded at all. Using various means, members of this class are often able to conceal a significant part of their actual income from tax officials. Despite some progress, both tax evasion and tax avoidance are still widespread, primarily due to poor tax administration and low ethical standards among emerging capitalists and a part of the middle class. While creating an effective fiscal order and an efficient tax collection system is a long-lasting process, taxation is often considered a form of punishment. Taxation is often believed to limit the business sector's ability to expand. It is rarely seen as a fair and rational instrument of income redistribution.

The extent of the informal sector depends on the maturity of institutional arrangements and developments in the real economy. In economies with relatively more advanced market institutions and a higher market culture – such as in the countries which joined the EU in 2004 – the scope of tax evasion is much smaller. Although it is difficult to measure and impossible to quantify, it seems feasible to claim that the shadow economy is larger in Ukraine than in Poland, in Armenia than in Latvia, in Romania than in Hungary, and in Macedonia than in Slovenia.

As for real developments, the tendencies are mixed. In the fast-growing countries, at least part of the expansion is due to vigorous activities in the parallel economy, thus its impact on income levels and its structure is greater. As output rises, more people considered jobless make ends meet by working in the shadow economy than by collecting unemployment benefits. The business communities are able to take greater advantage of soaring shadow markets, while weak regulations allow them to hide part of their actual revenue. In the countries with continuing recessions, an increasing number of people are looking for opportunities to earn money wherever they can, including in the shadow economy, but they have fewer opportunities than in a growing economy.

The outcome of what has happened thus far is a puzzle and can only be roughly estimated. While the shadow economy is known to contribute to higher income for all social classes, it is impossible to estimate precisely how it influences the final distribution of net disposable real income. Although the informal sector contributes to higher production and welfare as a whole, it also transfers income from some households to others. Because these income flows cannot be precisely mapped, only broad conclusions can be drawn.

Income redistribution is not a zero-sum game. It is conducted within the boundaries of the parallel economy – as well as between the parallel and the official economy – and can enhance overall growth. Thus, in the long run, it can contribute to a higher standard of living for the whole society. It seems, in any case, that the parallel economy – through its contribution to actual national income and its impact on its redistribution – does raise inequality. Moreover, in the transition economies, as well as in other emerging markets, the difference between the official and the true picture of income distribution – if one takes into account the shadow economy – may be much greater than in the highly developed market economies.

CHANGING INCOME DISTRIBUTION PATTERNS

Income distribution has changed qualitatively during the transition. Particularly important is that most government subsidies and allowances have been radically reduced or eliminated completely. Various international organizations, especially the International Monetary Fund (IMF), from the start of transition considered the elimination of subsidies to be an absolute necessity. The IMF was willing to back only structural adjustment polices that led to the liquidation of all subsidies. This external pressure was mixed with domestic tugs-of-war between economic traditionalists and free-market zealots.

Depending on the social and political situation, as well as on the chosen path of price liberalization and adjustment, the way the subsidies were removed influenced income dispersion. The more radical the subsidy cuts, the deeper the shift in income inequality. Whereas some shortages did indeed disappear rather quickly (*the shops were full of goods...*), the real income and money balances of households shrank even faster (*...because the consumers' pockets became almost empty*). Consequently, the ultimate effect of slashing subsidies and price liberalization did contribute to fiscal improvements and helped introduce a market-clearing mechanism, but these were achieved at the cost of growing inequality.

In the meantime, however, the unavoidable part of transition – price liberalization together with far-reaching subsidy reductions – has been causing high inflation. Often, the first thing to rise is the basic cost of living: the prices of food, housing, utilities and public transport. Inflationary income redistribution – executed by adjusting real income downward by different rates per household group – significantly increased income inequality in the early 1990s. With extremely high inflation, real income distribution depended on the indexation procedures used at the time of the stabilization policy. Because of this unequal indexation, inequality continues to fuel social tensions. Since this problem is far from solved in any transition economy, the ongoing change in relative wages will continue to cause political friction.

As a result, income shifts between certain groups will also continue, regardless of how these groups' contributions to the national welfare change. In terms of inequity, these changes will cause certain shifts in the existing pattern of income distribution, mainly in the relative position of some professional groups *vis-à-vis* others. While some segments of the given country are becoming a part of the global labor market – with all its implications for income distribution – most of the labor market is not directly or deeply involved in such exchange. The trade between the former centrally planned economies is still relatively high, despite their ongoing trade liberalization (Figure 7.2).

The countries that are transforming faster are also absorbing a larger part of the foreign direct investment, what is raising further their competitiveness due to better technologies, management and marketing (Figure 7.3).

Economic reforms also liberalized the wage structure in the state sector. Regardless of the initial pace of privatization, by the early 2000s, more than three-quarters of the labor force in most transition economies earned their salaries in the private sector. Thus, income has become more tightly linked to qualifications, experience and performance. The transition has meant a closer relation between an individual's past investment in his or her own human capital and his or her current remuneration. That, in turn, has led to still greater wage dispersion. Because the quality of human capital varied more than did salaries under central planning, realigning wages with human capital levels has increased income inequality.

Even more significant for rising income inequality is the shift of labor from the state to the private sector. Not only is the wage dispersion in the private sector larger than in the state sector, but average income earned is higher. This is a consequence of the higher labor productivity in the private sector; the state still controls a number of obsolete, noncompetitive industries, and poorly managed, low-paid services, such as education, health care and government administration. Because of the meager budgetary situation, these sectors have not been able to compete with the salaries offered by private industries, which perform more profitably. Therefore, as more workers shift to the rapidly growing private sector, income inequality rises. This reflects the market adjustment to accommodate higher quality labor. Nevertheless, the salary ratio remains somewhat distorted in transition economies, because their labor markets are still quite rigid and far from perfect.

When an economy moves from central planning to free markets, the most revolutionary and fundamental changes take place in asset ownership. The basic features of emerging capitalism after socialism are denationalization, privatization, property restitution, foreign direct and portfolio investment and financial intermediaries emerge to accompany private-sector expansion. These events have a major impact on changes in income distribution and, of course, growing inequality. As a result the share of wages and social transfers in total household income decreases, while the share of capital gains (profits, dividends, interest and rents) – increases. This process itself contributes significantly to growing inequality. Market reforms inevitably result in some unfair redistribution, as it is an unavoidable byproduct of the transition process. Whereas limiting the range of the post-socialist redistribution is a matter of sound policies, containing it entirely is simply impossible.

The fundamental shift of assets from state to private hands has been followed by a shift in the income earned on these assets in the same direction. Obviously, these changes also increase inequality. Therefore, policymakers must decide how to transfer property rights and how to manage the process. The two options range from selling state property to any investor to freely distributing all assets among all eligible citizens.[6] In the real world, some combination of the two techniques is needed. Hungary chose a path closer to the first option, the Czech Republic closer to the latter, and Poland between the two. The implications for corporate governance and microeconomic efficiency differ in both options, but so do the consequences for income inequality in the long run. The choice between the two options is not simple. More unequal

Figure 7.2 Direction of Export in Transition Countries (2002)

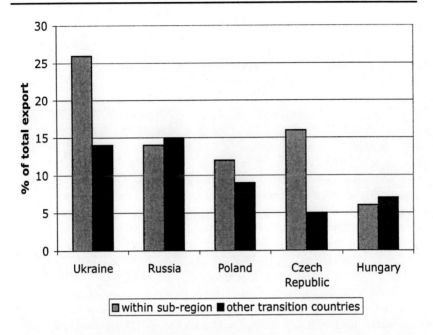

Notes: 'Sub-region' implies in the case of Russia and Ukraine the CIS and for Czech Republic, Hungary and Poland the East–Central European countries.

Source: EBRD (2003).

privatization, by selling to strategic investors, favors competitiveness and hence the income level, whereas more egalitarian asset distribution favors income equity but does not necessarily improve efficiency.

The populist mainstream in both economics and politics has suggested that mass privatization through the free distribution of shares can offset the hardship caused by structural adjustment, especially growing unemployment and falling real earnings and pensions. This may be true, but the effect is only partial and temporary. In fact, in several countries, workers have gone on strike – not against privatization but in favor of it. These strikers were not free-market zealots; they just wanted the quasi-money – the shares, vouchers, certificates or coupons, which they felt was rightly theirs. Poor people often found themselves in the bizarre position of having no access to an adequate social safety net, yet owning one or two shares of a privatized enterprise. This poverty and lack of social protection did not accord with the vision of a market

Figure 7.3 Cumulative (1989–2003) FDI Inflow Per Capita

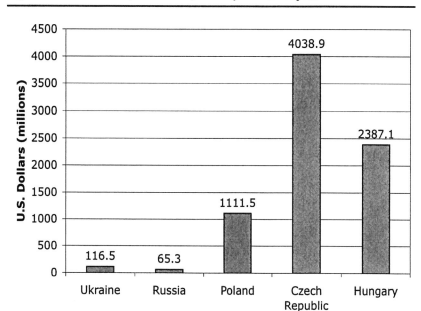

Source: EBRD (2003).

economy under 'people's capitalism. It also barely reduced inequality and the resulting tension.

The problem of equality versus inequality is even more serious. The basic issue is not the change in the income distribution pattern in the first post-socialist decade, but the irreversible foundation that has been laid for income distribution in the future. This change is the result of the stormy and indeed poorly regulated process of asset distribution linked to privatization. While some citizens were fighting for a fairer indexation of their modest income (i.e., the current flow), the more cautious were trying to acquire as much property as possible (i.e., stock, or future income).

In conclusion, the flow of income alone cannot accurately answer questions about the scope, direction or pace of inequality shifts. People that are, in fact, rich (owning many assets) may report very little income, whereas somebody else – a relatively poorer person – can pay the highest possible taxes. To properly measure inequality in an emerging post-socialist market economy requires analyzing not how the flow of income is dispersed, but how it is distributed and how denationalized assets are divided. Otherwise, the picture will be distorted, if not false altogether. Unfortunately, there is not even a rough statistical basis for such considerations. Most income flows are registered, but asset transfers are not. This data gap exists rather deliberately, since the actual policymakers – under tremendous pressure from interest groups and the media – are not very keen to know the truth.

The introduction of comprehensive taxation systems has changed the income–distribution mechanism and its final outcome. Fiscal order in transition countries is not yet the same as in the mature market economies. The personal income tax – for some countries, an entirely new phenomenon – is in most cases progressive, although the brackets and scales vary by country and can change in either direction. Because higher income is taxed at a higher margin, such taxation – unlike a handful of countries with a flat tax[7] – decreases the gap between the net disposable income of better- and worse-remunerated people and, subsequently, narrows the scope of inequality.

In transition economies, the fiscal regimes and policies are not stable and hence neither is the equalizing effect of fiscal policy. There are continuous debates and political battles between parties on raising and lowering taxes. Most recently, however, the fashionable approach seems to favor cutting taxes, even if it causes still larger fiscal deficits. Again, the true system is never a masterpiece of public finance theory and reasonable, long–term-oriented policy, but always a political compromise.

CONCLUSION

The core of the transition process is changing a centrally planned regime to a market economy that will be able to expand and compete internationally. In the era of contemporary globalization this transformation is more difficult – and more important – than ever. Other issues, including income and wealth distribution, are often seen as secondary goals or byproducts of the systemic changes. In fact, transition economies often contain a frantic process of wealth buildup. People soon get the message that capitalism cannot be restored or created without capital and capitalists – and the inherent consequences for inequality. The conclusions are obvious. During the transition inequality will rise, and policymakers should try to shape such inequality in a way which facilitates the transition's goals.

From social and political points of view, it is a challenge to permit any meaningful shift of income from the bottom to the top quintile, even under robust growth. Certainly, it is much more difficult to do so during a period of collapsing output or when growth is sluggish. For the transition economies, the latter has been the case for a number of years. Therefore, in considering the issue of inequality, policymakers must distinguish between the stages of contraction and growth. Contraction phases have lasted from a relatively short period of three years in Poland to a staggering ten years in Ukraine. The problem became still more serious when average income was declining and policy favored a new middle class. Under such conditions poverty must also increase. Hence, during the longer periods of contraction, the redistribution mechanisms transferred even more of the poor's already diminished income to the rich.

This is the picture from a macroeconomic perspective. On the micro level, however, the changing pattern of income flow mainly reflects the shift in certain population groups' contributions to gross domestic product (GDP). This product unfortunately shrank during the first few years of transition. The poor were getting poorer because their contribution to a declining national pie was falling faster that the contributions of other groups. The shorter this extremely difficult period was and the smaller the fall in output, the better. Arguably, both the scope and the length of the transitional recession could have been reduced if not avoided altogether (Kolodko 1992, 2000).

Fortunately, all transition economies eventually started to grow. In 2003 the average rate of GDP growth hovered around 4.5 per cent (EBRD 2003) and this pace can be sustained for many years to come. When an economy is on the rise, the issues of inequity and inequality can be addressed in a different way. During a recession, the question is how can the loss of income be shared? How can particular social groups participate in its decline? Under an expansion, the question can be modified: how should growing income be distributed? How should the increment in national income be divided between population groups? Even in the most advanced market economies, policy affects how income is shared, as it cannot be left exclusively to spontaneous market forces (Stiglitz 2002, 2003). This is even more appropriate in transition countries, where market forces are, by definition, in the making. The best policy guideline for the government is to intervene only to guarantee a compromise between the interests of particular income groups and provide sufficient incentives for capital formation to facilitate development and growth in the standard of living for all.

Thus far, transition has brought mixed results. That is true also for the issues related to income inequality. The biggest challenge for policymakers is how to deal with growing inequality and the simultaneous widening of poverty. This challenge is made more difficult by the interrelationship between the two as well as by the aftermath of a severe, long-lasting recession, which has brought the GDP per person in most post-socialist countries to the level that even in 2004 is lower than pre-1989 levels. Hence, growing inequality is not only a political issue that will provoke tensions and conflicts, but one that creates an economic obstacle to durable growth (Tanzi and Chu 1998).

When a policymaker trying to catch up with a more advanced world faces a trade-off between faster growth with higher inequality (but less poverty) and slower growth with lower inequality (but widening poverty), he can be happy because his choice is clear. Policy should facilitate fast growth and sustained development, and income policy should support these obvious goals (Kanbur 1998). Then, in the longer run, everyone's standard of living may improve. After the initial surge of inequality, and when the economy is on the rise, it may be even possible to reduce disparity without harming the ability to expand. This seems to be even truer for inequity. Therefore, the more the transition advances and the stronger the foundations for fast and durable growth, the weaker is the trade-off between equity and efficiency.

Globalization is not an obstacle to ambitious targets such as equitable growth. It can make it more difficult to accomplish, yet under certain conditions it can help. The latter, however, can happen only if the government policy is properly involved in the process of growth and income distribution. Neither too much liberalism, nor too much interventionism makes for good guidance. Hence, the quest for the optimum combination between the two must continue. This is certainly the case of the post-socialist emerging markets during the era of globalization, because the existing pattern of income distribution is not yet final. It will change and fluctuate far into the future.

NOTES

1. In some international analyses, certain countries are occasionally included in two groups simultaneously. For instance, Hong Kong, South Korea, Singapore and Taiwan have been treated by the IMF and the World Bank as advanced economies, whereas global investment banks still classify them as emerging markets.

2. For instance, in Poland in 1989, about 20 per cent of GDP was from the private sector, of which about one-third was nonagricultural. Undoubtedly, such legacy from the reformed centrally planned regime was quite helpful for the implementation of the structural changes this time leading to the full-fledged market system. This legacy explains also – to a certain extent – the relatively better performance of the Polish economy during the initial years of transition, despite the failure of ill-advised 'shock without therapy' in 1989–92 (Kolodko 2002).

3. It is said in a 'socialist economy', because by all means it had not deserved to be referred to as a 'centrally planned economy', since it was not led at that time any more by a discipline of a central plan.

4. According to the EU Commission and Eurostat estimates, the GDP per capita on a purchasing power party (PPP) basis in accession countries hovers below 50 per cent of the EU-15 average. This is indeed a very large gap.
5. For the advanced market economies, the scope of the shadow economy is estimated at about 15 percent of GDP for the EU countries and below 10 per cent for the United States.
6. The point is that assets distributed on the primary market – for free or for a nominal, symbolic fee – are sooner or later redistributed on the secondary market. Again, people are free to do so, but in the end it leads to the accumulation of these assets by only a few, with all the consequences for growing inequality.
7. In a few countries, such as Russia and more recently Slovakia, a flat personal income tax has been introduced. For obvious reason, it will contribute to growing inequality. Not only for this reason such fiscal policy will fail and in due time will be replaced by the progressive taxation system. It is only a matter of time. And – as it happens strangely also in economic policy – a matter of fashion.

REFERENCES

Atkinson, Anthony B. and John Micklewright (1992), *Economic Transformation in Eastern Europe and the Distribution of Income*, New York: Cambridge University Press.

Atkinson, Anthony B. Lee Rainwater and Timothy M. Smeeding (1995), 'Income Distribution in Advanced Economies: Evidence from the Luxembourg Income Study', Luxembourg, Luxembourg Income Study Working Paper No. 120.

Cornia, Giovanni Andrea (1996), 'Transition and Income Distribution: Theory, Evidence and Initial Interpretation', Helsinki, United Nations University, World Institute for Development Economics Research (WIDER) Research in Progress No. 1.

Deininger, Klaus and Lyn Squire (1996), 'A new data set measuring income inequality', *World Bank Economic Review,* **10** (3), 565–91.

European Bank for Reconstruction and Development (2003), *Transition Report 2003: Integration and Regional Cooperation*, London: European Bank for Reconstruction and Development.

Garten, Jeffrey E. (1998), *The Big Ten: The Big Emerging Markets and How They Will Change Our Lives*, New York: Basic Books.

Gilpin, Robert (2001), *Global Political Economy: Understanding the International Economic Order*, Princeton, NJ: Princeton University Press.

Kanbur, Ravi (1998), 'Income Distribution and Growth', Washington, DC, World Bank Working Paper No. 98–13.

Kolodko, Grzegorz W. (1986), 'Repressed Inflation and Inflationary Overhang Under Socialism', Urbana-Champaign, Illinois, University of Illinois, Bureau of Economic and Business Research, Faculty Working Paper No. 1228.

Kolodko, Grzegorz W. (1989), 'Reform, stabilization policies and economic adjustment in Poland', Helsinki, United Nations University, World Institute for Development Economics Research (WIDER) Working Paper No. 51.

Kolodko, Grzegorz W. (1992), 'Economics of Transition: From Shortageflation to Stagflation: The Case of Poland', in Armand Clesse and Rudolf Tokes (eds), *Preventing a New East–West Divide: The Economic and Social Imperatives of the Future Europe*, Baden-Baden: Nomos Verlagsgesellschaft, pp. 172–81.

Kolodko, Grzegorz W. (1996), *Poland 2000: The New Economic Strategy*, Warsaw: Poltext.

Kolodko, Grzegorz W. (2000), *Post-Communist Transition: The Thorny Road*, Rochester, NY: University of Rochester Press.

Kolodko, Grzegorz W. (2002), *Globalization and Catching-up in Transition Economies*, Rochester, NY: University of Rochester Press.

Kolodko, Grzegorz W. (ed.) (2003), *Emerging Market Economies: Globalization and Development*, Aldershot, England, and Burlington, VT: Ashgate Publishing.

Kolodko, Grzegorz W. and Walter W. McMahon (1987), 'Stagflation and shortageflation: a comparative approach', *Kyklos*, **40** (2), 176–97.

Kolodko, Grzegorz W. and D. Mario Nuti (1997), 'The Polish Alternative: Old Myths, Hard Facts and New Strategies in the Successful Transformation of the Polish Economy', Helsinki, United Nations University, World Institute for Development Economics Research (WIDER) Research for Action Paper No. 33.

Kornai, János (1980), *Economics of Shortage*, Amsterdam and New York: North-Holland Publishing Co.

Milanovic, Branko (1998), *Income, Inequality, and Poverty During the Transition from Planned to Market Economy*, Washington, DC: World Bank.

Mobius, J. Mark (1996), *On Emerging Markets*, London: Pitman Publishing.

North, Douglass C. (2002), 'Understanding Economic Change and Economic Growth', Warsaw: Leon Kozminski Academy of Entrepreneurship and Management Distinguished Lectures Series No. 7.

Nuti, D. Mario (1989), 'Hidden and Repressed Inflation in Soviet-type Economies: Definitions, Measurements and Stabilization', in Christopher Davis and Wojciech Charemza (eds), *Models of Disequilibrium and Shortage in Centrally Planned Economies*, London and New York: Chapman and Hall, pp. 101–46.

Poznanski, Kazimierz (1996), *Poland's Protracted Transition: Institutional Change and Economic Growth*, New York: Cambridge University Press.

Shorrocks, Antony and Rolph van der Hoeven (eds) (2004), *Growth, Inequality, and Poverty: Prospect for Pro-poor Economic Development*, New York: Oxford University Press.

Stiglitz, Joseph E. (2002), *Globalization and Its Discontents*, New York: W.W. Norton.

Stiglitz, Joseph E. (2003), *The Roaring Nineties: A New History of the World's Most Prosperous Decade*, New York: W. W. Norton.

Tanzi, Vito and Ke-young Chu (eds) (1998), *Income Distribution and High-quality Growth*, Cambridge, MA: Massachusetts Institute of Technology Press.

Tanzi, Vito, Ke-young Chu and Sanjeev Gupta (eds) (1999), *Economic Policy and Equity*, Washington, DC: International Monetary Fund.

United Nations Development Programme (1996), *Human Development Report 1996*, New York: Oxford University Press.

United Nations Development Programme (2002), *Human Development Report 2002*, New York: Oxford University Press.

World Bank (2002), *Globalization, Growth and Poverty: Building an Inclusive World Economy*, New York: Oxford University Press.

World Bank (2003), *World Development Report 2004: Making Services Work for the Poorest People*, New York: Oxford University Press.

8. Globalization and Equity: A Latin American Perspective

Roberto Bouzas and Ricardo Ffrench-Davis

Much of the economic debate in Latin America at the beginning of the twenty-first century concerns how globalization and structural reform affect economic growth and equity. While scholars and policymakers agree that deeper integration into the world economy raises the potential for economic growth, the recent experience of Latin America suggests that such potential may not be realized. The effects of globalization on equity are subject to more debate, but the Latin American record is also far from encouraging. During the last ten years poverty and equity have actually worsened in many countries of the region, breeding discontent regarding the effects of globalization and economic reform on poverty and income distribution. Although the causal links between globalization and economic growth and equity are far from straightforward, the Latin American record suggests that domestic institutions and policies are critical ingredients for reaping the benefits of deeper integration into the world economy.

This chapter reviews recent literature on globalization and equity in Latin America. Evaluating the distributive effects of globalization has more than academic merit. Designing and implementing policies to prevent or moderate the negative effects that globalization and liberalization may have on equity would not only improve economic performance, but also increase the political support required to make outward-oriented reforms sustainable. This chapter begins by introducing a distinction between globalization as a market phenomenon and as a policy phenomenon. It then provides an overview of the evolution of inequality in Latin America in the last decades, followed by a discussion of the conventional transmission channels through which globalization can affect equity and income distribution, and presents data about Latin America. Next the chapter focuses on the macroeconomic dimensions of the link between globalization, growth and equity before offering some conclusions based on the preceding discussion.

GLOBALIZATION: MARKETS AND POLITICS

The concept of globalization usually enters public policy debates from two separate perspectives. One aspect is 'positive' and refers to structural trends in technology and their effects on economic distance. The other view is 'normative' and takes the shape of policy recommendations. The two versions of globalization appear frequently mixed in policy debates. Distinguishing among them is not always easy (Bouzas and Ffrench-Davis 1998).

As a market phenomenon, globalization is driven by the falling cost of moving goods, services, money, people and information. The reduction in economic distance made possible by technical progress enables the exploitation of arbitrage opportunities in goods, services and factor markets, reducing (but not eliminating) the importance of geography and the effectiveness of policy and institutional barriers. As a market phenomenon, globalization has increased firms' ability to fragment the production process across different geographical locations, thus contributing to the steady growth of international trade (especially in manufactures and services) and foreign direct investment (FDI).

Although globalization is a major feature of the contemporary international economy, there is widespread disagreement over its extent and depth. According to one view, globalization triggers pressures towards convergence in performance and institutions (the familiar 'race to the bottom'). An alternative perspective, however, emphasizes the uneven and incomplete nature of globalization. While it is accepted that mobility is very high in certain sectors (such as financial markets), integration is far from complete. In goods or labor markets the degree of integration is even shallower. Similarly, idiosyncratic features still dominate in areas such as infrastructure, basic societal principles or institutions (Garrett 1999).

But globalization is not simply a market phenomenon. Public policies, such as removing administrative barriers and harmonizing national policies and institutions, also play an important role in fostering international integration. Policy decisions may deepen market integration, speed up the pace towards globalization and promote convergence between national practices and institutions. This process, however, takes place in the context of an international system shaped by power asymmetries. In this global environment, some agents (public and private) are more successful than others in promoting their preferences and values, which may then appear as universal

Table 8.1 Median Gini Coefficients by Region and Decade

Region	1960s	1970s	1980s	1990s
Eastern Europe	0.251	0.246	0.250	0.289
South Asia	0.362	0.339	0.350	0.319
OECD and high-income countries	0.350	0.348	0.332	0.337
Middle East and North Africa	0.414	0.419	0.405	0.380
East Asia and Pacific	0.374	0.399	0.387	0.381
Sub-Saharan Africa	0.499	0.482	0.435	0.469
Latin America	0.532	0.491	0.497	0.493

Source: Deininger and Squire (1996).

(Lawrence et al. 1996). Thus, policymaking in developing countries must deal not only with the challenges posed by globalization as a market phenomenon, but also with the pressures arising from a policy agenda that asymmetrically reflects preferences and vested interests.

INEQUALITY IN LATIN AMERICA: AN OVERVIEW

Income distribution in Latin America is the most unequal in the world. This is not a new phenomenon: at least since the 1960s Latin America has displayed the highest Gini coefficient in the world, followed closely by Sub-Saharan Africa (Table 8.1). In contrast to other regions, and despite the high levels of inequality recorded in the 1960s and 1970s, Latin America failed to improve equity indicators in the 1980s and 1990s. Most studies of Latin America confirm either that inequality has remained relatively stable in the last twenty years (Deininger and Squire 1996) or that it has increased slightly (Morley, 2001a; Londoño and Székely 1997). Considering that most Latin American countries experienced an economic recovery during the early 1990s following a decade of deep recession and structural adjustment, it is very surprising that inequality remained practically unchanged.[1] This result may be explained by the fact that while economic recessions worsen income distribution, economic recoveries may not improve it to an equivalent extent. Moreover, slow economic growth may be compatible with a worsening income distribution.

During the last two decades Latin America as a region did not experience a substantial change in income distribution, but individual countries did.[2] The resilience of income inequality in Latin America was apparent despite a significant increase in the Gini coefficient in Argentina and Venezuela, and an increase in Brazil and Mexico in the 1980s and stabilization thereafter (Morley 2001a). Uruguay, by contrast, showed a significant fall in inequality, followed by Peru, where equality improved during the last decade. Taking a longer-term horizon, in Chile there was a sharp worsening of income distribution in the 1970s and a further worsening in the 1980s. The situation improved somewhat between 1990 and 1997, with a moderate step-back as the Asian economic crisis spread. All in all, income distribution is currently somewhat better than in the 1980s, but significantly more regressive than in the 1960s (Ffrench-Davis 2002, chapter 9).

The cross-country disparities of the Gini coefficients imply significant differences in each income group's share in national income. Recent data indicate that by the end of the 1990s, the percentage of total income that accrued to the richest decile more than tripled the percentage of the poorest 40 per cent in Brazil, Bolivia, Colombia and Honduras[3] (CEPAL, 2002b). For Brazil that ratio was 4.6 times. At the other extreme, Uruguay and Costa Rica displayed ratios of 1.25 and 1.9, respectively (see Table 8.2).

Wage inequality is a major determinant of income inequality in Latin America. In other words, high inequality is not just a consequence of the gap that exists between labor and property income, but of income differences among workers as well. Wage differentials, in turn, are largely the result of an unequal distribution in the quantity and the quality of education[4] (Morley 2001a; Behrman et al. 2001), a feature particularly prominent in Latin America. According to the Inter-American Development Bank (IADB 1998), the second richest decile of the Latin American population has, on average, three years less of education than the richest decile. For the lowest 30 per cent this education gap rises to nearly seven years.

Despite the policy relevance of the subject, there is scant information on wage differentials according to education levels across Latin America. Some studies have attempted to harmonize the information collected by household surveys (e.g. Inter-American Development Bank, 1998). Morley (2001a) compared the average wage of white-collar workers (typically more educated) with those of blue-collar workers (typically less educated). As shown in Figure 8.1, the ratio between these two groups' incomes is higher in Latin America than in other regions of the world. Moreover, while this ratio contracted in the rest of the world after 1982, in Latin America it actually increased after 1988.

An alternative procedure for estimating wage differentials according to education is to run statistical regressions using education, gender, work experience and other relevant factors as independent variables and then use the resulting coefficients to calculate rates of return per level of education. Available evidence suggests that in Latin America the rate of return of post-

Table 8.2 Household Income Distribution, 1990–2000

| | | Share in total income of | | | |
| | | Poorest | Next | Next | Richest |
Country	Year	40%	30%	20%	10%
Argentina	1990	14.9	23.6	26.7	34.8
	1997	14.9	22.3	27.1	35.8
	1999	15.4	21.6	26.1	37.0
Bolivia	1989	12.1	22.0	27.9	38.2
	1997	9.4	22.0	27.9	40.7
	1999	9.2	24.0	29.6	37.2
Brazil	1990	9.5	18.6	28.0	43.9
	1996	9.9	17.7	26.5	46.0
	1999	10.1	17.3	25.5	47.1
Chile	1990	13.2	20.8	25.4	40.7
	1996	13.1	20.5	26.2	40.2
	2000	13.8	20.8	25.1	40.3
Colombia	1994	10.0	21.3	26.9	41.8
	1997	12.5	21.7	25.7	40.1
	1999	12.3	21.6	26.0	40.1
Costa Rica	1990	16.7	27.4	30.2	25.6
	1997	16.5	26.8	29.4	27.3
	1999	15.3	25.7	29.7	29.4
Ecuador	1990	17.1	25.4	27.0	30.5
	1997	17.0	24.7	26.4	31.9
	1999	14.1	22.8	26.5	36.6
	1999	13.1	23.0	27.8	36.2

Table 8.2 continued

Country	Year	Share in total income of			
		Poorest 40%	Next 30%	Next 20%	Richest 10%
Honduras	1990	10.1	19.7	27.0	43.1
	1997	12.6	22.5	27.3	37.7
	1999	11.8	22.9	28.9	36.5
Mexico	1989	15.8	22.5	25.1	36.6
	1994	15.3	22.9	26.1	35.6
	2000	14.6	22.5	26.5	36.4
Panama	1991	12.5	22.9	28.8	35.9
	1997	12.4	21.5	27.5	38.6
	1999	12.9	22.4	27.7	37.1
Paraguay	1990	18.6	25.7	26.9	28.9
	1996	16.7	24.6	25.3	33.4
	1999	13.1	23.0	27.8	36.2
Uruguay	1990	20.1	24.6	24.1	31.2
	1997	22.0	26.1	26.1	25.8
	1999	21.6	25.5	25.9	27.0
Venezuela	1990	16.7	25.7	28.9	28.7
	1997	14.7	24.0	28.6	32.8
	1999	14.6	25.1	29.0	31.4

Source: CEPAL (2002b).

Figure 8.1 Relative Wages: White Collar versus Blue Collar, 1982–97

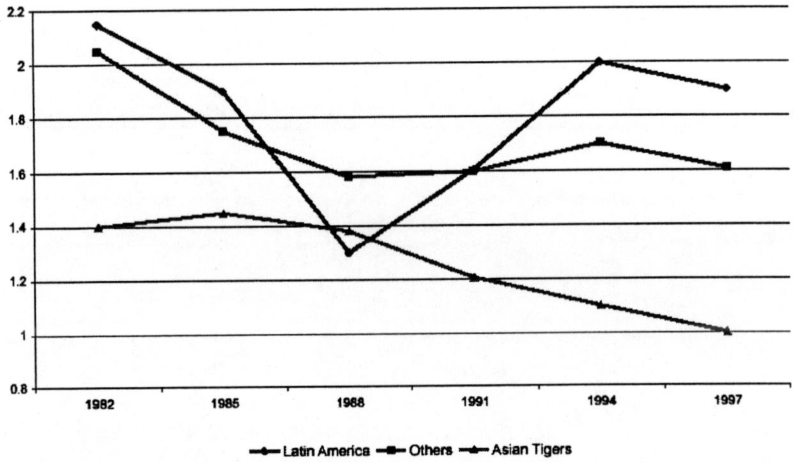

Source: Morley (2001a).

secondary education is very high (compared with Asia and other industrial regions) (Inter-American Development Bank, 1998) and that it increased further in the 1990s. Behrman et al. (2001), for example, estimated that the return of an additional year of study increased during the 1990s by nearly 7 per cent. When disaggregated by level of education, their estimates show that this income rise was almost entirely due to a significant increase in the marginal return of higher education. This means that the relative returns of primary and secondary education fell compared to those of higher education. Computing hourly wages for each educational category,[5] the gap between workers with post-secondary education and the rest increased notably during the 1990s (Berhmann et al. 2001). The gap between higher and primary education increased significantly during the early 1990s, but fell by nearly 13 per cent between 1994 and 1998.

It is not easy to account for the large and persistent income disparity by level of education that prevails in Latin America. These differences cannot be accounted for by the relative scarcity of university graduates, since Latin America has a larger share of university graduates than the typical Asian economy[6] (Morley 2001a). Moreover, since the 1970s the share of university graduates in the labor force has increased significantly in Latin America. One possible hypothesis is that the effects of globalization on the demand for qualifications in Latin America have helped to maintain large wage differentials.

Thus the causal links between globalization and equity are far from straightforward. Higher mobility of goods, factors of production and technology will affect relative prices and factor returns, thus influencing equity, but the direction of the effect is policy-dependent. The next two sections explore the 'micro' and 'macro' dimensions of the links between globalization and equity.

TRANSMISSION CHANNELS

As a market phenomenon globalization manifests itself in the increasing mobility of goods, services, technology and factors of production. In the last two decades international trade and FDI have increased much faster than real output (see Table 8.3). In effect, since 1983 annual output growth averaged 2.8 per cent (a slower pace than in previous decades), while merchandise trade rose by 5.7 per cent per year and FDI by a remarkable 16.2 per cent. The higher international mobility of output and factors of production (particularly capital) has affected the return rates of different factors of production. This section briefly reviews the major transmission channels as treated in the literature.

Mobility of Goods

According to neoclassical trade theory, summarized in the Heckscher–Ohlin and Stolper–Samuelson theorems, international trade can act as a substitute for factor mobility to equalize factor payments across multiple countries. With two factors of production (unskilled labor and capital or skilled labor), trade liberalization in developing countries (where unskilled labor is abundant) will raise the demand for that factor, as well as its price. Since the poor are owners of unskilled labor, trade liberalization should raise their welfare in absolute as well as in relative terms.

The opposite will take place in developed countries, where skilled labor or capital is abundant. In developed countries the owners of capital or skilled labor will see their price rise, while the income of unskilled labor will contract. Without trade barriers, factor prices will tend to converge in both regions. According to this simplified account, given two factors of production, globalization (understood as trade liberalization) will reduce income differentials in developing countries and widen them in the developed world. The implications are clear: trade liberalization in developing countries will bring not only higher efficiency, but also greater equality.

This scenario, however, rests on a number of assumptions that do not fully apply to Latin America. First, the model assumes only two factors of production and developing countries are taken to be a homogeneous group in which unskilled labor is unambiguously abundant. However, Leamer (1984) suggests that the most abundant factor in Latin America is not unskilled labor but natural resources such as arable land, minerals or oil. Data collected in a classic study on the factor content of foreign trade (Bowen et al. 1987) show a similar picture. Moreover, trade liberalization in Latin America was implemented at the same time that China and other large economies with abundant unskilled labor moved into the world economy.

The second critical assumption is the absence of factor-intensity reversal. However, factor-intensity reversals were detected long ago when comparing rice production in Asia and the United States (Arrow et al. 1961). If this is the case, even if unskilled labor is the abundant factor, it will be impossible to predict that trade liberalization will produce a higher demand for unskilled labor.[7]

And last, the statement that trade liberalization will reduce income differentials in unskilled labor-abundant countries requires technology change to be neutral. If technology change is biased against unskilled labor and, in addition, technological development takes place mainly in the developed world (where unskilled labor is scarce), the importation of technology embodied in capital goods may have unexpected effects.

In sum, the assumptions of classic trade theory may be inappropriate to make a prediction about the effects of trade liberalization on factor earnings and equity in many Latin American economies. If so, trade liberalization may not lead to an improvement in income distribution, but to the reverse. This may demand the implementation of mechanisms to cope with the undesired effects of trade liberalization on equity.

Indeed, according to Morley (2000) the prediction that trade reform will reduce wage differentials and lead to a more equitable distribution of income in Latin America did not materialize.[8] Two possible explanations for this result may be precisely that the region's comparative advantages do not lie in unskilled labor-intensive activities or that trade liberalization has favored the importation of capital-intensive or skills-intensive technologies (generally embodied in imported capital goods). Rama (2001) also claims that the 'China effect' may have contributed to a growing skills premium in Latin America. Many Southeast Asian and Asian economies have larger pools of cheap unskilled labor than does Latin America. Trade liberalization and Asian (particularly China's) fast integration into the world economy encouraged a massive importation of Asian products which may have lowered considerably the demand for unskilled labor in Latin America.

Table 8.3 Globalization: Stylized Facts, 1983–2001 (indices, 1983=100, and percentages)

| Year | World GDP | World trade(a) | | Real world FDI (b) | Mergers and acquisitions as % of world FDI |
		Total	Manu-facturing		
1983	100.0	100.0	100.0	100.0	n.a.
1985	108.3	110.8	116.1	116.6	n.a.
1990	128.3	147.4	160.9	337.4	74.4
1995	138.4	195.8	218.5	558.4	56.4
2001	163.4	270.3	310.6	1487.3	80.8
	Annual average growth (%)				Average (1987–2001)
	2.8	5.7	6.5	16.2	62.5

Notes:

a. Merchandise export volume.

b. Based on inflows, deflated by unit price of world imports, published by the IMF.

n.a.: not available.

Source: Trade and world GDP from WTO; FDI figures from UNCTAD.

But Morley's findings about the effects of trade reform on wage differentials are not consensual. Behrman et al. (2001) collected data on wage differentials for eighteen Latin American countries over the last two decades.[9] Based on this information they performed panel cross-section regressions using structural reform indexes as explanatory variables [this chapter and Morley (2000) use the structural reform indexes developed in Inter-American Development Bank (1997)].[10] In contrast to Morley (2000), these authors found no reliable relationship between trade liberalization and wage differentials.[11] Rather, their regressions suggest that trade reform slightly reduced incomes inequality, albeit with a lag.[12] However, they stop short of attributing their results to trade liberalization per se, as the latter may open the door to multiple forces with counterbalancing effects.[13] Using national data, Acosta and Rojas (2002) found that trade liberalization accounted for only a minor fraction of the increase in Mexico's skills premium (decreasing through time), and even a smaller share in Argentina.[14] In the case of Argentina, the increase in the skills premium induced by trade reform may have been a result of the factor content of imports (intensive in unskilled labor), the relative abundance of skilled labor as compared to its regional trade partners (that gained preferential market access through Mercosur) and/or a contraction in the share of manufacturing in total output experienced during the 1990s (traditionally, important low-tech manufacturing – such as textiles, food and tobacco – employed a relatively high share of unskilled labor).[15]

Apart from the effects on the skills premium, trade liberalization has had significant effects on employment. Dismantling the protectionist policies that prevailed during most of the import-substitution period produced significant job losses across Latin America. Although the reforms also created new jobs, they were not ready substitutes for the lost jobs. In effect, while old jobs were destroyed very fast, the new jobs took longer to emerge. Mexico, the Latin American country that went probably the farthest in the process of globalization, illustrates this case. According to Rama (2001), a 20 per cent cut in Mexico's average tariffs reduced wages by an estimated 5 per cent. Industrial restructuring also shifted workers previously employed in non-competitive industries towards the low productivity rural sector or the informal labor market. Although industrial restructuring led to the creation of new job places in export-oriented activities (such as the *maquiladora* industry), they may have lower wages and less job security than lost jobs. If job security matters, the new jobs may result in a welfare loss (Ferranti et al. 2000). Of course, the alternative to these new jobs may be unemployment, the informal labor market or poverty.[16] On the whole, this outcome may have been aggravated by the macroeconomic context and the specific content of the reforms implemented, which may have encouraged faster net import de-substitution as opposed to a net increase in exports (Ffrench-Davis 2000, chapters 1–3).

Factor Mobility

If factors of production can move freely, they will leave locations where they are poorly paid in favor of those in which they are highly paid. Consequently, the outflow of unskilled labor from unskilled labor-abundant countries will raise its price in the latter and lower it in skilled labor or capital-abundant countries. Skilled labor or capital will flow in the opposite direction, raising skilled labor or capital incomes in developed countries and lowering them in the developing world.[17] As a result, income inequality will rise in developed countries and fall in developing countries (Culpeper 2002).

However, one of the major features of the current phase of globalization is the asymmetry between the high mobility of capital and the widespread restrictions on labor mobility. Indeed, it is somewhat paradoxical that the widespread political consensus about the benefits of the free movement of goods, services and capital does not extend into the free movement of persons

(Solimano 2001a; Martínez 2000). As Rodrik (1997) points out, this gives rise to asymmetries in income distribution that hurt the less mobile factors (especially unskilled labor). The lower mobility of unskilled labor also contributes to an excess supply of unskilled labor-intensive products (where developing countries have comparative advantages), lowering their price in the world marketplace (CEPAL 2002a). Most importantly, restrictions on unskilled labor mobility reduce world output, since they inhibit labor from moving from low to high productivity regions.

In contrast, skilled labor has much higher mobility. The 'brain drain' towards developed countries may create an additional burden on developing countries. This burden tends to increase after a major macroeconomic crisis, as human capital flees in search of more stable environments. This trend may worsen the long-term growth potential of developing countries, particularly the poorer ones (Solimano, 2001b).

The high mobility of physical capital also changes the relative productivity of skilled and unskilled labor, altering the wage structure. In particular, the facts that capital and skilled labor are often complementary and that incorporated technical change has a pro-skilled labor bias mean that there may be positive correlations between mobility, the incorporation of productive capital and the skills premium. (Acosta and Gasparini 2002)

The naïve view that factor mobility will reduce income inequality in developing countries must also be qualified by other real-world facts. In many Latin American countries trade and capital-account liberalization coincided with periods of euphoria in international capital markets. As a result, trade liberalization was accompanied by a significant real appreciation of the domestic currency (CEPAL 1998; Ffrench-Davis 2000). A currency appreciation will reduce the incentives of trade liberalization to shift resources from non-exportables to exportable-producing sectors, moderating the effects of freer trade on factor prices, reducing the rate of factor utilization and discouraging net employment in the production of tradables. Yet, the most negative effects of higher capital mobility may not be a result of their level, but of their volatility – an issue addressed in more detail in the next section.

As opposed to his findings on trade reform, Morley (2000) found that capital-account liberalization had progressive effects on income distribution. His results suggest that when barriers to capital inflows are dismantled, new capital inflows reduce profits and raise labor demand.[18] By contrast, according to Berhman et al. (2001) capital-account liberalization had regressive effects on income distribution, although they contracted sharply across time. This result is consistent with the findings of Rama (2001), for whom the effects of capital inflows on the skills premium (and particularly FDI) were positive and stronger than those of trade liberalization.[19] These findings are consistent with the previous work of Feenstra and Hanson (1997) based on microeconomic data for the Mexican *maquiladora* industry. Acosta and Gasparini (2002) offer evidence supporting the hypothesis that capital and skilled labor are complements in the case of Argentina. Using disaggregated data, they show that the skills premium for workers with higher education increased in those sectors where the incorporation of physical capital was more intense.[20]

Moreover, a more detailed assessment of the impact of capital flows on income distribution would need to distinguish among flows of greenfield FDI, mergers and acquisitions and financial flows. These effects would also be very dependent on the macroeconomic environment in which these flows would take place. Titelman and Uthoff (1998) show that capital surges have tended to crowd out domestic savings and to weaken macroeconomic sustainability. On the contrary, flows that are both more stable and more directly linked to capital formation can crowd in domestic savings and enhance capital formation and macroeconomic sustainability. Since economic cycles have asymmetric effects on employment and earnings, capital surges may end up worsening equity. The composition of capital inflows can also be traced to the kind of domestic policies implemented, particularly concerning capital-account liberalization *vis-à-vis* prudent macroeconomic regulation of capital flows (Ffrench-Davis 2002, chapters 9–10).

Movements of Technology

The effects of technical change on income distribution depend on how new technologies affect the use of factors of production. Unskilled labor-intensive technologies will increase the demand for unskilled labor and thus raise its income. Capital-intensive or skilled labor-intensive technologies will do the same with the demand for capital and skilled labor and raise their returns. Consequently, the effects of technical change on equality will depend on the bias of a specific technology. Most of the literature on technical change in the developed world agrees that during the last decades wages and the rate of return to education have been consistent with skills-biased technical change. Technological innovations such as computers and telecommunications tend to raise the productivity of the best trained and most flexible workers. Consequently, in periods of rapid technical change – such as the last two decades – the education premium should be expected to increase (Acemoglu 2002).[21]

Trade and investment liberalization in Latin America fostered significant, albeit heterogeneous, technological modernization. Although the relative abundance of unskilled labor in Latin America (as compared to industrial countries) should favor the adoption of unskilled labor-intensive technologies, the limited resources channeled to indigenous research and development means that technology is mostly imported embodied in new capital goods. The concentration of technical progress in developed countries is one of the most important sources of international asymmetries (CEPAL 2002a). In effect, quite apart from the inadequacy of technical progress to developing countries' factor endowments and its effects on equity, the limited development of technical progress in Latin America can act as a constraint on development (technical progress being a major factor behind economic growth). Unlike Southeast Asia, few technology-related activities have located in Latin America, except for some *maquila* activities in northern Mexico. Although the spread of new information technologies has broadened the sources of freely available information, stricter protection of intellectual property rights has slowed down the rate of technology transfer and led to higher innovation rents. This is likely to have had regressive international distributive effects.

Trade liberalization in Latin America sharply reduced the relative price of capital goods, stimulating imports and the incorporation of new technologies embodied in production equipment. This fact, combined with sizable FDI inflows towards the region, stimulated technological modernization.[22] However, this technical changes has been biased towards skilled labor, a fact which partly accounts for the increase in the skills premium (Cornia 1999).

The results of Berhman et al. (2001) suggest that for those Latin American countries engaged in trade and structural reform during the last two decades, technical progress rather than trade accounted for most of the increase in the skills premium. However, it is hard to differentiate these effects because much of the technical progress is transmitted through trade, as it is embodied in high-technology capital and intermediate goods. For Acosta and Rojas (2002) technical change was the main element responsible for the increase in the skills premium in Argentina, a result consistent with the previous work by Bebczuk and Gasparini (2001).[23] Acosta and Rojas (2002) report similar effects in Mexico. In summary, since trade liberalization has been a potent stimulus for upgrading technology, trade reform may have had significant indirect effects.

THE MACROECONOMIC DIMENSION

Globalization also has macroeconomic dimensions that deeply affect how transmission channels operate and are closely dependent on policy choice. These dimensions include: the links between globalization, trade and growth, volatility and discretion in national economic policymaking.

Globalization, Trade and Growth

The links between globalization and equity must take into consideration the issue of economic growth. The conventional view holds that the rationale for globalization (and for policies which foster liberalization and structural reform) rests on its positive effects on economic efficiency and growth. Although this view is deeply rooted in academic and policy circles, there is enough evidence to challenge the strength of the relationship as well as the implied causal links (Rodrik 1999; Rodríguez and Rodrik 2001). Moreover, even if a strong causal relationship between openness and growth were established, the issue of whether economic growth is neutral in terms of income distribution would remain open.[24] It is also important to take account of the often neglected effects of liberalization and globalization during the transitional phase. In effect, even accepting the existence of long-term beneficial consequences in terms of efficiency and growth, attention needs to be paid to transition costs and how these will affect the final outcome. The optimists maintain that any negative effects can be counterbalanced by social policies and will be eventually more than compensated by faster economic growth. Skeptics, by contrast, emphasize that it may be difficult to effectively address transition costs in a context characterized by fragile and underdeveloped institutions. They also point out that these negative trends may give rise to negative, path-dependent outcomes.

Since the 1990s, the foreign trade of Latin American countries has grown rather vigorously, both exports and imports. In fact, the rate of growth of export volume has averaged 7.4 per cent, slightly higher than that of world trade. Yet this has not translated into faster economic growth. That the exports-to-gross domestic product (GDP) ratio accounted for scarcely one-fifth of GDP may help to account for the fact that relatively rapid export growth between 1990 and 2002 coexisted with a meager growth of GDP of 2.4 per cent per year (see Table 8.4).[25]

Comparative research in Latin America has shown four intertwined policy features which can make a significant difference for the growth and equity outcome of globalization and liberalization. The first issue is whether trade liberalization is led by import liberalization or export promotion. Agosin and Ffrench-Davis (1993) show that, depending on the nature of the trade reform process, the effects of liberalization on growth and employment can differ markedly. The second issue concerns the behavior of the capital account and the exchange rate during trade liberalization. A liberalization process undertaken simultaneously with complete capital-account liberalization – particularly if this is done under abundant international liquidity – will lead to a real appreciation of the domestic currency which will stimulate underinvestment in the production of tradables. This will have negative long-run effects on the sustainability of the liberalization drive and will jeopardize outward orientation. The third issue is the macroeconomic environment which prevails abroad and domestically during the process of trade liberalization. In effect, a vigorous external environment characterized by fast import growth in major trade partners will imply faster and easier export growth. Similarly, a domestic macroeconomic environment characterized by an economy working along the production frontier (at full employment) will make it easier to reallocate factors from import substitution towards the rest of the economy. Finally, the effects of trade liberalization can be quite different depending on the extent and coherence of complementary policies geared to complete markets, particularly long-term capital, technology diffusion, management practices and labor training (CEPAL 1998; Ffrench-Davis 2000, chapters 2, 3, 6 and 10).

Imported Volatility

Closer integration into the world economy offers new opportunities for developing countries, but also new challenges and risks. The Latin American countries have been traditionally subject to large shocks stemming from terms-of-trade fluctuations. These shocks have been amplified by the heavy dependence of export earnings on a limited number of natural resource-intensive products. This long-standing feature did not change in the 1990s, although Mexico and some Central American states succeeded in diversifying their exports towards manufactured products.[26] For the rest, however, commodities continue to account for the bulk of export earnings.

Deeper integration into the world economy should facilitate risk diversification and ease adjustment to external shocks. In theory, developing countries should be able to diversify their terms-of-trade risks by hedging in international financial markets. In practice, however, domestic and foreign financial markets are not deep enough. They usually operate with such short-term horizons that they cannot protect domestic economies from the longer cycles which prevail in goods and financial markets. Moreover, capital flows tend to parallel trade shocks, amplifying the fluctuations of the international business cycle. Consequently, shifts in capital flows have compounded the traditional sources of imported volatility.

In an inter-linked world economy, any adverse global, regional or local shock propagates rapidly to other economies. Such 'contagion' can be transmitted through either a decline of import volumes and/or changes in commodity prices. But influences can be also channeled through asset markets. Portfolio shifts can affect the exchange rate, interest rates and economic activity levels. This external source of financial volatility was largely absent in the 1950s, 1960s and early 1970s, when multilateral lending, foreign aid and FDI dominated global capital movements (Solimano 1999).

The volatility of capital flows and domestic policies is higher in Latin America than in the industrial world or even other developing regions, such as the East Asian tigers (Ferranti et al. 2000).[27] The Latin American experience during the 1990s shows that in periods of financial euphoria, domestic credit and liquidity expands too much. Similarly, during 'dry seasons' liquidity contracts too sharply. These powerful financial amplifiers lead to sharper expansions, but also to deeper busts. Volatile financial flows, coupled with unstable growth rates, have negatively affected incentives to invest and damaged the long-run growth potential.

Figures 8.2 and 8.3 show the marked instability of net transfers between Latin America and the rest of the world during the last quarter of a century, and the huge fluctuations of economic activity levels in the region. The overall evolution of GDP in Latin America in recent decades has been systematically anticipated by changes in aggregate demand. Comparing Figures 8.2 and 8.3 reveals that changes in aggregate demand have been closely associated with changes in net foreign transfers.

The economic impact of international disturbances is magnified by Latin America's thin domestic financial markets, which lag very far behind the rest of the world. Despite recent progress towards developing new international financial instruments (such as contingent credit lines, which were of little help for Argentina), world financial markets still offer limited opportunities for risk diversification and insurance against global disturbances. The combination of shallow domestic financial markets, high volatility of international capital flows and a deficient international financial architecture has led to a growing (but still far from unanimous) consensus that full capital-account convertibility may not be an optimal policy.[28] Critics of unrestricted integration into world capital markets underline the desirability of counting on instruments for prudential regulation of international capital flows, whether direct (such as mandatory reserves, taxes on foreign capital or quantitative limits to FDI) or indirect (such as tax regulations). The regulatory regimes adopted by Chile (Agosin and Ffrench-Davis 2001; Ffrench-Davis 2002) and Colombia (Ocampo 2003) in the 1990s are good examples of the suggested practices.

Volatility imported by globalization may have negative effects on equity if the performance of income distribution throughout the business cycle is not symmetrical. In effect, if there are lagged effects, the worsening of income distribution during economic downturns may not be fully compensated by subsequent upswings.

Table 8.4 Latin America (19 countries): GDP Growth, 1990–2002 (annual percentages)

Year	Total GDP	Exported GDP	Non-exported GDP
1990–94	2.9	6.4	2.4
1995–97	3.3	10.9	2.0
1998–2002	1.2	6.3	0.1
1990–2002	2.4	7.4	1.5

Source: Authors' calculations based on official data, provided by ECLAC. Preliminary data for 2002.

Loss of Discretion in Macroeconomic Policymaking

One explanation for the evolution of inequality in the last two decades is that globalization has limited the power of governments to follow certain policies. Undoubtedly globalization, and especially the ability to move money rapidly from one place to the other, has limited policy discretion for governments and has taken certain policy issues, such as land reform or expropriations of any kind, virtually off the agenda. The constraints posed by globalization have led to a shared consensus that sustainability of 'populist' policies becomes much more fragile in a more integrated world. Some authors and policymakers would go one step further and argue that governments are no longer able to implement the kind of redistributive and compensatory policies that may be desirable to reduce inequality. However, despite the growing influence of these views, reduction in policy discretion has been uneven across countries and has varied according to circumstances. Based on an analysis of Organization for Economic Co-operation and Development (OECD) economies, Garrett (1999) showed that the loss of policy discretion has been far from homogeneous. He also found no evidence of a 'generalized race towards the bottom' as predicted by the proponents of globalization as an all-encompassing process. This does not invalidate the view, however, that developing countries are now more vulnerable to volatile flows as well as to changes in expectations and market sentiment than in the past.

Some loss of policy discretion may not be necessarily a bad thing. According to Solimano (1999) and Rodrik (1999), the constraints on domestic policies posed by some international agreements (such as the World Trade Organization) may help developing countries by boosting the credibility and

Figure 8.2 Latin America: Net Foreign Transfers, 1970–2002 (% of GDP)

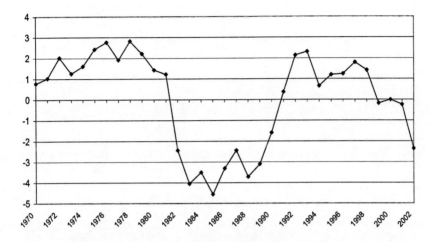

Source: ECLAC. Net foreign transfers are equal to net capital inflows minus net factor payments (interest plus profit remittances).

sustainability of their own domestic policies and by reducing the scope for rent-seeking practices. Examples of these are prudent regulation of financial markets, limits to budget deficits, efforts at tax harmonization and compliance with basic labor rights. However, whether these constraints will exert positive or negative influences on performance will ultimately depend on the nature of the constraints and the incentives associated with them. There is nothing intrinsically good or bad in reducing or increasing policy discretion. What matters is the way in which policy discretion is exercised or the kind of constraints that the outer world imposes on local authorities. As argued above, opening the capital account may actually lead emerging economies to import external financial instability, with capital inflows worsening macroeconomic fundamentals, rather than to higher investment rates. Similarly, international market discipline may not be an efficient check on domestic sources of instability, given the whims of opinion and expectations characteristic of financial markets. Financial markets may inaccurately perceive some domestic policies as inadequate and, even more importantly, may actually induce key variables (such as the exchange rate) to deviate from sustainable levels for relatively long periods of time. In such circumstances, market sentiment may (and will) generate incentives for emerging economies to enter a 'vulnerability zone' during the booms.

Figure 8.3 Latin America (20 countries): GDP and Aggregate Demand, 1990–2001 (annual growth rates, %)

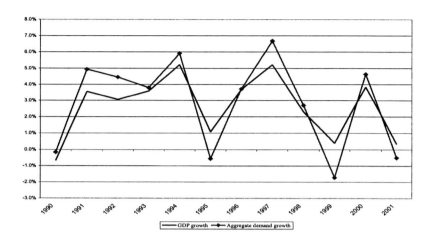

Source: ECLAC, based on official figures in constant 1995 dollars.

Globalization limits the capacity of using economic policy as a counter-cyclical instrument geared to maintaining full employment. To the extent that the loss of discretion to use monetary, exchange rate and fiscal policies either to absorb external shocks – financial or real – or to smooth the business cycle is genuine, a larger share of the adjustment burden will fall on real output and the labor market. Since nominal wages are not fully flexible, the adjustment process will eventually affect output and employment levels (CEPAL 2002a; Ocampo 2003; Rama 2001). However, the extent of this loss of policy discretion may have been exaggerated, as revealed by the performance of some Latin American countries in the last decade. The idea that governments cannot use capital controls to restrict the inflow or outflow of all or certain types of capital, thus leaving the domestic economy vulnerable to the ebbs and flows of international capital markets, may hold some truth (particularly at times of crisis), but less than what is often believed. The Chilean experience with controls on portfolio-capital inflows illustrates the fact that there is scope to adopt compensatory policies in the context of a market-oriented policy framework (Ffrench-Davis 2002; Williamson 2000). Indeed, the loss of policy discretion may derive more from the fact that policymakers lacking intellectual independence or credibility may want to please 'market sentiment', rather than from some irreversible trend.

It is generally accepted that international financial markets are sensitive to the fiscal policy stance of individual countries, particularly at times of crisis. Such fiscal stance can also be taken as an indicator of how 'responsible' the government is in managing its macroeconomy (Solimano 1999). This may encourage governments to implement pro-cyclical fiscal policies, cutting government spending or raising taxes in economic downturns, thus amplifying an economic slowdown or recession (with the ensuing loss in employment and real incomes).

One related issue, troubling for democratic governance, is the growing duality in the constituencies that policymakers must take into consideration. The increasing complexity and globalization of the world economy has widened the gap between policymakers and financial agents, on one side, and those who bear the consequences (workers and firms) of their actions. At least in some Latin American countries, an excessive concentration on financial-market preferences has had a major influence on the evolution of the countries' macroeconomy and productive systems.

Capital-market integration has remarkable implications for domestic policies and constituencies. Most leaders in emerging countries are experiencing a 'dual constituency syndrome' (Pietrobelli and Zamagni 2000): although they are elected by their countries' voters, they must also seek the support of those who 'vote' through the financial markets. Recent financial cycles have revealed significant contradictions between the two roles, in what has become a negative-sum game. A more positive outcome may require policies which actively foster consistency between the level and composition of financial flows and the sustainability of key macroeconomic indicators.

CONCLUSION

We still know relatively little about the linkages between globalization and economic reform and welfare and equity. There are no obvious or universal conclusions that can be offered as ready-to-use policy recipes. Thus it may be wiser to adopt a more balanced and careful approach than the one that prevailed in academic and policy circles for most of the last two decades. The Latin American experience offers several generalizations.

The effect of globalization and structural reforms on equity remains a hotly debated issue. Empirical works frequently reach opposite conclusions. For example, while trade liberalization had regressive effects for Morley (2000), Berhman et al. (2001) did not find a significant relationship between the two phenomena. There is no consensus on the factors that explain the increase in the skills premium in Latin America, a fact that contradicts the predictions of conventional theory. Several hypotheses have been offered, such as the 'China effect' or the fact that unskilled labor was heavily protected prior to the reforms. More recently, however, a growing consensus has emerged about the potential role of biased technical change.

One topic that needs more research is the role of domestic policies and institutions in transmitting the effects of globalization. Based on a large sample of developing countries, Rama (2001) concluded that globalization can have negative or positive effects on income distribution, depending on variables such as the level of public sector spending or investment in education. There is also little knowledge about the effects of globalization on phenomena such as the incomes gap produced by differences in gender or the use of child labor, factors than can significantly affect large sections of the population. In this case, the causal links are more tenuous, since child labor and production for self-sufficiency are not directly related to globalization (except for forms of sexual tourism)

The distinction between the market and policy components of globalization does not always come out clearly in the policy debate. This creates a grey area in which policy prescriptions are presented as optimal responses to market constraints, although they are in reality a result of preferences and vested interests. The search for simplified policy recipes, instead of a more transparent and more pluralistic policy debate, may have been a significant factor behind the disappointing economic and equity performance of Latin America since the 1990s.

It is beyond dispute that globalization restricts the range of policy choices at the disposal of policymakers. However, not all countries are affected in the same way and with the same intensity. Consequently, rather than making general statements about the policy constraints imposed by globalization, a more careful analysis of the factors that shape national differences can help to identify policies and institutions that may increase the resilience of developing countries to negative external shocks and enhance the room for indigenous policy choice.

There is a need to know more about how to cope with the problem of the 'globalization of financial volatility' and macro sustainability. More research and understanding on the need and the direction of international financial institutional reform is required. More and better knowledge is also required on how to make sure that developing countries have enough room to make responsible but active counter-cyclical monetary, fiscal, exchange-rate and capital-account policies. Finally, more research would be welcome on the critical issues of how to compensate for or deal with the negative effects of pro-market reforms and globalization, whenever these negative effects (transitional or otherwise) are proved to exist.

NOTES

The authors wish to thank Emiliano Pagnotta for his able research assistance. We would also like to acknowledge the insightful comments made by Gary McMahon, Nancy Birdsall, John Williamson and anonymous referees. Any remaining errors of fact or interpretation are our own responsibility.

1. The frustration regarding the reduction of inequality extends into poverty reduction. According to CEPAL (2003), in 2002, there were 220 million Latin Americans living in poverty, accounting for 43 per cent of the population.
2. Despite different national performances, by the late 1990s virtually all the large economies of the region displayed Gini coefficients higher or close to 50 per cent, among the highest in the world. Only in Uruguay and Costa Rica was inequality comparable to that of developed countries.
3. The first decile is critical to characterize income distribution inequality in Latin America. If the first decile is excluded, the Gini coefficient for most Latin American countries is not substantially different from that of the United States (Birdsall 2002).
4. Apart from education, the literature typically takes into account factors such as gender, labor market fragmentation between formal and informal employment and rural and urban employment.
5. The data refers to male workers 30–55 years old and employed in urban regions.
6. This is not the case with secondary education. No Latin American country has a higher rate of secondary school graduates than Korea, Malaysia or Taiwan. According to Morley (2001b), the contrasting educational strategies pursued by the countries of the two regions since the 1970s – the extension of secondary education in Asia and the increase in the coverage of higher education in Latin America (even at the expense of a high rate of drop-outs in secondary and tertiary education) help to account for the different performance of inequality. Educational strategies affect the distribution of one of the scarce factors in most developing countries (i.e., human capital). Although educational strategies can help to account for the distribution of the costs and benefits of deeper integration into the world economy, an examination of this interesting connection goes beyond the scope of this chapter, which is more focused on the impact of globalization and economic reform policies on equity.
7. There is evidence, for example, that while agriculture (more specifically corn production) is labor-intensive in Mexico, it is capital-intensive in the United States. Moreover, in a two-good, two-factor model, if the autarky relative price of corn, say in Mexico, is higher than the free trade price, trade liberalization will lead to a lower demand of unskilled labor at initial factor prices. This may help to account for the fact that Mexico has been so cautious regarding the liberalization of agriculture.
8. This standard prediction was based on the assumption that Latin America had comparative advantages in unskilled labor-intensive products and/or neutral technology. Indeed, the record of Southeast Asian countries during the 1960s and 1970s supported the view that deeper

integration into the world economy would reduce wage differentials between skilled and unskilled labor in the developing world as a whole (Wood 1997).

9. The sample used by the authors includes urban male workers aged 30–55. This groups accounts for approximately one-fifth of the total employed population.

10. The proposed trade-reform index is based on a simple average of average tariff rates and average dispersion. One shortcoming of this indicator is that it does not take into account the incidence of non-tariff measures. However, in contrast to other usual indicators (such as the export plus import to GDP ratio) it refers exclusively to policies and it is not contaminated by the agents' response to those policies.

11. This work focuses on wage differentials, not on income distribution or per-capita income. As Morley (2001b) points out, these three variables may not move in the same direction due to structural changes in the supply of labor, the effect of transfer payments or unemployment.

12. Galiani and Sanguinetti (2003) studied the relationship between wage differentials and trade opening up in urban Buenos Aires between 1992 and 1999. Their results suggest that the gap between workers with complete superior education and the rest widened most markedly in those sectors in which import penetration was higher.

13. When interpreting these results, readers should recall that their authors use different dependent variables. Morley (2000), for example, uses the Gini coefficient. Behrman et al. (2001), in turn, use wage differentials for different groups of individuals, controlling for age and educational level. Although these variables are closely linked to inequality, they do not measure the same concept. These methodological differences suggest that the results must be interpreted with care. In particular, differences in the estimated sign for some specific reform variables should not be automatically interpreted as contradictory.

14. To assess the effect of trade liberalization on the education premium, Acosta and Rojas (2002) regress workers' wages (in log form) against, among other factors, age and educational levels (personal characteristics), as well as the interaction between the skills level and the relative importance of exports and imports for each sector.

15. Beckzuk and Gasparini (2001) argue that in the case of Argentina, 'The fall of industry during the whole period [1980–98] seems to be the main determinant of the collapse of the demand for individuals with high school degree or less'.

16. In the case of Mexico the sizable impact of the 1994 'tequila' crisis shows in the fact that average wages fell by 15 per cent.

17. This prediction neglects the impact of agglomeration effects.

18. An alternative interpretation may be that capital-account liberalization was implemented during a period of abundant international liquidity and after Latin America had suffered many years of a binding external constraint. Consequently, inflows appear associated to the economic recovery that effectively took place in 1990–97.

19. This result is verified not only in Latin America, but also in other developing regions.

20. Acosta and Gasparini (2002) estimate a series of models in which workers' hourly wages (in log form) depend, among other factors, on variables capturing the relationship between their educational level and the incorporation of machinery and equipment (as a share of

value added) in their sectors of activity. They cover 1992–99 and use information for twenty Argentine urban conglomerates.

21. Since the education premium makes investment in human capital more attractive, the supply of this type of labor should increase over the longer term. Thus, in the long term the effects of technology change could even be progressive (Morley 2001b), by inducing socially desirable investments in education and fostering a rise in productivity and average wages.

22. The positive contribution of technical change was not reflected in vigorous GDP growth because capital formation remained depressed and domestic demand unstable.

23. Beckzuk and Gasparini (2001) estimate that more than two-thirds of the increase in the skills premium is accounted for by technical change, while only 15 per cent can be attributed to the effects of trade liberalization.

24. The neutrality of economic growth in terms of income distribution has given rise to a lengthy literature. See, for example, Aghion and Howitt (1998); Forbes (2000) and Bertola (2000).

25. For an analysis of the effects of trade reforms on trade performance, see Bouzas and Keifman (2003).

26. In 1999 manufactures accounted for 84 per cent of total Mexican exports, as compared to just 27 per cent one decade earlier. In the case of the Central American Common Market, the share of manufactures in total exports increased from 39 to 54 per cent over the same period.

27. In the years preceding their crises, East Asian nations became 'Latin-Americanized', in the sense of allowing increased external deficits, mounting outstanding debt and currency and maturity mismatches, thus entering vulnerability zones (Ffrench-Davis and Ocampo, 2001).

28. See, among others, Ffrench-Davis (2000); Ocampo (2003); Palma (2002) and Solimano (1999).

REFERENCES

Acemoglu, Daron (2002), 'Technical change, inequality and the labor market', *Journal of Economic Literature*, **40** (1), 7–72.

Acosta, Pablo and Leonardo Gasparini (2002), 'Incorporación de capital y brecha salarial: una nota sobre la industria manufacturera en la Argentina de los noventa', [Incorporation of capital and the wage gap: a note on the manufacturing industry of Argentina in the 1990s], *Anales de la AAEP* (26 August).

Acosta, Pablo and Gabriel Rojas (2002), 'Trade reform, technological change and inequality: the case of Mexico and Argentina in the 1990s', Department of Economics, University of San Andrés, www.udesa.edu.ar/departamentos/economia/seminarios/2002/montes_rojas.pdf.

Aghion, Philippe and Peter Howitt (1998), *Endogenous Growth Theory*, Cambridge, MA: MIT Press.

Agosin, Manuel and Ricardo Ffrench-Davis (1993), 'Trade liberalization in Latin America', *CEPAL Review*, 50 (August), 41–62.

Agosin, Manuel and Ricardo Ffrench-Davis (2001), 'Managing Capital Inflows in Chile', in Stephany Griffith-Jones, Manuel F. Montes and Anwar Nasution (eds), *Short-term Capital Flows and Economic Crises,* London: Oxford University Press, ch. 9.

Arrow, Kenneth J., Hollis B. Chenery, Bagicha Singh Minhas and Robert M. Solow (1961), 'Capital-labor substitution and economic efficiency', *Review of Economics and Statistics*, **43**, 225–50.

Bebczuk, Ricardo and Leonardo Gasparini (2001), 'Globalization and inequality: the case of Argentina', Department of Economics, Universidad Nacional de La Plata, www.depeco.econo.unlp.edu.ar/public02.htm (July).

Behrman Jere R., Nancy Birdsall and Miguel Székely (2001), 'Economic Reform and Wage Differentials in Latin America', Washington, DC, Inter-American Development Bank Working Paper No. 435.

Bertola, Giuseppe (2000), 'Macroeconomics of distribution and growth', in Anthony B. Atkinson and François Bourguignon (eds), *Handbook of Income Distribution*, Amsterdam and New York: Elsevier Science, pp. 477–540.

Birdsall, Nancy (2002), 'From Social Policy to an Open-Economy Social Contract in Latin America', Paper presented at the Brazilian National Bank for Economic and Social Development 50th anniversary conference, Rio de Janeiro.

Bouzas, Roberto and Saúl Keifman (2003), 'Making Trade Liberalization Work', in Pedro-Pablo Kuczynski and John Williamson (eds), *After the Washington Consensus: Restarting Growth and Reform in Latin America,* Washington, DC: Institute for International Economics, pp. 157–79.

Bouzas, Roberto and Ricardo Ffrench-Davis (1998), 'La globalización y la gobernabilidad de los países en desarrollo' [Globalization and governability in Developing Countries], *CEPAL Review*, special issue (October), 125–37.

Bowen, Harry, Edward Leamer and Leo Sveikauskas (1987), 'Multicountry, multifactor tests of the factor abundance theory', *American Economic Review*, **77** (5). 791–809.

CEPAL (1998), *Políticas para mejorar la inserción en la economía mundial* [Policies to Improve Linkages with the Global Economy] 2nd edn., Santiago, Chile: Fondo de Cultura Económica.

CEPAL (2002a), *Globalization and Development*, Santiago, Chile.

CEPAL (2002b), *Panorama Social de América Latina y el Caribe 2001–2002*, Santiago, Chile.

CEPAL (2003), *Panorama Social de América Latina y el Caribe 2002–2003*, Santiago, Chile.

Cornia, Giovanni A. (1999), 'Liberalization, Globalization and Income Distribution', Helsinki, United Nations University, World Institute for Development Economics Research (WIDER) Working Paper No. 157.

Culpeper, Roy (2002), 'Approaches to Globalization and Inequality within the International System', www.nsi-ins.ca/ensi/publications/policy_briefs.html.

Deininger, Klaus and Lyn Squire (1996) 'A new data set measuring income inequality', *World Bank Economic Review*, **10** (3), 565–91.

Feenstra, Robert C. and Gordon H. Hanson (1997), 'Foreign direct investment and relative wages: evidence from Mexico's maquiladoras', *Journal of International Economics*, **42**, 371–94.

Ffrench-Davis, Ricardo (2000), *Reforming the Reforms in Latin America: Macroeconomics, Trade, Finance*, London: Macmillan/Palgrave and New York: St. Martin's Press.

Ffrench-Davis, Ricardo (2002), *Economic Reforms in Chile: from Dictatorship to Democracy*, Ann Arbor, MI: University of Michigan Press.

Ffrench-Davis, Ricardo and José Antonio Ocampo (2001), 'The Globalization of Financial Volatility', in Ricardo Ffrench-Davis (ed.), *Financial Crises in 'Successful' Emerging Economies*, Washington, DC: Brookings Institution.

de Ferranti David, Guillermo E. Perry, Indermit S. Gill and Luis Serven (2000), *Securing our Future in a Global Economy*, Washington, DC: World Bank.

Forbes, Kristin J. (2000), 'A reassessment of the relationship between inequality and growth', *American Economic Review*, **90** (4), 869–87.

Galiani, Sebastián and Pablo Sanguinetti (2003), 'The impact of trade liberalization on wage inequality: evidence from Argentina', *Journal of Development Economics*, **72** (2), 497–513.

Garrett, Geoffrey (1999), 'Mercados globales y política nacional: ¿colisión inevitable o círculo virtuoso?' *Desarrollo Económico*, **38** (152), 883–924.

Inter-American Development Bank (1997), *Latin America After a Decade of Reforms: Economic and Social Progress*, Baltimore, MD: Johns Hopkins University Press.

Inter-American Development Bank (1998), *Facing up to Inequality in Latin America: Economic and Social Progress in Latin America 1998–99*, Baltimore, MD: Johns Hopkins University Press.

Lawrence, Robert Z., Albert Bressand and Takatoshi Ito (1996), *A Vision for the World Economy: Openness, Diversity and Cohesion*, Washington, DC: Brookings Institution.

Leamer, Edward E. (1984), *Sources of International Comparative Advantage: Theory and Evidence*, Cambridge, MA: MIT Press.

Londoño, Juan Luis and Miguel Székely (1997), 'Persistent Poverty and Excess Inequality: Latin America, 1970–1995', Washington, DC, Inter-American Development Bank, Office of the Chief Economist, Working Paper No. 357.

Martínez, Jorge (2000), 'Migración Internacional y el Desarrollo en la Era de la Globalización e Integración: temas para una agenda regional' [trans] CEPAL, Serie Población y Desarrollo No. 10.

Morley, Samuel (2000), 'The effect of growth and economic reform on income distribution in Latin America', *CEPAL Review*, 71 (August).

Morley, Samuel (2001a), *The Income Distribution Problem in Latin America and the Caribbean*, Santiago, Chile: UN Economic Commission for Latin America and the Caribbean.

Morley, Samuel (2001b), 'Distribution and Growth in Latin America in an Era of Structural Reform', Washington, DC: International Food Policy Research Institute, Trade and Macroeconomics Division, Discussion Paper No. 66.

Ocampo, José Antonio (2003), 'Capital Account and Counter-cyclical Prudential Regulations in Developing Countries', in Ricardo Ffrench-Davis and Stephany Griffith-Jones (eds), *From Capital Surges to Drought*, London: Palgrave/ Macmillan.

Palma, Gabriel (2002), 'The Three Routes to Financial Crises: The Need for Capital Controls', in John Eatwell and Lance Taylor (eds), *International Capital Markets: Systems in Transition*, New York: Oxford University Press, pp. 297–338.

Pietrobelli, Carlo and Stefano Zamagni (2000), 'The Emerging Economies in the Global Financial Market: Some Concluding Remarks', in José Antonio Ocampo, Stefano Zamagni, Ricardo Ffrench-Davis and Carlo Pietrobelli (eds), *Financial Globalization and the Emerging Economies,* Santiago: ECLAC/Jacques Maritain Institute, pp. 313–25.

Rama, Martín (2001), 'Globalization and Workers in Developing Countries', Washington, DC: World Bank Project on 'Globalization, Growth and Poverty: Building an Inclusive World Economy'.

Rodríguez, Francisco and Dani Rodrik (2001), 'Trade Policy and Economic Growth: A Skeptic's Guide to the Cross National Evidence', Cambridge, MA: National Bureau of Economic Research Working Paper No. 7081.

Rodrik, Dani (1997), *Has Globalization Gone Too Far?* Washington, DC: Institute for International Economics.

Rodrik, Dani (1999), *The New Global Economy and the Developing Countries: Making Openness Work*, Baltimore, MD: Johns Hopkins University Press.

Solimano, Andrés (1999), 'Globalization and National Development at the End of 20th Century: Tensions and Challenges', World Bank Working Paper No. 2137.

Solimano, Andrés (2001a) 'International Migration and the Global Economy: An Overview', World Bank Working Paper No. 2720.

Solimano, Andrés (2001b), 'Globalizing talent and human capital: implications for developing countries', CEPAL, *Serie Macroeconomía del Desarrollo*, no. 15.

Titelman, Daniel and Andras Uthoff (1998), 'The Relationship between Foreign and Domestic Savings under Financial Liberalization', in Ricardo Ffrench-Davis and Helmut Reisen (eds), *Capital Flows and Investment Performance*, Paris and Santiago: OECD/ECLAC.

Williamson, John (2000), *Exchange Rate Regimes for Emerging Markets: Reviving the Intermediate Option*, Washington, DC: Institute for International Economics.

Wood, Adrian (1997), 'Openness and wage inequality in developing countries: the Latin American challenge to East Asian conventional wisdom', *World Bank Economic Review*, **11** (1), 33–57.

Index